7/08

J. Campbell

STOICISM AND EMOTION

STOICISM & EMOTION

MARGARET R. GRAVER

The University of Chicago Press
Chicago & London

Margaret R. Graver is associate professor of classics at Dartmouth College.

The University of Chicago Press, Chicago 60637
The University of Chicago Press, Ltd., London
© 2007 by The University of Chicago
All rights reserved. Published 2007
Printed in the United States of America
16 15 14 13 12 11 10 09 08 07   1 2 3 4 5

ISBN-13: 978-0-226-30557-8 (cloth)
ISBN-10: 0-226-30557-0 (cloth)

Library of Congress Cataloging-in-Publication Data

Graver, Margaret.
    Stoicism and emotion / Margaret R. Graver.
        p.   cm.
    Includes bibliographical references and index.
    ISBN-13: 978-0-226-30557-8 (cloth : alk. paper)
    ISBN-10: 0-226-30577-0 (cloth : alk. paper)
    1. Stoics. 2. Emotions (Philosophy). I. Title. II. Title: Stoicism and emotion.
    B528.G73 2007
    128'.37093—dc22

                                                                    2007015185

B.E.G.
round the griefs of the ages

CONTENTS

ACKNOWLEDGMENTS

Financial support for this project was provided by a sabbatical fellowship from the American Philosophical Society and a Senior Faculty Fellowship from Dartmouth College. Tad Brennan, Brad Inwood, Bob Kaster, and an anonymous reader for the University of Chicago Press provided me with detailed comments on the entire manuscript. I wish to thank them for their patience, clearsightedness, and not least for their continued resistance to certain of my contentions. Numerous others, including especially David Konstan, Burton Cooper, and Jim Tatum, but also Howard Hughes, Adina Roskies, Christine Thomas, and Stephen White, read portions of the work in draft; their comments, too, have been very helpful. Others have contributed by working through ideas with me in conversation; among these, I would mention especially Martha Nussbaum, whose teaching and advising at Brown University gave me my first introduction to the subject, and also Victor Caston, Christopher Gill, Stephen Menn, Anthony Price, David Sedley, and Nancy Sherman. I also wish to acknowledge the contributions of seminar members and audiences at various locations where portions of this work have been delivered orally, and to thank the institutions whose sponsorship has made these exchanges possible, including Brown University, Cornell University, Dartmouth College, Northwestern University, the University of California at Davis, the University of Colorado, the University of Crete, the University of North Carolina at Chapel Hill, the University of Notre Dame, the University of Texas at Austin, and the

University of Toronto. A different kind of gratitude is owing to Bruce, Sarah, and Nicolas Graver, who have given me the strength to get through this as well as many other endeavors.

INTRODUCTION
Emotion and Norms for Emotion

The title *Stoicism and Emotion* seems on the face of it to represent a contradiction in terms. "Stoicism" in today's English means "absence of emotion," and this usage takes for granted that the Stoics of ancient Greece advocated an across-the-board suppression of feeling. It is no wonder, then, that people interested in the study of emotion have frequently regarded the ancient Stoics with suspicion, even hostility. Most of us believe, reasonably enough, that the capacity for emotions is an important and in any case an ineliminable part of being human. Most of us hold, also, that it would be wrong to conflate emotions with beliefs, as if there were no difference between merely thinking someone unfortunate and feeling pity, or thinking oneself harmed and feeling anger. Our intuitions tell us that a good theory of emotion must give some consideration to the chemical and biological bases of our feelings; that it must say something about childhood and the way our emotional dispositions evolve over time; at the most basic level, that it must treat human beings as living creatures and not minds only. When we hear that Stoics defined emotions as a species of judgment, and that the aim of Stoic ethics is to attain a condition in which one is completely free of emotion, we seem to be dealing with an account which is not only not admirable, but indeed scarcely credible as a description of what anyone actually experiences.

If these are our reasons for turning away from Stoic thought on this subject, then it is time for us to take another look. Stoicism is not a quick study: we have copious source materials, but these materials are of very mixed quality, and the more ancient and authoritative witnesses are also the ones that require the most specialized knowledge to evaluate properly. The main outlines of this ancient position do, however, emerge with increasing clarity, and they are well worth seeing. The founders of the Stoic school did not set out to suppress or deny our natural feelings; rather, it was their endeavor, in psychology as in ethics, to determine what the natural feelings of humans really are. With the emotions we most often experience they were certainly dissatisfied; their aim, however, was not to eliminate feelings as such from human life, but to understand what sorts of affective responses a person would have who was free of false belief. Further, they sought to develop plausible psychological explanations for affective responses, explanations which would register the observed facts of human behavior while preserving their own intuitions about causal necessity and the material bases of psychological events. These same explanations were integrated into a larger psychological theory which explored the relations between emotions and involuntary feelings, emotions and insanity, emotions and moral development. This large-scale project is not the work of philosophers who regard emotions as unimportant, a nonessential field of study which can safely be skirted by serious ethicists. That it also refuses to treat emotions as essentially harmless but rather demands that they be examined, corrected, purified—this indeed presents a challenge to many modern ways of thinking. But it is not a challenge we have a right to ignore.

Linguistic equivalents are rarely exact: if we are to speak about Stoic thought on "emotions" (the English word), we had best begin by getting clear about what kinds of responses the Hellenistic Stoics have in mind when they use their word *pathos* (plural *pathē*). By itself, the word *pathos* is not very helpful; it means generally something like "experience" or "affected-ness," with its more exact sense being indicated by context. Stoic definitions are available, but definitions can be frustrating: they place a term within a system without necessarily telling us where in our lived experience the term was thought to apply. What we need are examples, narratives of human behavior that can show us, rather than tell us, what kinds of experience are assumed to count as *pathē*. I appeal, therefore, to a group of examples given in two treatises by Chrysippus of Soli, the third leader of the school at Athens and the most influential Stoic writer of antiquity. These treatises were titled *On Emotions* and *On the Psyche;* we do not have full texts, but a detailed description of them by the medical writer Galen indicates what examples were cited and for what purposes. Here, then, is a series of anecdotes, all taken by the philosopher, as was customary, from works of Greek literature.[1]

- *Iliad* 10.9–10: The army of Troy has advanced to a position very near the Greek camp, intending to burn the ships beached there and so cut off all retreat. Seeing this, the Greek commander Agamemnon is terribly frightened; his heart pounds, and he cries out.
- *Iliad* 4.24: Hera has spent ten years and much personal toil marshaling the Greek forces against Troy. Now as the gods sit in counsel, Hera's husband deliberately offends both her and Athena by suggesting a truce. Athena remains silent, but Hera cannot contain herself; she bursts out with a torrent of angry words.
- *Iliad* 13.494: Aeneas is preparing to engage an enemy leader whose men have massed closely about him. Calling to his own men, he sees them flock to his side, and his heart is glad.
- *Iliad* 14.315–16: Hera has put on her most alluring garments and has offered herself to her husband in a flowery meadow. The longing Zeus experiences seems to him greater than ever before.
- *Odyssey* 4.113: Veterans of the Trojan War sit at table with their families while a bard recites the events of their own recent past. All present are seized with a desire for lamentation; their weeping fills the room.
- Euripides, *Andromache* 629–30: In the midst of the sack of Troy, Menelaus encounters Helen, who had been his wife. In justified retribution, he raises his hand to strike her dead—but then her garment falls open to reveal her breast, and a wave of tenderness obliterates his resolve.
- Euripides, *Medea* 1078–79: Desiring above all to punish Jason, Medea resolves to kill the children she has borne to him, even though she understands that doing so will cause tremendous pain to herself.

Chrysippus mentions all of these stories as instances of what he, in his language, calls *pathē*. *Pathos*, then, is his collective term for experiences of this general kind, experiences for which the poets themselves use more specific terms such as *cholos*, *penthos*, or *himeros*. An English speaker will easily render those more specific terms with our words "anger," "grief," "desire," and so on, keeping in mind the narratives associated with them. Correspondingly, if asked to name the class to which all these experiences belong, an English speaker will be hard put not to say "emotion." It is for this reason that I have used the word "emotion," rather than "passion," "sentiment," or any alternative term, throughout this book.[2]

It is important to realize, though, that not every experience which is called an "emotion" in our language will necessarily fall within the extension of the ancient term. While the textbook examples of Stoic *pathē* are recognizable as core instances of what we call emotions, there are also important varieties of affective response which are not meant to be included in claims about the *pathē*. Chief among these are certain affective responses which the Stoic theory accepts as entirely rational and good, terming them not *pathē* but *eupatheiai*. These include, at the very least, awe and reverence, certain forms of joy and gladness, certain particular kinds of love and friendship, and some powerful types of longing or wishing. To determine what exactly these responses are, what criteria constitute them as a class, and how they differ from the core instances of emotion is a central task of this book. For it is these, above all, that tell us what affective responses are for and what they ought to be like.

In addition, there are some feelings which Stoics count as strictly involuntary, below-threshold responses. These include not only low-level physiological events such as blanching or shuddering but even some feelings manifested in tears or laughter and, remarkably, many responses to literature, music, and the visual arts. And just as there are below-threshold responses which are not yet emotions, so also there are over-the-top responses which are no longer emotions but belong rather to the category of mental illness. These, too, need to be treated separately. Each of these forms of affectivity will concern us at some point; meanwhile, we should proceed on the understanding that the Stoic claims about emotion do not apply to everything in the affective realm but do apply to those experiences that are cited by Chrysippus from Greek literature: the fear of Agamemnon, the wrath of Hera, the delight of Aeneas, and other responses of the same kind.

Of all the assertions Stoics make about emotion, the one that has attracted most attention in recent years is the claim that emotions are defined by their propositional content; i.e., that every instance of emotion is in its very essence a judgment concerning some present or potential state of affairs.[3] Agamemnon's fear for the ships implies and, in a way, *is* a judgment on his part that a bad thing, the sort of thing one ought to feel strongly about, is about to happen. This is not to say that there is not also a particular feeling or set of feelings that are characteristic of fear. The sweating palms, the pounding heart, the lump in the throat seem to everyone to belong to the experience of fear, and the Stoic position does allow that if Agamemnon was afraid, he must have felt something of this kind. But the sensations we associate with fear would not be identified as fear if they did not result from a judgment of impending evil. For these same sensations might be produced in us in other ways, either by affectless physiological causes (running, certain medications) or by other kinds of judgments: a pounding heart, for instance, might be a manifestation of happy excitement rather than fear. Hence it will often be necessary for us to uphold a distinction between felt sensations in themselves and felt sensations as produced by particular kinds of judgment; in effect, between what it *feels like* to be afraid and what it *is* to be afraid.

But it was not merely for the purposes of description that Stoic philosophers sought to define response types in terms of their propositional content rather than their corporeal manifestations. By approaching the subject in this way, they were also establishing a set of norms for the affective realm. Judgments, as such, are either true or false. If it should turn out that a particular type of response always implies a false judgment, then that is a response we should seek to eliminate, not because we wish to be unresponsive but because we wish to avoid believing what is false. And the Stoics' chief claim about emotions, properly so called, is that they do imply false judgments—that Agamemnon's fear and Hera's wrath depend on ways of seeing the world that are demonstrably mistaken. One cannot comprehend the Stoics' position, let alone respond adequately to it, until one engages fully with their reasons for asserting this. An informative study of Stoic psychology is thus required to consider certain points in Stoic ethics as well. Above all, we need to give careful attention to the theory of value, which states the criteria by which objects are to be considered beneficial or harmful. Only then can we follow the reasoning by which impassivity (*apatheia*) becomes a psychological norm.

The analysis of emotions and emotional behaviors in terms of judgments implies a strong position on moral responsibility. In this ethical system, the making of any judgment goes hand in hand with responsibility: people are held accountable for what they do just insofar as they are reasoning beings, ones that possess concepts, make judgments, and act on the basis of linguistically formulable reasons. Not every creature is capable of acting responsibly: subrational animals, very young children, and the mentally impaired are not, and accordingly these are not accountable for the feelings they have either. But the full-scale affective responses of mature, unimpaired human beings are 'up to us' in exactly the same way as our actions are up to us: we do have reasons for them, even if we are not always fully aware of what those reasons are. Indeed, the Stoic position is that genuine affective responses are one kind of voluntary action. It will still be true that our experience of them is frequently an experience of being overwhelmed or carried away against our will, and this point will require explanation. But this psychology does not understand the human mind in a way that allows the usual mechanisms of volitional behavior to be replaced on occasion by other, nonvolitional mechanisms or mysterious forces. So there is no recourse to emotion as a means of discounting or lessening responsibility for actions taken by reasoning adults. The motivation for some violent act may well have been experienced as a surge of overwhelming anger, but this does not make the perpetrator any less accountable for what was done.

The volitional nature of particular acts of judgment is in turn grounded in the character of the individual. Both Hera and Athena are provoked by Zeus, but Athena holds her peace; Hera cannot. Presumably there is something about Hera herself that explains this difference, some disposition to respond in this way which belongs to her over a long enough time that one would want to call it a trait of character. Such traits of character seem to offer a better opening for analysis than do isolated episodes of feeling. In Stoicism, tendencies toward particular classes of emotion are described in terms of deep-seated beliefs: misogyny, for instance, is a deep-seated belief in the badness of women and manifests itself in a range of emotions concerned with women. Individual responsibility for emotions is thus bound up with the history of a person's intellectual development. In order to explain why powerful and sometimes destructive responses often seem to arise in us of their own accord, one has to appeal to a long succession of causes that have operated on a person over time. These will necessarily include such external factors as early upbringing, education, and cultural influences, as well as prior emotional experience. For the Stoics as for Aristotle, such causes can be identified without obscuring the contribution each individual makes to his or her own emotional formation.

Finally, we need to keep in mind that true judgments, as well as false ones, can be responsible for powerful feelings. The affective responses of the normative human being are generated on the basis of knowledge; these actually count as goods within the Stoic system of value. And while a perfectly reliable judgment, one whose every premise is thoroughly justified and in harmony with other elements of belief, seems hardly possible to attain, still it could be the case that even our ordinary emotional experiences have in them some elements of true belief. These elements should be ratified rather than rejected, and with them any components of feeling generated by them. On this basis I think it is possible to find a Stoic justification for some dimensions of our emotional lives which common moral intuitions are unwilling to give up: our purest affections, our most justified aversions, our most profound desires, even our regrets. There will still be much that has to be eliminated, for erroneous ways of thinking pervade every area of human experience. But affectivity itself will still be an essential part of human nature.

✖

The first three chapters of this study provide an overview of Stoic emotion theory as framed within more general claims about the nature of mental events, of affective responses generally, and of responsibility for action. As background to the essential cognitive analysis, the first chapter gives a sketch of Stoic views on the corporeal basis of emotions and the relation between material and intentional accounts of psychic function. In this chapter, as throughout the book, I maintain a distinction between feelings, or sensed psychophysical changes, and affective responses themselves, which require particular kinds of judgment. For the Stoics, who insisted on the physical nature of all events, emotions and other affective responses are always constituted by some kind of psychophysical change. But while that change does explain the way the emotion feels, the affective response is not simply reducible to its psychophysical description. Responses which are very similar in terms of feeling can be classified quite differently because of differences in content. The content of affective judgments is reserved for chapter 2, which spells out the intellectual components of the various classes of response and explains the Stoics' crucial distinction between ordinary emotions and normative or 'eupathic' versions of affect. Chapter 3 then turns more specifically to problems of causation, in order to clarify what is implied by the school's notorious claim that emotions are volitional. Responsibility, I argue, is not incompatible with Stoic determinism, nor does it leave Stoics without recourse to explain the common experience of being overridden or run away with by one's emotion. For it is possible to act voluntarily and yet be unable to stop oneself from acting.

But understanding what the Stoic claims are is not of much use unless one also understands how those claims were meant to be applied. We need to consider not only the content of the crucial definitions but also their extension, how they match up to the various kinds of experience a person can undergo. Chapters 4 and 5 seek to specify that extension by collecting some examples of feelings which Stoics explicitly refuse to count as emotions, either because they occur without any judgment or because they belong to 'melancholic' or insane states of mind. The former, sometimes called 'pre-emotions,' are below-threshold responses in rational beings, ones that stop short of an act of assent. These include many feelings which have been cited, in the current debate and also in antiquity, as evidence that emotions are involuntary in nature. The feelings of the insane are excluded from the definition for a different reason: because they belong to persons whose capacity for mental processing is impaired, they are not even candidates to be considered as forms of rational response. Genuine affective responses may be 'irrational' in the sense of being ill-advised or disorderly, but they are still the responses of reasoning beings. Deranged responses are not like this and are accordingly exempt from moral responsibility. They are comparable rather to instinctive behaviors in animals.

We then turn away from single episodes of emotion to examine the account of long-term emotional characteristics of persons; that is, from events such as angry feelings or behaviors to the relatively stable conditions which figure in an emotional personality. The idea that a person may be disposed by individual traits of character to experience some emotions rather than others is fundamental to the Stoic position on responsibility. Chapter 6 offers evidence that the Stoics, despite the absolutist tendencies of their thought on virtue and vice, also put forward a more nuanced account of personalities, identifying and describing long-term behavioral dispositions in both the wise and the nonwise condition. Chapter 7 then considers how emotive dispositions develop over time within the life history of the individual. The choices of the individual play a role in the development of character, and so also in a different way do factors beyond individual control such as heredity and place of origin. The latter assertion raises concerns about the role of luck in moral development; I argue, however, that these concerns do not threaten the integrity of the system.

The final chapters continue the study of moral development even as they return to the issue of normative affect. Chapter 8 argues that Zeno's conception of healthy relations between persons and within social groups incorporates a robust role for what we can recognize as genuine love, affection, and friendship; chapter 9, that the Stoic system not only allows but actually requires the retention of many dimensions of affectivity in ordinary persons, including even the painful feelings of sorrow and remorse. Both points are directly concerned with moral development. Eupathic love has an educative dimension as the person of perfect understanding seeks to share that understanding with another. More broadly, the very idea of affection as it exists among the wise can be transformative for our ways of thinking about ordinary social interactions. Regret for misdeeds is edifying in a different way, in that it alienates imperfect people from their present condition and so motivates one to replace perverted patterns of behavior with others that more nearly approximate the norm. A Stoic account of Socrates' efforts to educate the gorgeously flawed young Alcibiades should not downplay the erotic dimensions of the relationship, and neither should it fail to mention the emotional pain that is the cost of that education to the pupil.

✌

The ideas presented here are primarily those of the Athenian Stoa as first propounded by Zeno of Citium and expanded upon by Chrysippus of Soli in the mid- to late third century B.C.E. It was in this early period that the view on emotions was developed most extensively in conjunction with other elements of Stoic thought. Specifically on the subject of emotion there were at least five treatises written during the third century; these will not have been identical in content, but they do seem to have shared a set of important claims and a standard terminology originating with Zeno. The work to gain the widest circulation was Chrysippus's *On Emotions:* it was still available in libraries in the second century C.E. So widely known was Chrysippus's work that his views are regularly mentioned by other ancient authors as being *the* Stoic views, along with those of Zeno from which they were derived. And because references to Chrysippus's thought are very numerous and frequently corroborate each other, we have the wherewithal to reconstruct his position in some detail.

My interest in recovering the Zenonian and Chrysippan account, rather than later adaptations of it, expresses itself in definite choices I have made in the handling of source materials.[4] Where possible I have given preference to the actual words of the Stoic founders as quoted by later authors, or to paraphrases in which there is a clear intention to paraphrase accurately. Some of our best evidence in fact comes from authors hostile to Stoicism who, in their eagerness to refute some point of doctrine, sometimes make a grand show of quoting the exact wording they find offensive. Authors who have proved helpful in this way include Plutarch and Galen, both self-styled Platonists, the skeptical philosopher Sextus Empiricus, Alexander of Aphrodisias the commentator on Aristotle, and also the Neoplatonist Simplicius in the sixth century A.D. These reports have to be used cautiously, for all these authors also have their own philosophical objectives and characteristic modes of thought. Care must be taken not only to work around their biases but also to see beyond the dialectical frame they tend to impose on the material, their tendency to find sharp dichotomies between the Stoa and other schools where there may in fact have been only subtle gradations of emphasis.[5]

A case in point is an important work by Galen, the medical writer of the second century C.E., entitled *On the Precepts of Hippocrates and Plato*. Galen's purpose is to defend his own account of the physiology of voluntary action, based in part on dissection studies and the older medical literature and in part on his understanding of Plato's tripartite psychology in the *Republic* and *Timaeus*. Because this account is in conflict with the more unified Stoic psychology, which enjoyed great prestige among his contemporaries, Galen makes a consistent effort to refute the arguments which support the Stoic position. In so doing he reports in detail and with frequent quotation a considerable portion of the content of Chrysippus's treatises *On the Psyche* and *On Emotions*. The report is not entirely trustworthy, since Galen is no doubt being selective in his presentation of the evidence, and also because it is not always clear what words belong to which author, or what position was actually taken by Posidonius of Rhodes, to whom Galen repeatedly appeals for support. Used with care, however, Galen's book can provide a wealth of information on early Stoic psychology.

For fuller exposition and the overall structure of the thought one often has to turn to the so-called doxographic tradition, encyclopedia-style summaries put together from earlier sources. The most important of these are the review of Stoic doctrines included by Diogenes Laertius in his biography of Zeno, written in the early third century, and a careful account of Stoic ethics which is quoted by the Byzantine-era compiler Johannes Stobaeus. The latter is of particular interest because of internal evidence which suggests it was composed in the first century B.C.E., perhaps by the philosopher Arius who was an associate of Augustus Caesar.[6] These summary accounts tend to be dry and schematic in the manner of presentation; connections and explanations are frequently omitted, and the purpose of argumentation is not always clear. On the other hand, because these works are not motivated by any pretensions to philosophical achievement, they can generally be trusted not to alter or embellish what was in their own sources. For terminology and for the wording of definitions these are often our best sources.

I refer often to the works of Cicero, whose philosophical writings provide us with our earliest continuous accounts of Stoic thought. Cicero at one time kept a Stoic philosopher, Diodotus, as his private tutor, and had met Posidonius in his home at Rhodes. More important, he had read deeply in the large literature of Greek Stoicism; when a relevant work was not available in his own library, he would ask his friend Atticus to find him a copy. In his own works he seeks to present philosophical ideas accurately

	300	200	100	B.C.E.	C.E.	100	200	300
above	ZENO *CLEANTHES*	*Diogenes* *Apollodorus* *Panaetius*	Cicero Philodemus		Philo Seneca	Gellius Galen Sextus	Diogenes Laertius Origen	Calcidius Nemesius
below		*CHRYSIPPUS* *Sphaerus* *Persaeus*	*Posidonius* *Hecato*	*Arius* (?)	*Epictetus* *Hierocles* Plutarch *Aetius*		Athenaeus Alexander Clement	Eusebius Didymus Caecus

Figure 1. Approximate dates of major Stoic authors and sources. Italic indicates authors whose works survive only in fragments.

in a variety of styles, sometimes advocating for a Stoic view, sometimes maintaining a critical distance by the use of embedded narrators. Sometimes, too, he mingles Stoic ideas with ideas adapted from Plato or other ancient traditions. For my purposes, the most useful passages are those in which he gives a plain exposition of what he has read, especially where portions of his Latin account match closely with the later accounts we have in Greek.

Of particular importance among Cicero's works is his extended account of Stoic views on grief and other emotions in the third and fourth *Tusculan Disputations.* Here he speaks in his own voice, but the position he defends is mainly that of Chrysippus in his work *On Emotions.* We know this not only because he mentions Chrysippus frequently by name but because the terms and concepts he presents match closely with what we know from other sources about that philosopher's characteristic interests and emphases.[7] Even so caution is needed, for Cicero knows the writings of many philosophers and also adds some arguments of his own devising. With critical reading, though, it is usually possible to make the necessary distinctions and so to develop a fuller and more detailed picture of the central Stoic assertions than would otherwise be possible.

With Seneca and Epictetus in the following century I have taken a somewhat different approach. Both were well read in Stoic treatises of the Hellenistic period and sought to present that received doctrine accurately as well as effectively. But both are also independent thinkers whose personal commitment to Stoic ethics has plenty of room for original contributions, and it would carry me too far afield to attend to the particular interests and emphases of each as fully as they deserve. Where they quote or paraphrase from the older tradition I have used them freely, and I have also found them helpful for illustrations and examples of points most Stoics had in common. In chapters 4 and 5 I do give close attention to points for which Seneca provides the principal evidence, trying to discern his intent; even here, though, I am interested in his views because I believe them to have been developed in harmony with the views of the Stoic founders, which he, like Cicero, had studied extensively in Greek.

Occasionally one finds good evidence for early Stoic thought in quite odd places. The notebooks of the Epicurean scholar Philodemus, recovered with great labor from the buried city of Herculaneum, supply a missing link in the terminology of volition. A textbook by Hierocles, an orthodox Stoic of the Roman Empire, was found buried in sand at Hermopolis in Upper Egypt. A scriptural commentary by the Jewish scholar Philo of Alexandria eventually made its way to Armenia; from it we recover evidence of the early Stoic terminology of 'pre-emotions' or involuntary feelings. In this as in some other instances, a careful consideration of the relations among our various sources can result in a significant reinterpretation of Stoic thought.

My aims are those of the interpreter; in some sense even those of the translator. It is not my intention either to advocate for the Stoic position or to demonstrate that it is mistaken; rather, I have been concerned to understand the appeal that this body of thought undeniably had for intelligent persons in its own time.[8] To that end a sympathetic presentation can be very helpful, and in that spirit I have consistently sought to understand Stoic thought from the perspective of its proponents, rather than its detractors, pondering its motivations and considering how the more obvious objections might be answered. But this is not a project in neo-Stoic thought. I do not mean to claim that other ways of thinking about emotion are invalidated by the one studied here, and I do not, like Nussbaum (2001) and Becker (1998, 2004), seek to update or modify the ancient position in order to render it acceptable to modern readers.[9] For me, Stoicism remains a historical subject.

At the same time, I would not be writing this book if I did not feel that Zeno and Chrysippus were good philosophers whose views deserve our respect. Their positions may not be ones that would work for us: we have discovered much that they never dreamed of, in biological science and also in philosophy, and have opened new possibilities for the medical treatment of behavioral disorders that once belonged only to the realm of ethics. Were the ancient Stoics able to take cognizance of these discoveries, they would undoubtedly wish to modify their own thinking in significant ways. But we also can learn from them, for their effort at sustained and rigorous thinking on questions of affectivity and morality sets an example that even in a changed world we may well seek to emulate.

I

A Science of the Mind

Present-day research on emotion takes place primarily in the context of the physical sciences. A study of anger, for instance, might derive some of its premises from careful measurement of autonomic adjustments in heart rate, diastolic pressure, and body temperature or from the analysis of videotaped changes in facial expression. Philosophers as well as neuroscientists have been fascinated by the possibility of using resonance imaging techniques to pinpoint the location of specific brain structures that regulate the various modes of emotional response.[1] Animal research, too, has yielded valuable results, on the assumption that affective responses may be homologous across multiple species. Jaak Panksepp offers an example from his own research. Replicating an older experiment by J. P. Flynn, Panksepp fed a tiny charge to an electrode implanted in the medial hypothalamus of a cat. In an instant, the quiet animal was transformed. Hissing and spitting, teeth and claws bared, it leapt directly at Panksepp's head and was only prevented from doing him serious harm by the Plexiglass screen that stood between them. Panksepp cites verbal reports from human subjects stimulated at the same brain sites to corroborate his assumption that the cat had experienced something like what we know as a subjective feeling of rage.[2]

It would of course be a mistake to think that the corporeal realization of an emotion—what Panksepp activated in the cat—is the only object worthy of study. Few would deny that the emotions we experience involve, perhaps even require, the formation of beliefs with certain kinds of propositional content, such as *that the speaker has failed to show up* or *that the operation is today.* For the purposes of ordinary life and ethics, accounts that spell out that content—what phi-losophers call "intentional terms" accounts—provide us with our most efficient and useful ways of talking about emotion. Yet even when we proceed to that more properly mental description of mental experience, we do not suppose that we are somehow invalidating the results of con-temporary brain research. We do not believe ourselves to be describing disembodied processes that need no biological realization at all. Rather, we proceed on the understanding that a single mental event, such as the recognition of a threat, is analyzable on two different levels, a physiologi-cal level as investigated by the neuroscientist and an intentional level as investigated by the cognitive psychologist. The relative utility of one or the other analysis will depend on the context and purpose of the investi-gation.

Stoic psychology is on the whole very different from modern affective neuroscience. Its primary emphases are on the propositional content of our mental experience and on the norms that arise from logical analysis of our evaluative judgments. However, Stoic thought is also like our own in that it considers the mind to be necessarily a material thing and mental events to be of necessity physical changes in the world. Just as we turn to biological research to bolster our confidence that sensation and thought do bear some decipherable relation to a material substrate, so Stoic ratio-nalism seeks to undergird its intentionalist account with a low-level expla-nation based on the theoretical physics of that era.

The possibility that one might attend to both the biological perspective and the discursive or logical perspective had been recognized already by Aristotle. In sketching out the basis for his inquiry into the nature of the psyche, Aristotle notes that one and the same emotion may be defined dif-ferently from the standpoint of different branches of intellectual inquiry.

> The natural scientist would define each of them differently from the dia-lectician. For instance, there is the question what anger is. One person will define it as "a desire for retribution" or something of that kind, another as "the boiling of the blood and warm stuff around the heart." One of these tells the material, the other the reasoning; that is, the form.[3]

Aristotle's point is that neither of the accounts mentioned here, the strictly material and the strictly intentional, need displace the other. Either may be sufficient for its own type of investigation, and both may be true in their own way. Moreover the *physikos* or natural scientist—Aristotle has

no word for "psychologist"—has need of both: he is the student of 'en-
mattered principles.' He will investigate the nature of thought, desire, and
intention, but not as subjects for abstract science: for him, they are of
interest as characteristic functions of living creatures.

Aristotle's methodological presupposition is matched by the assumption which seems to have prevailed in the early Stoa that events in the
mind—impressions, judgments, emotional responses—can in theory be
understood either in intentional terms, by verbalizing the propositions
which are their contents, or in physical terms, by specifying some material
change at some spatial location. For most purposes, in naming causes or
in predicting, producing, evaluating, or managing the emotions, the Stoics
give priority to explanations cast in intentional terms. Yet a serious effort is
also made to account for the causal efficacy of the mind in physical terms
by describing the material of which it is composed and the temporal and
spatial dimensions of its activities. The psyche is thus made continuous
with a universal system of nature which is entirely governed by scientific
principles—principles which are by nature investigable, whether or not
human beings have yet succeeded in describing them adequately.[4]

Given the empirical limitations of ancient Greek physiology, it might
appear that the details of the physical account would be of interest only
as a historical curiosity. Nonetheless it is important to the purposes of this
study to review what is known about Stoic thought on this subject. This
is for several reasons. First, the way the mind material is conceived helps
to account for the readiness of Stoic philosophers to assume a connection
between human rationality and divine purpose. For the substance they
call *pneuma*, 'breath' or 'spirit,' incorporates within itself a set of structural principles which are linked to the structure and organization of the
universe as a whole. In addition, the constraints imposed by the nature
of the material are occasionally called upon to serve certain explanatory
needs. We will see in chapter 5 how an appeal to the physical is used to explain behavioral aberrations in those labeled insane, and in chapter 7 how
a similar appeal helps in explaining differences in individual temperament.
Meanwhile it is of more than passing interest to see that Stoic accounts of
the subjective feelings we experience in emotion are grounded in the animate being's functional sensitivity to its own corporeal states, in a manner
not unlike that proposed by William James in 1884 and recently revitalized
by Antonio Damasio and others.[5]

In this chapter, then, I seek to identify those notions in Stoic thought
which correspond in the ancient context to what a neuroscientist like Panksepp seeks to understand about animal and human responses. Through a

few surviving discussions, many occasional references, and some significant choices regarding terminology, it is possible to trace out a rudimentary physiology of mind and emotion which is consistent with basic tenets
of Stoic natural science. At issue is a whole group of functional capacities
recognized as specific to the psyche, not only emotion but also perception,
thought, judgment, and conscious action. For the purposes of this book,
the particular point of interest is in the nature of the affective response itself, both the sort of physical events that are said to be involved and the relation of those events to the content of our beliefs. In order to make sense
of what our sources tell us on these points, however, we need to begin at
a more fundamental level, with the place of the rational living creature
within the Stoic universe. For it will turn out that human affectivity is not,
after all, a peculiarity of vice but is continuous with basic life function in
us and even with yet more basic attributes such as the cohesiveness of our
flesh. At the same time, it is set apart by its dependence on those cognitive
abilities which qualify us as rational beings.

The psychic material

It is axiomatic for Stoicism, as it is for most present-day philosophy, that
the mind is necessarily a material thing and that mental states and events
are also physical facts or changes in the world. Arguments to this effect are
reported already for the earliest scholarchs, Zeno of Citium at the beginning of the third century B.C.E. and Zeno's immediate successor, Cleanthes. The best of these arguments are premised on the claim that anything
which interacts with a body must itself be corporeal. After all, the very
notion of interaction would seem to require some sort of contact, and
it is hard to see how anything can come into contact with a body unless
it, too, has the attributes of body—that is, unless it both extends in three
dimensions and offers some form of resistance to its surroundings.[6] But
the mind does interact with the body. When you cut your finger, it hurts,
and pain, even the crudest physical pain, is a kind of awareness. Likewise
bodily illness is often accompanied by mental lowness or confusion. Conversely, some experiences that seem to belong to the mind have obvious
effects on the body. People who are angry or embarrassed grow red in the
face; people who are afraid may turn pale; anxiety and erotic desire have
unmistakable physiological components.[7] None of this could happen, the
Stoics reason, if thoughts and emotions were not also alterations in some
kind of psychic material.

Considering the tasks that the mind material has to do, its composition turns out to be surprisingly simple. Called "fine-textured" and "an exhalation of the solid body," it would seem to be a kind of gas, mingled with other body components but capable of separating itself from them.[8] In fact, a gas is exactly what it is, for we are told by many sources that the animating mind-stuff consists of *pneuma,* a highly energized gaseous material which is mentioned very often in Stoic physics. In one sense *pneuma* is nothing other than a mix of fire and air, two of the primary elements or basic stuffs in the old four-element scheme.[9] Yet this mixture, simple as it sounds, turns out to possess remarkable properties which enable it to endow bodies with all the capacities needed for life, perception, and voluntary movement.

To follow the Stoics' thinking on the activities of *pneuma* it is helpful to reflect in a general way on the structure and cohesiveness of things around us. We say that a log is more highly structured than a pile of ashes, and a quartz crystal is more highly organized than a heap of sand; we say also, in the language of our own physics, that the organization of the log or the crystal has something to do with the amount of energy that is stored in it. So, too, at a further level of complexity, one can say that a living creature is better organized than a corpse: it is alive by virtue of a complex set of systems that work together harmoniously to maintain its life functions. Working from similar observations, Zeno assigned a central cosmological role to what he called the 'designing fire.' This fire is first and foremost the heat that is in all things, animate and inanimate; however, it also, perhaps equivalently, supplies the 'seminal principles' which explain the structural and functional properties of all things. In living things, the seminal principles are literally the principles contained in seeds or semen, by which the properties of parent organisms are passed on to the offspring.[10] But nonliving things, too, receive their organizational principles from the designing fire, and indeed the universe as a whole exhibits a structural and functional complexity like that of living things because of the presence of the designing fire in it.[11] Zeno's rationalist theology identifies this organizing power with Zeus, the divine progenitor and wielder of the lightning of governance. But it is this same designing fire that is mingled with air in the warm breath of living animals.

The elements air and fire are like each other in that both are considered 'active' elements which work together upon the two 'passive' elements, water and earth. But fire and air are also opposed to each other as hot element to cold element and outward-moving to inward-moving force. The combination of the two produces 'tension' (*tonos*) by the balance of opposed forces, and this tension may vary in intensity, like the varying vibrations in the strings of a musical instrument.[12] It is variations in tension, and not the properties of air and fire alone, that explain differences in the qualities imparted by *pneuma* to things: hardness to stones, whiteness to silver, and at higher levels the sophisticated properties of plants and animals.[13] Living things differ across the board from the nonliving in that they have much greater complexity in structure and function, and animals also differ from plants in that their more elaborate body structures and life functions require a higher level of tension to support them. The special characteristics that set humans apart have their physical explanation in yet another level. Indeed the *pneuma* in a human being at his or her optimal level of functioning is characterized by such a high level of tension that it is capable of maintaining its cohesion after the body's death.[14] By contrast animal souls and those of imperfect humans simply die with the body.

Even within a single human being there is more than one level of pneumatic tension at work. Human beings, in addition to their intellectual capacities, also have some capacities of the same kinds as are in all living things—metabolism and growth, for instance—and some properties like those of nonliving things, including shape, coloration, and the varying density of our bones and tissues. All of these must be imparted by one and the same stretch of *pneuma;* there is no other. So it must be possible for *pneuma* to confer several different kinds of property at once. It may be that the inward and outward movements that constitute *tonos* occur in complex and overlapping patterns, like radio waves modulated in amplitude or frequency as well as in the overall strength of the signal. Those properties which we usually think of as belonging to our bodies are grounded in low-tensional or, as it were, low-frequency background patterns of pneumatic vibration, while our thoughts and feelings are grounded in high-tensional vibrations of the same medium.

The range of tasks performed by the *pneuma* in a person is thus very broad. Every life function and every physical characteristic a person has is conferred by the inherent *pneuma.* Very little remains that can be said with any theoretical rigor about the body as distinct from its admixture of *pneuma;* it is just a certain amount of earthy and / or watery material. However it is still reasonable for Stoic authors to draw a distinction between mind and body. If pressed to explain that distinction, it is available for them to say that the relevant contrast is one of functions: functions characteristic of humans (such as speech and reasoning) or of animals generally (such as perception and movement) are being contrasted with whatever else is present that either enables those functions or constrains them.[15] Thus while the Greek word *psuchē* refers in physical terms to the entire stretch of *pneuma* present in a human or animal, it is commonly used in a more restricted way, to refer to that centralized portion of *pneuma* which is responsible for what we would call the psychological functions.[16]

In this book I generally avoid the word "soul." That more theological rendering does have some advantages in that the *psuchē*, being composed of *pneuma*, serves as a vehicle for the divine fire. But our word "soul" suggests rather more in the way of theological or mystical implications than Stoic philosophers meant their term to convey. The Stoic *psuchē* is not a zone of miraculous possibility; it is as much subject to the laws of physics, and as accessible to scientific investigation, as everything else in the universe. 'Mind' or 'psyche' is often a better rendering, for it is the *psuchē* that performs the functions English speakers assign to the mind. It is important to remember, though, that the *psuchē* is in some ways more like the nervous system as a whole than it is like what we think of as the mind. Chrysippus's treatise *On the Psyche* was, like Aristotle's, a project in biology as much as in psychology.[17]

The central directive faculty

The most basic characteristic of *psuchē* as such is its capacity for perception. Definitions originating with Zeno make it 'perceptive *pneuma*' or a 'perceptive exhalation.'[18] What makes some *pneuma* sensitive to stimuli is not fully explained; if pressed, Stoic thinkers would presumably have said that this is one of the properties imparted by pneumatic tension. Probably, too, perceptivity is related to a greater admixture of fire than is found in plants, for animal *pneuma* is especially warm.[19]

But the functional capacities that set animals apart cannot be explained only by the possession of some basic property of sensitivity. The capacities above all of perception and local movement impose further theoretical requirements. What is registered by the eyes or ears needs to be of use to the organism as a whole, not only to the sense organs themselves, and if there are multiple senses, their input needs to be combined. Further, there is a need for locomotion and other motor functions to be coordinated with perception (the animal needs to see where it is walking) and for multiple movements to be coordinated with one another (both feet need to walk in the same direction).[20] To explain this integration of function, the Stoics posited what they called the 'directive faculty' or *hēgemonikon*, a kind of clearing house to which sensations are referred and in which behaviors are initiated. This is the most specific terminological equivalent in Stoicism for our word "mind."

The directive faculty is located in the chest, where it receives input from, and sends out instructions to, other portions of the psychic material extending into the sense organs and limbs. Chrysippus describes it as being like a spring with numerous distributaries or a tree with numerous branches, or, again, like a ruler with a network of spies.

> The parts of the *psuchē* flow from their seat, which is the heart, like a spring from its source, and are extended throughout the entire body: they fill all the limbs all over with vital breath and rule and govern them with countless different virtues, by nourishing them, making them grow, moving them from place to place, equipping them with sense and impelling them to action. And the entire psyche spreads out from the directive part to the senses, which are its functions, like branches from a trunk, to be messengers of the things they sense, while [the directive faculty] itself passes judgment like a king on the things they report.[21]

The hierarchy is very clear. Perception and response do belong to the entire organism, but not to all parts in the same way: they belong principally to the directive faculty, and to the sense organs and limbs only in a subordinate way, by virtue of their being in communication with the directive faculty.

The localization of the directive faculty in the chest was a natural choice in view of the Greeks' limited understanding of human physiology. Chrysippus's notion of signals carried by tentacle-like extensions of the sensitive material is grounded in observations of the characteristics of people and animals, not in any particular study of anatomy; still, to the extent that he was interested in anatomical details, he could look to what was known of the vascular system, with its easily visible network of branching pathways leading outward from the heart to the extremities.[22] Chest localization of the directive faculty also accorded well with simple observations about respiration and heartbeat. "Surely," says Chrysippus, "that by which we breathe is one and the same with that by which we live."[23] Retaining a long-accepted Greek etymology, the Stoics held that the newborn infant acquires its *psuchē* by the cooling action (*psuxis*) of its first intake of air on the fiery principle within the fetus.[24] The 'natural breath' of respiration then sustains the psyche throughout life.[25] It is not surprising, then, that the region around the heart was assumed by the Stoics, as by Aristotle, to be the primary locus of psychic function. As a theoretical construct, however, their account of psychic function did not depend on any particular physiology. Given a more detailed knowledge of the workings of the central nervous system, a Stoic theorist should have had no difficulty in transferring to the brain the role that Chrysippus in fact gave to the heart.[26] What could not be given up was the commitment to centralization in and of itself, the insistence that psychic activity has to belong to some single organ: not vision to the eyes, anger to the spleen, and worry to the gut, but all to the directive faculty, wherever that faculty might be located.

Further, this central faculty must on theoretical grounds be credited with some means of self-perception by which it can register information concerning the animate being's own states. Without this, it could neither register the perceptions of the senses nor direct the animal's movements. Walking, for instance, is next to impossible without proprioception, or a general awareness of the position of one's limbs. And something like proprioception is required for perception as well. Merely being affected by something in one's surroundings is not perception: a camera or tape recorder does that much, and so does a writing tablet. One needs also to be aware of one's own affectedness, that there is a change taking place in one's perceptual apparatus. So Aristotle notes that in order to explain perception one must also explain how it is that we "see" that we are seeing. He concludes, reasonably enough, that perceiving by sight is "not just one thing": it includes both awareness of some object and awareness of one's own states.[27] Stoic psychology makes uses of the same insight, but on the basis of a material psyche.

Especially interesting in this regard is a papyrus text by Hierocles, who is tentatively dated to the early second century C.E. Like earlier Stoics, Hierocles stresses the material nature of psyche and its presence in every part of the body. But his account is especially valuable in that it applies what is posited about the properties of *psuchē* to the problem of consciousness:

> Since the animal is composed of both body and *psuchē,* both being things that can be touched, pressed, and generally pushed around, and since they are mixed through and through, and one of them is a perceptive capacity and that same also undergoes alteration as I have demonstrated, it is clear that the animal would continuously perceive itself. For the *psuchē,* by stretching out and relaxing, presses upon all parts of the body, and since it is also mixed with all parts, when it presses it is also pressed by them in return. For the body is such as to offer resistance, and so also is the *psuchē.* And the feeling is a matter of their pushing on each other and at the same time pushing back. And signaling from the outmost parts inward toward the directive faculty . . ., it is taken up, so that there comes about a consciousness

of all parts of the body and also of all parts of the *psuchē*. And this is what
it is for the animal to perceive itself.[28]

Because *psuchē* and body are amalgamated in what is called a 'through
and through mixture,' some bit of *psuchē* will be able to sense the position
of even the tiniest bit of body; in addition, psyche will be able to sense its
own movements through the resistance they encounter from the body. So
the animal's awareness is not only a matter of a centrally located directive
faculty receiving signals from the periphery—'mind' communicating with
'body' as it were. Rather the directive part of the psyche is directly aware
of the nonpneumatic components and indirectly aware of its own movements amidst those components. In this way we can sense any change
in our own psyches, though we may not necessarily recognize the exact
nature of those changes.[29]

Thought, belief, and action

The Stoic founders also attempted to provide psychophysical explanations for those subtle psychic events in which information is conceptualized, interpreted, and translated into action. The simplest such event is
termed an 'impression.' An impression (*phantasia*) is an alteration of the
psuchē through which something seems (*phainetai*) to be present or to be
the case. In having an impression, the mind registers some state of affairs
prior to forming an opinion about it one way or another. Animals, too,
have impressions, though of a 'nonrational' kind, since animals were not
thought to conceptualize their impressions in the way humans do.[30] For
the present, though, our concern is only with rational impressions.

In this context, the word 'rational' (*logikos*) does not carry any normative implications; it merely refers to the capacity for complex reasoning
and speech. In a rational being, then, the content of an impression is propositional; that is, it is the same sort of thing as the meaning of a sentence.[31]
For instance, one may have an impression *that it is night*. This is different
from merely becoming aware of a change in one's visual field; it is informative in a way that raw sense data are not. Thus an impression can be
considered a specifically mental event, one which involves some awareness of intentional objects.

At the same time, however, every impression is necessarily also a physical event. To refer to the physical basis of impressions, Zeno spoke of
an 'imprinting' (*tupōsis*) in the psyche, a term which suggested to Greeks

the familiar act of pressing a signet ring into wax.[32] The image is a sophisticated one. Wax seals were the usual form of signature for contracts
and letters, the imprint of the ring certifying that the ring's owner was
responsible for the contents of the document. In speaking of an imprint,
Zeno calls to mind the property of significance that wax acquires when
put in a certain spatial configuration. The seal is constituted by the wax
and certainly does not exist apart from the wax, and yet it is not reducible
to its constituent material. What matters about it *as an imprint* cannot be
conveyed without referring to features independent of that particular material realization, features that would be the same even if constituted by
some other suitable matter.

Taken literally, the imprint model presents certain difficulties. A sheet
of wax cannot easily show even two imprints at a time, whereas the mind
may be aware of many objects at once. To give the Stoic account more
credibility, Chrysippus dismisses the notion of a planar surface with ridges
and indentations, the account given by his immediate predecessor Cleanthes.[33] The only thing one should be committed to, he says, is that there
is an alteration of *some* kind in the psychic material. He continues with an
analogy of his own:

> Just as the air, when many people are speaking at once, receives at one time
> innumerable impacts of different kinds and immediately sustains many
> modifications, so also the directive faculty will undergo something analo-
> gous when it takes on complicated impressions.[34]

This model is not fundamentally different from Zeno's version: air replaces
wax, voices the signet ring, and 'modifications' the imprint. However, in
that it makes the substrate three-dimensional and vastly more subtle and
fine-grained than wax or clay, it goes much further toward reassuring the
skeptic that materials do exist which are capable of bearing the complex
sorts of alterations that constitute mental activity. It is an advantage also
that the air in the analogy is a material very similar to the warm air which
constitutes the psyche itself. If air can transmit the sounds of utterance, it
seems reasonable that *pneuma* should be able to sustain the multiple modifications that would be needed to explain our thought processes.

In many cases an impression will concern some object in one's surroundings, either a simple percept—the standard example is "a white
thing"—or a percept under some particular description such as "horse"
or "dog."[35] With this sort of impression one can say, straightforwardly,

that the impression is "an experience in the psyche which reveals both itself and what made it."[36] The impression is made, i.e., caused, by some material thing, which, by impinging upon the sense organs, brings about an alteration in the material psyche, and that alteration "reveals itself" together with its object through the psyche's awareness of its own movements. But impressions may also be of that kind for which the object is more properly described as an actual or hypothetical state of affairs, i.e., a proposition. Here there is a difficulty, for a proposition, being incorporeal, can hardly be said to have caused the impression—at least not by Stoics, for causes in Stoicism are always corporeal. For this sort of impression the Stoic account seems to have been that they arise 'by combination from within'; that is, that they represent their objects through combinations of the mind's own stock of concepts.[37] Physical causation for the impression must come from within the person: the mind material—which is after all a living substance, very different from wax or clay—forms *itself* into configurations that correspond to various propositions. In this sense what should be named as causes are the previous configurations of mind material which are substrate to various thoughts and beliefs already resident in the mind. One could say this and still hold that these causes operate in virtue of their intentional properties.

An impression is what one might call a mere thought, a linguistically formulable notion that one entertains without necessarily being committed to it. What converts thought into belief is a further mental event which is termed variously 'assent' (*sunkatathesis*), 'judgment' (*krisis*), or 'forming an opinion' (*doxazein*).[38] Assent is defined in intentional terms: it is that event in which one either accepts an impression as true or rejects it as false. That assent also has a physical description comes across most clearly in those texts which treat the conditioning factors for assent, whether or not it occurs in any given instance. For those conditioning factors are described both in intentional terms, e.g., as the extent to which the person recognizes valid inferences, and in physical terms as a certain level of tension in the mind material. Thus several sources claim that assent in the person of perfect understanding is characterized by 'strength' or 'good tension,' while the less reliable assents of ordinary persons are 'weak.'[39] The ordinary mind is, as it were, a pushover, yielding easily to impressions which the wise person would resist.

One particularly important class of assents is those called *hormai*, impulses or action tendencies. From a psychological and moral perspective what matters about action is the mental event that initiates it, and this event can be described as a special form of assent; that is, assent to a proposition of a particular 'impulsory' kind. According to the summary in Stobaeus,

> What sets impulse in motion is nothing other than an 'impulsory' impression of something's being immediately appropriate.[40]

Walking, for instance, is assent to an impression that moving the feet in a certain way is appropriate just at this moment (that is, that it suits some present need; no strong notion of duty or obligation is implied). The assent need not be conscious or deliberate; it does not have to be said that one always verbalizes the impulsory impression, even in thought.[41] But the Stoic claim is that in order for us to say a person is walking (not, say, stumbling forward when pushed), this very thought must pass through his or her mind and be endorsed.

A further Stoic definition of impulse makes it 'a motion of psyche toward something,' namely, toward the predicate contained in the endorsed proposition.[42] For instance, the motion of the psyche which is an impulse to walk would be a change in the psychic material such as would cause me to satisfy the predicate "walk." The signal from my heart to my legs and the actual movement of my legs and other body parts are all included in the one event which is my motion toward walking. Meanwhile, because of the proprioceptive capacity of psyche, I both feel my legs moving and am conscious that walking is what I mean to be doing.

The Stoic approach to action thus classifies the responses of the animate being according to the intentional characteristics of psychic events rather than by the expression of those events in observable behavior. The behavior per se is not synonymous with the action: it is what happens when one acts, but to say what action is being performed, one has to make reference to what happens in the mind. For this reason Chrysippus objects to an earlier Stoic definition of walking as 'an extension of *pneuma* from the directive faculty to the feet.' For Chrysippus, walking can be defined without any mention of the feet at all; it is just 'the directive faculty itself,' i.e., a certain event in it.[43] The importance of this assertion is that it allows behaviors which are very similar from the standpoint of the observer to be analyzed differently in ethics. Similar sets of foot and leg movements, for instance, need not be counted as instances of the same action type if they do not express the same sort of assent. My dog does not ever walk in the way that I walk when I participate in a protest march. For similar reasons, the wise person's 'prudent walking' is evaluated differently from an ordinary person's walking, in that it represents a different sort of judgment.

It does not differ at all, however, in the way the feet move or in what the walker feels going on in his or her body.

Affective events

We can now consider more specifically how emotions and related affective phenomena fit into the Stoic account of mental functioning. The standard definition is of some help here. Emotions are defined by Zeno as 'excessive impulses,' that is, as action tendencies of a certain powerful kind. Since every impulse involves assenting to some impulsory impression, the definition implies that emotions, too, depend on our formulating and ratifying certain propositions about ourselves and our surroundings. The precise content of an emotion qua judgment will be the subject of chapter 2. But the definition also implies that an emotion is, like every impulse, a motion of the psyche toward some predicate. To understand emotions at the physical level, we need to identify as best we can what sort of movement this might be. If emotions are impulses, what are they impulses to do?

A useful starting point is again in the Stobaean summary, where we are given what seem to be standard definitions for the broad emotion types "distress" and "delight."

> Distress is a contraction of psyche which is disobedient to reason, and its cause is a fresh believing that some evil is present toward which it is appropriate to be contracted. Delight is an elevation of psyche which is disobedient to reason, and its cause is a fresh believing that some good is present toward which it is appropriate to be elevated.[44]

The phrases 'it is appropriate to be contracted' and 'it is appropriate to be elevated' correspond exactly to the description of the impulsory impression as spelled out earlier in the Stobaean account. Just as in impulse generally the psyche sees some predicate as appropriate and moves to fulfill it, so in the specific impulse called distress one sees 'being contracted' as appropriate and therefore experiences the type of movement called a *sustolē* or contraction. Likewise in delight one sees 'being elevated' as appropriate and therefore experiences the type of movement called an *eparsis* or elevation.[45] These movements differ from, say, raising a finger, in that they are movements 'of the psyche,' ones in which the main event is that the psyche itself is undergoing some change. That change, whatever it is, will also be sensed by the distressed or delighted person, through the continuous perception that *psuchē* has of its own movements.

Additional detail is provided by the physician-philosopher Galen, who claims to derive his knowledge directly from the writings of Chrysippus. In Galen's report of Stoic psychology we find mention of a whole list of psychic events which are distinguished from the judgments involved in emotion and yet regularly co-occur with them. Galen associates this discussion especially with the psychology of Zeno; his report makes it clear, however, that Chrysippus used the same terminology in his work.

> Zeno held that emotions are not the judgments themselves, but the contractions and pourings and elevations and lowerings of the psyche that follow upon the judgments.

> Zeno and many other Stoics do not consider the emotions to be the judgments of the psyche themselves, but rather the irrational contractions and lowerings and bitings and elevations and outpourings in relation to them.

> In some of the definitions that follow . . . he [Chrysippus] defines distress as a shrinking at what is thought to be a thing to shun, delight as an elevation at what is thought to be a choiceworthy. And . . . he also mentions contractions and outpourings.[46]

Of note in these passages is not only the expanded list of affective movements—'contractions,' '(out)pourings,' 'elevations,' 'lowerings,' 'bitings,' and 'shrinkings'—but also the fact that they are alterations specifically 'of the psyche.' Zeno's collective term for them is 'things which follow upon judgments,' where the verb "follow upon" (*epigignesthai*) might also be translated "supervene on." We will return to this term in a moment; meanwhile, we should consider the psychic movements themselves.

Some of the terms reported by Galen had been long established in Greek usage as ways of speaking about emotion: 'biting,' in particular, is a metaphor of long standing for the pain of grief, and the verbs meaning 'to be contracted' and 'to be elevated' are attested in connection with sorrow and pleasure respectively.[47] Whether we should also interpret these words literally, as descriptions of the physical movements of the psyche, is harder to say. It may be significant that with the exception of 'biting,' all of them are verbal nouns suggesting changes in size, shape, or location. In choosing them the Stoic founders may have meant to indicate that the *pneuma* in the heart region does move in these and similar ways. But the exact nature of the alteration is not particularly important at the level of theory, as long as it is agreed that there must be *some* physical change underlying each feeling.

In that vein it is of interest to note that all six of the movements mentioned here are associated with either delight or distress. Clearly there has been some effort to name many different movements, perhaps to correspond with many different reported feeling-tones. If anguish *feels* different from, say, worry, there should be a different physical alteration underlying it.

The above material from Galen should be compared carefully with the following sentence from Cicero's detailed report of Stoic emotion theory in Tusculan Disputation 4:

> Further, they say that it is not only the emotions which consist in the judgments and opinions which I have mentioned, but also the things brought about by emotions. For instance, distress brings about a kind of biting pain, fear a sort of withdrawing and fleeing of spirit, gladness an outpouring of hilarity, desire an unbridled reaching.[48]

Cicero's language corresponds closely to what Galen reports for Zeno and Chrysippus. As my translation indicates, his words 'biting' and 'out-pouring' are Latin equivalents for Greek terms attested by Galen. Also, his expression "things brought about by emotions" (*illa quae efficiuntur per-turbationibus*) is very close to the Greek phrase "things that follow upon judgments" (*ta epigignomena krisesi*), especially since he has just indicated that emotions consist in judgments. Earlier in the same paragraph Cicero also supplies Latin equivalents for the terms 'lower,' 'contract,' and 'elevate,' from the definitions of distress and delight.[49] His knowledge of this Stoic terminology, then, is as detailed as Galen's.

Where Cicero's report differs from Galen's is in supplying terms also for the psychic movements which occur in two other broad emotion types: 'a withdrawing and fleeing of spirit' as the effect of fear, and 'an unbridled reaching' as the effect of desire. 'Withdrawing' (*recessus*) and 'reaching' (*adpetentia*) correspond to the Greek terms *ekklisis* and *orexis*, words used in the definitions of those emotions in the Stobaean account. Cicero's handling of these terms is significant. It is clear from the sentence quoted that he understands there to be a characteristic movement (which might also be a feeling) for each of the four emotions listed and not only for distress and delight, as Galen implies. Clearly, too, he believes his source to have said that retraction and extension are, like contraction and elevation, movements primarily 'of the spirit,' though this does not preclude there being some overt pursuit or avoidance behavior at the same time.

If Cicero's understanding is correct, then the Stoics were giving a somewhat altered role to two terms which already had an established role in

Greek philosophy. Aristotle regularly uses *orexis* and *ekklisis* for pursuit and avoidance generally, as when the lion springs or the deer darts away. But Aristotle also tends to assume that all pursuit and avoidance is driven by desire or fear, an assumption the Stoic founders did not share.[50] What Cicero says about 'withdrawing' and 'reaching' suggests a differently structured account, one which brings out the etymological sense of those words in the way indicated by my translation.[51] On this account, *ekklisis* or 'withdrawing' is the alteration of the psyche that characterizes fear as distinct from calm avoidance. So for instance Agamemnon, when he fears the Trojan encampment, takes aversive action as any general might, but in his case the aversive action is also an instance of a psychic retraction which he feels in the pounding of his heart and which others may observe in his facial expression and cries of alarm. In the same way, cases of desire involve extending one's psyche toward the object one has in mind. Actions which might otherwise be routine take on a new urgency as one hastens forward toward one's objective—the prize to be claimed, the offender to be punished, the lost child to be embraced at last. Subjectively it is as though one's entire self were pressing forward and outward until that objective is met.

Since the psyche normally has some proprioceptive awareness of its own movements, it is expected that we will be able to feel movements such as 'contraction,' though we may not recognize that it is specifically a contraction that we are experiencing. Effects might be felt throughout the body but should be most noticeable in the chest region, given that the directive faculty is located there. In anger, especially, we are said to have an internal sensation of "something evaporating from the heart and blowing outward toward the hands and face."[52] Indeed, the widespread agreement that the chest is the primary locus of emotion was taken by the Stoics to be good evidence that the old assumption about chest localization of psychic function was correct. Chrysippus's use of examples from poetry and ordinary speech suggests that on this point he considered the reports of nonphilosophers to be authoritative to some extent. If large numbers of people were found who felt love, anger, and fear in their elbows rather than around their hearts, that would be an indication that the theory was in need of amendment.

It is not required, though, that we should be able to sense the precise nature of the changes that are taking place. Assuming that self-perception works in the way Hierocles describes, one would actually expect people's account of their inner experience to be somewhat inexact. For the directive faculty's perception of the psyche's own movements is an indirect kind of perception, mediated by the resistance of the nonpneumatic components of the body. While introspection may indeed be authoritative inasmuch as it indicates that some psychic event is going on and where, it need not be authoritative as to the mechanics that are involved.

Considered as descriptions of feelings, the Stoics' affective predicates are bound to seem odd, even bizarre, especially to us, who do not have full access to the linguistic habits of ancient Greeks. Perhaps not everyone would describe his or her sensation of grief as precisely a 'shrinking'; perhaps not even very many people would do so. If terms like 'shrinking' are intended only to account for psychic change at the theoretical level, then the oddness of the language might not matter; if they are supposed to capture something of the way emotions feel, though, then the linguistic strain is surely a disadvantage. It may be, though, that the strain is inevitable. For feelings differ from judgments in that they resist intentional description. When trying to find words for how an emotion feels, we inevitably do one of two things: either we drop down to the physiological level of description, as when, referring to our own physiology, we speak of "touching a nerve" or "a surge of adrenaline"; or we make use of metaphors: the lump in the throat, the knot in the stomach, and so on. In all such cases we mean that there is some internal change which is perceived by the person who has the emotion, but we don't insist that it be perceived under that same description. The Stoic language offers a way of referring to a variety of feeling-tones without circularity (a feeling "of grief") or feeble deixis ("you know, *that* feeling").

It is important to be clear about the relation between the feelings involved in emotion and the judgments which are also involved. That relation is well described by the collective term 'things which follow upon judgments.' 'Follow upon' (*epigignesthai*), sometimes translated 'result from' or 'supervene,' is a verb widely used in philosophical Greek to express relations of one-way entailment: to say that B 'follows upon' A is to say that A entails B without implying the converse. In speaking of 'the things which follow upon the judgments,' Zeno and Chrysippus are saying that the judgments involved in emotion are sufficient conditions for the corresponding psychophysical changes, but not that they are necessary conditions. In other words, they are saying that while a judgment of this sort is always accompanied by the corresponding feeling, instances of the relevant feeling type might also occur without one's having made that particular judgment.

The same position is implied more succinctly in the short-form definitions of pleasure as an 'irrational elevation,' fear as an 'irrational withdrawing,' and so forth. Not every affective movement is an irrational movement, for there are also such things as 'well-reasoned elevation,' 'well-reasoned withdrawing,' and 'well-reasoned reaching,' which are affective responses but not emotions.[53] In each case, the supervenient movement is, again, like the movement of the feet in the walking case: it is not definitive of the action, since there are multiple reasoning processes which may result in a movement of that type. Considered merely as changes in the shape of the mind material and as felt sensations, all instances of, for instance, 'elevation' must be very much alike; considered as judgments, they may be very different.[54]

A careful reading of the important source material in Galen gives us reason to doubt the further assertion of that author that there was a substantive difference between Zeno and Chrysippus on the nature of emotion events. According to Galen, Zeno identified the emotions with the supervenient psychophysical changes, but Chrysippus subsequently revised that view to make the emotions simply 'the judgments themselves.' Galen may have reached this conclusion from the existence of two sets of Stoic definitions: an older, probably Zenonian, set making desire an 'irrational reaching,' delight an 'irrational elevation,' and so forth; and a second set formulated by Chrysippus, in which the emotion is a judgment such as will always produce the relevant movement. But while there is certainly a difference of wording, I question whether Zeno and Chrysippus had any marked difference of view as to what happens when a person has an emotion. Both clearly hold that having an emotion involves both the psychophysical change and the judgment, and both describe the relation between the two in very much the same way. For Zeno, the change supervenes on the judgment and would not be an emotion if it did not supervene on a judgment of this sort (i.e., an irrational judgment). For Chrysippus, the change is reliably produced by the judgment, which would not be an emotion if it did not produce a movement of this sort. The chief difference between the two philosophers is in the exact application of the term 'emotion' within the sequence. In reformulating the definition, Chrysippus seeks to bring out more clearly what was already implied in Zeno's version: that it is the nature of the judgment that defines what sort of impulse has occurred.[55]

This last is the essential point. On the model suggested by both the Zenonian and the Chrysippan definitions, there is a distinction to be made between the emotions or *pathē* understood as judgments (i.e., strictly for their intentional content, which may be either true or false), and the feeling one gets from a certain emotion. In itself, the feeling merely registers the physical event that is what happens when one has the emotion. More-over, because the felt psychophysical event merely supervenes on the emo-tional judgment, rather than being itself the emotion, feelings which are phenomenologically similar will not necessarily represent the same kind of affective response. It will be possible to experience something that feels like delight, anger, or fear but that is not one of those emotions because it does not meet the relevant intentional criteria. Raw feeling, the most intractable element in emotion, can come apart from the beliefs that are responsible for it.

The material we have seen in this chapter offers on behalf of the early Sto-ics a tightly unified conception of what it is to be a human being. To be a living person in this conception is to be able to feel with every indrawn and exhaled breath the vital energy of the self and of the sustaining cosmos. It is to be in a dynamic balance with that cosmos, as heat within the chest meets with the coolness of air from without and tempers it, establishing a rhythm that plays itself out in the vibrant energy of the heartbeat and other life functions. The *pneuma* around the heart is the very center of the person. It supplies not only the energizing nutriment we now associ-ate with oxygen but also the complex structuring and identity-making ca-pacities of DNA, the tensile power of the muscles and ligaments, even the very hardness of our bones. Meanwhile it is that same vital *pneuma* which sustains the modifications that constitute belief, decision, and action. It is no accident that speech emerges from the chest: the thoughts expressed in speech actually reside there.[56] In moments of excitement, then, when we feel the chest tighten and the breathing destabilize, the heart pound, the rush of heat to the face or cold to the extremities, what we are feeling is an event taking place at the core of our being. It is not a side effect of something going on in the brain but an alteration in the mind itself.

At the same time, Stoic thought insists that this profound stirring of a person's very self will sometimes run contrary to the fullest expression of human potential. The affective response is not always a natural response; in fact, as ordinarily experienced it is not at all what our nature is designed to do. To see why the founders held this position, we need now to turn our attention more directly to the role of judgment in emotion.

2

The Pathetic Syllogism

It has been my contention that in early Stoic thought, having an emotion is not quite the same as having a feeling. The feeling is our subjective awareness of a physical change in the psychic material; it is something that happens when one has an emotion, but the possibility is left open that it may also occur at other times and for other reasons. For instance, the uplifted feeling that we associate with delight or gladness need not be uniquely linked to that emotion. There may be other kinds of affective response which produce that same feeling but which are not instances of gladness.

This is a point that proves to be crucially important when we seek to understand the norm laid down in Stoic ethics for the optimization of our affective experience. For among the best-attested and most generally known claims of this ethical system is that the genuinely wise person exhibits *apatheia* or impassivity; that is, the absence of the *pathē*. Realizing the fullest of human potential means, for Stoics, not only that one becomes able to control or channel the emotions but that one actually ceases to experience emotions as we know them. The distinction between emotions and feelings therefore serves to open up an interpretive space around a central dictum of Stoic ethics. If the psychic sensations we experience in emotion are not simply identical with the *pathē*, then the norm of *apatheia* does not have to be cashed out as an injunction against every human feeling. One might be impassive in the Stoic sense and still remain subject to other categories of affective experience.

Indeed there is reason to doubt, prima facie, whether an objection to psychic feelings in themselves could be made consistent with Stoic naturalism. The Stoics were teleological thinkers. For them, the very fact that a significant structural or behavioral feature is regularly found in some species indicates that that feature is provided by nature for some good reason. The capacity to undergo a wide range of feelings is just such a regular feature, "hard-wired," as we would say, into the human psyche. Thus to deny any role for feeling in the life of the wise would be to claim that human beings are endowed by nature with psychic equipment for which we have no legitimate use.[1] As the endowment of nature plays a role in Stoicism analogous to that played by the evolutionary endowment in our own science, this would be equivalent to saying in a modern context that a creature has evolved capacities which do not promote its effective functioning in its environment. People would have something like a foot in the middle of their foreheads.

At least for some feelings there is evidence of exactly the opposite position. In book 3 of Cicero's *On Ends,* for instance, we are told that shrinking from pain is natural, and so is the love of parents for their children.[2] Most explicit and informative, though, is a passage from Cicero's redaction of Chrysippan emotion theory in the fourth Tusculan Disputation. Cicero is outlining Chrysippus's position on the psychological foundations of affective response. Significantly placed very near the beginning of this segment of his work is a strong statement of the role of nature in human affectivity. The occurrence of a 'reaching' feeling—the same feeling we experience in the emotion of desire—is here guaranteed an origin in nature:

> By nature, all people pursue those things which they think to be good and avoid their opposites. Therefore, as soon as a person receives an impression of some thing which he thinks is good, nature itself urges him to reach out after it.[3]

Similarly, in the continuation of the passage, there is said to be a natural origin for the movements of 'elevation' and 'withdrawing' and a way to experience these 'in accordance with reason.' For at least three important event types, then, the capacity to respond affectively to what one perceives as good or evil is not in itself problematic. It is a capacity that can be exercised improperly, and it is when we do so that we experience the 'irrational' reachings, elevations, and retractions that we recognize as desire, delight, and fear. But there is also a proper way to exercise that same capacity.

In order to understand the Stoic norm we need therefore to turn away from the supervenient psychic movements and address our attention directly to the content of emotions as judgments. For emotions have content: in their character as assents, they make certain claims about the world, although those claims are rarely if ever articulated in our minds in the actual moment of response. To grasp what emotions are for Stoics, we need to look closely at those implicit claims. We need to see how emotional reasoning works: what are its premises, its conclusions, its internal logic. Most of all, we need to compare the content implied in ordinary emotions with the sort of reasoning that might take place in a 'natural' or 'well-reasoned' version of affective response. Only then will we begin to be able to assess which portions of the bewilderingly complex affective domain fall under Stoic censure and which do not.

The view that cognitive elements—beliefs and judgments—play an essential role in the generation of emotions has been well established in modern philosophy of mind by the arguments of, especially, R.C. Solomon and Richard Lazarus.[4] These contemporary discussions focus most often on the status within emotion of evaluative beliefs or, more specifically, appraisals or construals. At minimum, they hold that part of what it is to have an emotion is to assess some object as being either beneficial or harmful for oneself. Fear, for instance, is held to be in its very essence an assessment of some thing or event as posing a significant danger of harm to oneself. The Stoics' interest in propositional content serves as an obvious point of contact with such views and has sometimes been influential in their formation. Contemporary in feel, also, is the distinction made in Chrysippan theory between *occurrent* and *dispositional* elements in emotional judgments; that is, between point-in-time events and relatively stable long-term commitments. However, the attested Stoic position is markedly different from any modern theory in the specific elements that it identifies as essential and in the way these are used to individuate emotion types by genus and species. A major enterprise of this chapter is to tease apart these dispositional and occurrent cognitive components and show how they fit together syllogistically to yield the occurrent judgments that are essential to affective response.

By far the most distinctive feature of the Stoic position, however, is its insistence that psychological claims about how emotions are generated must be integrated with other, prescriptive or normative claims as to the kinds of objects that can legitimately be valued. Armed with these ethical premises, the Stoics were prepared to take a definite position about the propriety or impropriety of the sorts of judgments that are characteristic of affective response. They were prepared to say that emotions are rational in that they make use of our mind's capacity to operate on the basis of reasons, and yet not rational in the sense of that word which implies that one's reasons are correct. The classification of affective responses proceeds accordingly: an ideal or 'eupathic' class for responses generated in a properly rational way, and an ordinary class for the imperfectly reasoned responses with which all of us are familiar.

In order to make sense of these distinctions, I will need in the course of this chapter to take up some points in Stoic ethics, in particular some points concerning the truth conditions for evaluations of various kinds of objects. First, though, let's consider how appraisals function in some broad categories of emotional response.

Emotions and ascriptions of value

The fact that emotions are defined as certain kinds of impulses tells us already that they must have thought-content. We saw in chapter 1 that impulses or *hormai* are defined in Stoic psychology as a subset of assents: to act is to endorse a certain kind of proposition, namely, the proposition that some predicate is appropriate to oneself at that moment. Our question is about the relation of the judgments involved in emotion to the particular type of judgment that I will call a *simple ascription of value;* that is, a judgment to the effect that 'X is good' or 'X is bad,' where X is an object type such as 'money' or (more properly) 'having money.'[5] There is no question that such judgments figure prominently in the Stoic account, but what exactly is their role in the emotion event?

For instance, would it be right to say that an emotion in Stoicism simply *is* a simple ascription of value? Should one say that what happens when a person has an emotion is fully captured by stating that he or she judges some external object to be either good or evil? Certainly this is not a position that matches our immediate intuitions about what an emotion could be. Anger, fear, desire, and grief surely do not seem very much like deciding that something is valuable; they seem like responses to events in our lives. Getting upset because you have just lost a fortune on the market clearly has something to do with a belief that money is important, but it is not plausible to say that you start believing money is important right in the very moment when you find you have lost the money. *That* belief is one you already had: what is new is just the realization that your particular circumstances have changed.

Besides, a strict identification of emotions with simple ascriptions of value would require us to abandon the widely attested Stoic definition that makes emotions a type of impulse or *hormē*. We know from texts presented in chapter 1 what kind of content an impulsory impression needs to have: it requires a predicate of which the agent can become the subject, an appropriateness term, and a time. A simple ascription of value includes none of these. Judgments with only the content 'X is good' would not satisfy the Stoic requirements for impulses, regardless of whether X is a general term ("having money") or a particular instance ("having *this* sum of money"). They might be necessary for the emotion to occur, but they could not be sufficient for it.

All the same, there is some reason to believe that Stoics did identify emotions with judgments of value. The account of Stoic ethics by Diogenes Laertius seems to say exactly that.

> They [the Stoics] think that the *pathē* are judgments, as Chrysippus says in his work *On Emotions*. For [he says that] fondness for money is a supposition that money is a fine thing, and similarly with drunkenness, stubbornness, and so forth.[6]

This report needs to be taken seriously, for Diogenes Laertius is widely (and correctly) regarded as a reliable witness, and the treatise he cites, Chrysippus's *On Emotions*, was the most influential Stoic work on the subject. However, there is an alternative explanation available for what Diogenes says here. We know from other fragments of this same treatise that Chrysippus sometimes used the word *pathē* to refer to a different, though related, item in Stoic moral psychology, namely, to the condition called a *nosēma* (sickness) or *arrōstēma* (infirmity).[7] Further, the usual definition of a *nosēma* is as a deeply held belief in the choiceworthiness of certain objects, and standard examples of it include 'fondness for money' and 'fondness for wine.' I therefore take the view (which has also been put forward by Tad Brennan) that the original passage in Chrysippus was never intended as a definition of emotion.[8] Diogenes Laertius used a good source but misunderstood what it was telling him. So this particular piece of evidence can safely be set aside for now. We will return to it in chapter 6, which treats the *nosēma* along with other dispositional traits of character.

Meanwhile there are other authoritative texts which state the judgment content of emotions rather differently. In these, what is said is not that an object is good or evil but that an object *already* recognized as good or evil is either present or near at hand. Galen, for instance, quotes Chrysippus as saying that the belief one has in distress is a belief 'that an evil is present to oneself' or, more briefly, a belief 'of the presence of evil.'[9] Cicero, too, gives the content in this form, together with corresponding formulations for desire, fear, and delight: fear, for instance, is or is caused by the belief "that some serious evil is impending."[10] What one decides is true in these formulations is not, for instance, *that a present thing is evil* but rather *that an evil thing is present*. The new or occurrent supposition, the one made in the moment of responding emotionally, is only that something either has just taken place (present object) or is likely to take place in the immediate future (object in prospect). The evaluative component comes in not because one decides, right then and there, that something is good or bad but because the occurrent supposition engages beliefs that are already in place as to the goodness or badness of certain kinds of objects. The latter are dispositional.

In order to link the occurrent, nonevaluative component with the dispositional, evaluative component, all that is required is that the agent recognize a simple type-token relation. Dispositional beliefs are typically about object types, as that all instances of personal bodily harm or financial loss are evils; occurrent judgments (of the kind we are concerned with here) are about tokens—*this* being-mugged or *this* winning-the-game. In order to make a judgment of the form attributed here to Chrysippus, one needs to recognize something in one's current situation as falling under some general type to which an evaluation has previously been assigned. This is part of the usual business of thinking: to process an impression at all, one has to arrange the details of occurrent experience under meaningful headings. It is not very different from what we do when we draw upon our stock of concepts to say, of some sense-impression, "This is a horse" or "This is a dog"; only it is at the next level of cognitive processing. I identify some new impression as a case of, say, a ball going into a glove, and I recognize it as coming under the heading of winning a game. I would not react emotionally, however, if I did not also believe that winning is a good thing for me. If I thought winning didn't matter, there would be no reason why this particular impression should get me excited. So my dispositional evaluative belief about the object type is a necessary condition for affective response in connection with objects of that type.

The formulation as we have it in this group of texts is therefore best analyzed as follows, using for convenience the parameters 'evil' and 'in prospect':

Objects of type T are evil.
Object O belongs to type T.
Object O is in prospect.

An evil is in prospect.

More briefly, one might assent to something like 'Object O, being of type T which is a bad type of thing to happen, is now in prospect.' A judgment of this kind is a necessary condition for the genus-emotion fear. One need not express such a belief, even to oneself, in order to be afraid; nonetheless a person who is frightened must have accepted that it is true.

Michael Frede offers a useful example of the way prior beliefs can convert a simple judgment of fact into an emotional response. Suppose you and I both happen to notice that Socrates is looking paler than usual today. Suppose, further, that you, having some medical knowledge and being a close friend of Socrates, take this paleness as an indication of fatal illness and become terribly anxious about it, while I note the change with perfect equanimity. It seems fair to say that the occurrent impression experienced by each of us has exactly the same content; it is just that 'Socrates looks pale.' The difference in our reactions is best explained by dispositional beliefs each of us brings to the occasion.[11] You, no doubt, believe already that (1) a paleness of this sort is a sure indication that Socrates' death is impending, and (2) Socrates' death is a grave misfortune for you. I, on the other hand, might lack one or both of these components. Perhaps I have believed all along that Socrates' death would be a matter of no importance or even a good thing for me, or perhaps I too regard it as an evil but see his paleness not as an indication of impending collapse but as a sign that he is thriving philosophically. In the one case, I have a different view about the value of the relevant object type ('signs of Socrates' death'); in the other, I accept the evaluation but do not recognize the occurrent impression as falling under that type. Without the necessary cognitive background, my occurrent judgment that he is pale fails to produce any anxiety.

Appropriateness

Something important is still missing. As long as the content of emotional judgments is specified only in terms of objects and their evaluation, it is far from clear how these judgments will be describable as impulses. For we know what the propositional content of an impulse ought to look like. We have already met the formula given in Stobaeus for the sort of impression which sets an impulse in motion: it is "nothing other than an impulsory impression of something's being immediately appropriate."[12] Formulations like 'a good is now present' make no mention of anything's being thought of as appropriate, nor do they indicate what particular action might be suggested by the impression. However, there are good sources which do spell out these logically necessary elements of emotional judgments.

The account which is most careful in terminology is the one in Stobaeus, which supplies a causal history of emotion events at the level of genus. A portion of the relevant passage was quoted in chapter 1 for its use of the affective predicates 'contract' and 'elevate.' Here is the same passage in full:

> Desire is a reaching which is disobedient to reason, and its cause is believing that a good is in prospect in the presence of which we will flourish, the belief itself including a disorderly and <fresh> motive element <as to that being genuinely a thing to reach for>.
>
> Fear is a withdrawing which is disobedient to reason, and its cause is believing that an evil is in prospect, the belief itself including a disorderly and fresh motive element as to that being genuinely a thing to avoid.
>
> Distress is a contraction of psyche which is disobedient to reason, and its cause is a fresh believing that some evil is present toward which it is appropriate to <be contracted.
>
> Delight is an elevation of psyche which is disobedient to reason, and its cause is a fresh believing that some good is present toward which it is appropriate to> be elevated.[13]

Both the third and the fourth genus make use of the expression 'is appropriate' (kathēkei), the exact expression we find in the Stobaean account of impulsory impressions. In the other two genera, kathēkei is replaced by a verbal adjective of similar force: orekton, 'to reach for,' means 'such as it is appropriate to reach for,' and pheukton, 'to avoid,' means 'such as it is appropriate to avoid.'[14] In all four cases, then, the person experiencing emotion is credited with a belief that a predicate like 'avoiding' or 'being elevated' is the appropriate thing to do under the circumstances. As we have seen, this is exactly the content one would expect to find in the sort of impression which, if endorsed, produces an impulse. Here, though, the predicate to which the action operator is attached is affective in nature. It may be either an internal change in the psyche like 'elevation' or 'contraction' or some observable action like striking someone or storming out of a room.

The role of appropriateness beliefs is stressed also by Cicero, when he treats the causes of distress in book 3 of the *Tusculan Disputations*. As mentioned above, distress is described in this work as "a belief that some serious evil is present." But there is also a second component:

> Fear is a belief that some serious evil is impending, distress a belief that a serious evil is present. Specifically, it is a fresh belief, and the evil is of such a nature that it seems right to be pained by it—seems so, at least, to the person who is suffering and who believes that it is appropriate for him to suffer.[15]

As his discussion proceeds, Cicero becomes even more explicit. What causes a person to be distressed at some event, he says, is not a single belief but a combination of two beliefs:

> But when our belief in the seriousness of our misfortune is combined with the further belief that it is right, and an appropriate and proper thing, to be upset by what has happened, then, and not before, there comes about that deep emotion which is distress.[16]

The claim is that given a suitable occurrent trigger, the combination of an evaluation with an appropriateness belief is sufficient for distress to occur, and moreover that each of those two components is necessary. Elimination of either would prevent the emotion from occurring.

This two-component analysis is reiterated with some frequency in Cicero's treatise, not only for distress but for other emotions as well. Some passages associate it especially with the name of Chrysippus, making it the basis of a characteristically Chrysippan method of consolation.[17] Considering the importance of Chrysippus to Cicero's account generally, we are safe in assuming the point was stressed by him as well. However, Chrysippus may not have been responsible for the heavily emphatic way Cicero states the appropriateness component when he says, "it is right, and an appropriate and proper thing" (*oportere, rectum esse, ad officium pertinere*). The redundancy is not paralleled in any of our other sources, and could be misleading if one took it to imply that grief occurs only when a person feels morally obliged to grieve. The Stoics' term *kathēkei*, when used in connection with impulsory impressions, does not have to convey any strong notion of duty or obligation. A reading more consistent with their usage finds in it only a loose notion of what is fitting under the circumstances—what is "called for," as we might say.[18] That is, one becomes distressed just when one comes to believe that distress is the response called for by one's present situation.

Now, the appropriateness component of emotional judgments is hardly unrelated to the evaluative beliefs considered above. Indeed, one way to think of that component is as registering the motivational aspect of evaluation. If my belief "this is a thing toward which it is appropriate to be elevated" were unrelated to my belief "this is a good thing," then considerations of value would not need to enter into my emotive reasoning at all. Merely recognizing the occurrent object as belonging to some class of objects which, when present, make elevation appropriate would be sufficient to trigger the affective response. But the Stoics' genus definitions clearly do require judgments of value. In order to spell out the relation between evaluation and appropriateness in the way Cicero assumes is correct, what one needs to specify for the appropriateness component is a conditional sentence like "If a good is present, it is appropriate for me to elevate my psyche." This is in accordance with familiar and obvious assumptions about the connection between goodness and choiceworthiness. Analogous specifications can be given for appropriateness beliefs about evils and about objects that are in prospect rather than present.

If we assume this form for the appropriateness component, it is easy to see how the several components mentioned in the standard genus definitions fit together to yield the expected impulsory impression. For a positive affect toward a present object one would have to reason internally:

1. Objects of type T are goods.
2. If a good is present, it is appropriate for me to elevate my psyche.
3. Object O, being of type T, is now present.
   It is now appropriate for me to elevate my psyche.

The premises labeled 1 and 2 are dispositional beliefs; only 3 is occurrent. And 3, while it does involve conceptualizing one's situation in a particular way, is likely to be relatively uncontroversial; it can be considered a simple matter of fact, like 'Socrates is pale.' Hence the language of causation is assigned not to the occurrent premise 3 but to the conjunct of premises 1 and 2. In times of strong feeling we do sometimes assume that the occurrent trigger has caused the emotion, saying for instance that Agamemnon is frightened *because* the Trojan camp is near. The Stoic position, though, is that Agamemnon's fear is caused by his belief that defeat is a bad thing, combined with a belief that one ought to have certain feelings when a bad thing is impending. The nearness of the camp is certainly part of the picture, but it is not the real cause. Only by identifying the two dispositional components can one explain how it is that the occurrent trigger produces this particular feeling rather than some other.

To be sure, no text spells out the pathetic syllogism in quite the form I have given here. But the syllogistic formulation merely makes explicit what is stated more succinctly in sources already mentioned. For the same reasoning can be laid out in the form of a single complex proposition, assent to which implies assent to the conclusion as stated above. Such a complex proposition might run roughly as follows:

> Object O—
> > which is of type T
> > > which is a good object-type
> > > > and thus, if an instance is present, makes elevation appropriate,
> > > > > —is now present.

Suitably varied for different situations and types of feeling, this is just what we have in the Stobaean and Ciceronian accounts.

How plausible is it that human beings regularly carry around with them a set of beliefs in the form of premise 2? No doubt very few of us ever articulate such beliefs to ourselves; on reflection, though, it seems likely enough that we are committed to them. An example is the criticism leveled against Demosthenes for participating in a sacrifice, typically a festive occasion, only six days after his daughter's death. What was in Demosthenes' mind is hard to say, but the fact that his opponent was able to make capital out of such an accusation shows clearly what a Greek audience could be expected to believe about the appropriateness of grief. In the same vein, Cicero observes that persons who have been bereaved will sometimes accuse themselves of misconduct if they experience any ordinary or cheerful feelings during the time of mourning. They also transmit the same attitudes to their children, disciplining them when they behave lightheartedly at funerals or other serious occasions.[19]

An analogous point could be made about the reaction many people have to emotionless figures like Mr. Spock of *Star Trek* or the cartoon-Stoic Cato of Lucan's *Civil War.* One feels that Cato, when he remarries Portia for her protection in time of war, *should* experience both love and sorrow; his nobility of purpose is not enough. When this Lucanian Cato proceeds to act as he does, in unruffled calm, I for one feel that something is missing which is of real moral significance. Words like "unnatural" and "inhuman" come to mind.[20] As an intuition about human nature, this reaction to the supposedly unfeeling sage is well worth noting. Not only does it tend to confirm a crucial part of Chrysippus's analysis, but it also suggests that beliefs concerning the appropriateness of affective response may be especially important to our notions of what it is to be a human being.

All the same, the validity of premise 2 does not go unchallenged. In a later part of this book we will consider evidence that one early Stoic, Chrysippus himself in fact, sometimes urged philosophical advisors to argue against the appropriateness premise as a therapeutic measure, to help people overcome an emotion in progress.[21] In view of some larger presuppositions of Stoic thought I question whether Chrysippus can have rejected premise 2 on his own account, at least as a general principle; his own preference for consistency should, I think, have prevented this. But that rather delicate issue does not need to occupy our attention just yet. For the core of Stoic thought on human affectivity was not in objections to premise 2 but in a challenging set of reflections on the nature of value in human life and on the kinds of evaluation humans regularly perform—in essence, on the meaning and status of premise 1. This is the original and indispensable version of the Stoics' position: if we are to follow their arguments further, we need to see what it was and how it was supported.

Evaluations and their objects

I begin this portion of the investigation by introducing, in an informal and provisional way, two distinctions that are fundamental to Stoic ethics. The first of these concerns the sorts of attitudes people take when they assign a positive or negative value to some object. It may be taken as a given that action, if it is really action and not just random movement of the limbs, presupposes evaluation. We could not engage in purposive behavior at all if we did not prefer some objects over others. It need not be assumed, however, that all our actions presume the same level of commitment to that evaluation. A person may value things, and accordingly pursue them, in the belief that those things are good—that is, that they are inherently beneficial, 'genuinely a thing to reach for,' the sort of thing anyone might want and that anyone would be better off having. We might describe them as ends in themselves or as somehow constitutive of our happiness. Conversely, in the negative case, one might disvalue and accordingly avoid something in the belief that it is intrinsically bad, 'genuinely a thing to avoid,' something to be prevented at all costs. Let us borrow a term from Terence Irwin and refer to this powerful sort of evaluation as an 'uncompromising' evaluation. It will be noted that on Stoic theory the emotions, properly so called, regularly depend on one's having assigned an uncompromising evaluation to some object.[22]

But many of our actions are performed without that kind of absolute commitment. We often evaluate things in a more restricted way, not regarding them as *inherently* beneficial or harmful but only as beneficial or harmful in this moment (but not at some other time), to this extent (but not in any amount), for ourselves (but not for people generally). That is, we think of these things not as somehow good or bad in themselves but only as advantageous or qualifiedly good, disadvantageous or qualifiedly bad. This is not to say that the pursuit of them must be lackadaisical. It may be energetic enough and yet imply nothing more in the way of evaluation than that this object is suited or not suited to our nature and needs in some limited set of circumstances. For the moment, I will refer to these as 'restricted' evaluations.

In addition to this difference in ways of evaluating, there is also a distinction to be made concerning the sorts of objects that become candidates for evaluation. An 'object,' in the sense intended here, is really a state of affairs: when we speak of pursuing food or a lover, what we mean is really "having food to eat" or "that my lover is near."[23] As such an object may have a cause, and the two broad categories that are of importance for Stoic ethics are distinguished in terms of their causation. Suppose I am in a meeting. What I say in the meeting depends on me, on my own character, motives, and judgments; things said by others do not depend on me, and neither do the temperature in the room, the quality of the furniture, or the likelihood of my catching cold from the person next to me. When I review the meeting later on, I am likely to evaluate my own role quite separately from those elements that were external to my agency. So also, in general, my own actions, states, and characteristics constitute a different class of objects from those determined by external factors such as my economic status, my social standing, my health, and the actions of my acquaintances. For while these latter may be influenced by my actions, that influence is very limited; the causes of them ultimately do not rest with me. For the moment, let us follow the older tradition of Greek ethics and call all such things 'external' objects, meaning not that they are external to one's physical boundaries but that they are external to one's sphere of control. Objects determined by oneself are designated by Plato and Aristotle as goods (or evils) 'of the psyche'; for our purposes, though, it will be less confusing to give them a term more clearly opposed to 'externals.' I will call them 'integral' objects.

Many integral objects, it should be noted, depend upon external objects for their realization. That someone else's property is in view is an external object, but only when such is the case can one either steal or refrain from stealing. An exercise of generosity involves having something to share; speaking one's mind requires having the use of one's vocal organs. To make matters clearer, one might prefer to speak of integrals as ways of handling externals or as dispositions to use externals in one way rather than another. The Stoic Aristo used the analogy of masks in the performance of drama. The mask might be of Agamemnon, a wealthy king, or Thersites, a lowly foot soldier, but we do not consider this when judging the actor; rather, we consider whether the performance was in accordance with the assigned part.[24] Stoic texts sometimes make use of adverbial formulations. Seneca speaks of the difference between holding an ambassadorship at all and holding it honorably, Diogenes Laertius of the difference between using externals at all and using them well or badly.[25] The adverb in each case expresses that aspect of the action which depends solely on the character of the agent.

The Stoic ethical stance

Now the chief insight of Stoic axiology could very well be expressed this way: that in a rational being, external objects never merit uncompromising evaluation but integral objects always do. Of course the ancient sources do not use the provisional terminology I have developed here. They speak most often of integral objects in terms of 'virtue' and 'vice' and of uncompromising evaluation in terms of what is seen as genuinely good or evil.[26] So the claim often appears in the form "virtue is the only good, vice the only evil." More precise treatments make it clear that the class of genuine goods and evils includes not only characteristics of persons but also any impulse that counts as an exercise of virtue or vice. The account in Stobaeus, for instance, lists 'prudent walking' as a good; analogously, a courageous utterance could count as a good object and a dishonest business dealing as an evil.[27]

Alternatively, one could say the same thing simply by referring to what I have called external objects with the Stoic term 'indifferents.' To call such objects 'indifferents' is not to say that one has to be indifferent to them; indeed, one might pursue them strenuously on the basis of a restricted evaluation, in what Stoics call 'selection' or 'disselection.'[28] But these are objects which do not in themselves make one's life different, turning a good life into a bad life or vice versa. What matters about them is only how they are used, the adverbial aspect, as it were, of our engagement with them. Virtues and faults must have something to work with if they are to be exercised. Fighting courageously in battle requires a battle to fight in; holding an ambassadorship honorably does not happen without the ambassadorship; acquiring money honestly means there was money to acquire. But in each case the elements of those activities that are external to the agent's control are not integral to the evaluation. If we think the fighting or the acquisition is good in itself, we are making a mistake.

One way of justifying this position on value comes from arguments about what is needed for a thing to be counted as intrinsically beneficial. An argument reported by Diogenes Laertius has clear Platonic antecedents, although it also gives a nod to Stoic physics by drawing an analogy with heat conceived as an elemental substance:

> Just as the proper characteristic of heat is heating and not cooling, so also that of the good is benefiting and not harming. But wealth and health are not any more beneficial than they are harmful; therefore wealth and health are not the good.[29]

In general, the 'proper characteristic' (*idion*) of a qualified thing is that which it must do if it has that property at all. If a thing is genuinely good, the reasoning goes, it must benefit us every time, not only on some occasions. So anything which harms us at all, even very infrequently, is not good in the requisite sense. Wealth, comfort, power, reputation, and other objects external to our control may be beneficial (in the ordinary sense) on some occasions, but there will always be cases in which each of these things turns out to be harmful. Not even health is beneficial all the time. If a brutal dictator is seeking to conscript you to become part of a death squad, then it is preferable *not* to be physically fit. (Seneca, who had some experience of dictators, recommends suicide in such instances.) For this reason, the Stoics argue, neither health nor wealth nor any other external object is truly beneficial at all, and neither are their opposites harmful. Genuine value does not come and go with the occasion.

Deeper motivations for the Stoic position lie within the structure of their own ethical system. Goodness in Stoic thought is essentially a notion of rightness or fit. Just as in mathematics the solution to a problem is right when it is in accordance with the system of thought which is mathematics as a whole, so in Stoic ethics a circumstance or event is good when it participates in some logically coherent system. For most things in the universe, the relevant larger system is just the universe itself, for the world as a whole operates according to underlying principles of regularity which admit of no exceptions, rather as we speak of the "laws of science." But the mind of an adult human, while it certainly participates in the larger world order, also has a frame of reference which is entirely its own. Because I am a rational being, capable of stating my beliefs and the reasons for what I do, there subsists right now, in relation to my mental contents, a large number of propositions or, as the Stoics term them, *axiōmata.* These can be interrelated in various ways: they may all be linked into a single coherent system, or (more likely) there may be some amount of internal contradiction. Thus my beliefs, actions, and affective responses are all capable of being evaluated not only in relation to universal reason but also in relation to my own harmonious or inharmonious system of belief. Such things belong to my own frame of reference; external objects or 'indifferents' do not.

The intellectual characteristics of humans thus serve to define what is good for the individual human being. Though we are born with the same allegiance to bodily needs as other animals have, we begin as we mature to develop the ability to think logically and to refer to our sense of what is logical when we act and when we form new beliefs.[30] This capacity for inference enables a more systematic understanding of the world and of ourselves, and this new understanding eventually wins our allegiance. We come to think of our own beliefs and actions in relation to one another, to the coherent pattern of belief that is developing in each of us, though rarely perfected in anyone. In theory it should be possible for a human to bring all of his or her beliefs into line with one another, achieving a full and consistent understanding of self and surroundings. If this should come about—and Stoic moralists maintain, for theoretical reasons, that it is not unheard of—then there would be in that person a harmonious order which resembles that of the universe or of Zeus. Such a state, variously called knowledge, wisdom, or virtue, is good for that human being in exactly the same way as the divinely ordained universe is good in itself; actions and feelings that belong to it are good by participation. Any epistemic condition which falls short of it is necessarily flawed, out of harmony with itself, and subject to error. This, the usual condition of ordinary people, is the condition of fault or 'vice'; actions and feelings that belong to it are bad in that they participate in an epistemic condition which is faulty overall.

It may seem an obvious objection that on this view, ordinary human beings are constantly confronted with evil in our own failings of reason and character and only rarely attain to the good, if indeed we ever do. But Stoic moralists do not appear to be troubled by this implication. Rather, they emphasize the richness of possibility that rationality confers on human life. A nonrational animal does not have its own good; neither does a plant or a rock; these only participate in the good of the natural order as a whole. Rational beings, though, have the opportunity to attain a good of their own in the perfection of their reason even as they continue to participate in the goodness of the cosmos. Alongside the dissatisfaction with our actual moral condition goes an extraordinary optimism about what we might achieve. The perfected human would resemble Zeus in goodness, though not in comprehensiveness; he or she would be practically a lesser divinity. It is only in comparison with this that our actual condition counts as evil for us.

Inconcinnity and fault is where we are; knowledge and virtue is where we might be. It would be missing the point of Stoic axiology, though, if we thought of virtue merely contrafactually, as something we could achieve if we were different. Features that are posited in the normative human develop naturally out of features that all unimpaired human beings exhibit. Courage, intelligence, fairness, and self-control are possibilities inherent in our rational nature, even if we in our current condition do not properly exemplify them. Becoming like the sage would be becoming more human, not less; it would be recognizable as human maturation.

Eupathic responses

For this very reason we should expect also that the person of perfect understanding will be capable of every feeling it is in human nature to have. And in fact we do find references in Stoic sources to a class of affects which belong specifically to the normative human. The collective term *eupatheiai*, 'good emotions' or 'proper feelings,' is attested from an early date and was probably the term used in the early treatises.[31] Cicero, rather surprisingly, offers the Latin term *constantiae* or 'consistencies.'[32] This may be a rendering of alternative Greek terminology which is now lost, or it may be creative translation: 'consistency' is one way to refer to the logically coherent state of mind which disposes one to experience these affects rather than ordinary emotions. To avoid confusion, I will retain the Greek term and speak of *eupatheiai* or eupathic responses. These responses are to ordinary emotions what the Stoic sage is to the ordinary person: they are the corrected version, the endpoint of development. We can think of them as normative affect.

As a normative response can hardly be dependent on any false belief, the evaluations that give rise to *eupatheiai* will necessarily be true. The objects at which they are directed must therefore be such objects as the person of perfect understanding can consider to be goods or evils. They may be bound up with externals in that actions and decisions have to be about something, but the external aspects of action would not be the real objects of the feeling. The real objects must be those integral goods and evils which are, as Seneca says, "real and the mind's own."[33] For instance, a wise person who meets with an opportunity to perform some generous or courageous action might feel a kind of yearning toward that action; conversely, she may be expected to experience a horrified aversion from anything shameful or wrong.

Phenomenologically the *eupatheiai* should resemble our familiar sensations of desire, anger, or fear, for at the psychophysical level of description they are instances of the same felt psychic movements. The *eupatheia* called 'wish,' for instance, is a 'well-reasoned reaching.' Generated by the same psychological mechanism as the emotions we know, they should have the same motive power and the same corporeal manifestations. If they differ at all at the level of feeling, it should be in that they are without any sense of conflict or contradiction. The reasoning processes of the normative mind work in a fully harmonious manner, with every judgment that is formed being logically consistent with the entirety of the belief-set. The *pathē*, by contrast, typically involve some discordance between the evaluations they presuppose and the agent's own background assumptions about what genuine goods ought to be like. If I may borrow a cant term which is particularly apposite to Stoic thought, the *pathē* are marked by "cognitive dissonance." Thus Cicero describes normative affect as being "quiet and consistent," while the feelings involved in desire, delight, and fear are said to be "too vigorous," "hollow," and even "swooning."[34] What Cicero does not say is that eupathic responses are less intense than ordinary emotions in the sense of being flat or unable to generate vigorous action. There is no reason we should believe this about the *eupatheiai*. They are corrected versions of human feelings, not diminished versions. We should think of them as being like the easy movements of a powerful athlete, forceful but without strain.

Preeminent among eupathic responses is the one called *chara* or joy. Joy is 'well-reasoned elevation,' corresponding on a feeling level to the happy excitement the ordinary person experiences on winning a raffle or leaving on vacation.[35] But joy differs from those feelings in being directed at genuine goods: a generous action, for instance, would be an occasion for joy, and the proper object of the feeling would be the generosity itself, as exercised on that occasion. Hence the person of perfect understanding, whose every action is an exercise of virtue, has reason to be joyful at every moment of the day. And this is a condition to which anyone may aspire. Seneca writes,

> Believe me, true joy is a serious matter. Do you think that it is with a re-laxed and cheerful countenance that one despises death, opens his home to poverty, reins in pleasure, and rehearses the endurance of pain? One who is pondering such things is experiencing a great joy, but hardly a soft or seduc-tive one. This is the joy I want you to possess: you will never run out of it, once you learn where it is to be found. . . . Cast aside those things that glit-ter on the outside, those things that are promised you by another or from another, and trample them underfoot. Look to your real good and rejoice in what is yours. What is it that is yours? Yourself; the best part of you.[36]

Seneca is writing as one ordinary, flawed human being to another: like other Stoic moralists, he does not claim to have perfect understanding on his own account, and he certainly does not assume that his addressee Lu-cilius will have achieved any such thing. We need to be careful, then, to refrain from reading his exhortation to joy as implying that joy is fully accessible to Lucilius in his current intellectual and ethical state. The 'real good' in which Lucilius must learn to rejoice is not his current self, as Michel Foucault's treatment of this letter could easily be taken to imply.[37] Rather, it is a good that is always present to one who has attained this en-tire fullness of human possibility. Lucilius's potential for virtue is the best part of him, but it is as yet only potential. He can learn to experience joy and the other *eupatheiai* only by transforming the self he now has.

Classification by genus

The difference between our ordinary emotional lives and the affective ex-perience of the wise comes out most sharply when affective responses are broken down by genus. For ordinary emotions, Stoics employ a simple fourfold analysis based on two parameters, perception as good or evil and perception as present or prospective. So, for instance, emotions of the ge-nus 'fear' are directed at objects perceived as evil and in prospect, while emotions of the genus 'delight' see their objects as good and present.[38] This fourfold classification is easily summarized in chart form (see fig. 2). For eupathic responses, by contrast, only three genera are posited: joy for present goods, 'caution' (or sometimes 'confidence') for prospective evils, and 'wish' (*boulēsis*) for prospective goods.[39] The fourth possible class of

	present	*in prospect*
good	DELIGHT	DESIRE
evil	DISTRESS	FEAR

Figure 2. The genus-emotions.

	present	*in prospect*
good	JOY	WISH
evil	——	CAUTION

Figure 3. The genus-*eupatheiai*.

objects, that of present evils, does not have any normative affect corresponding to it: it is apparently a "missing genus" of affective response (see fig. 3). Thus the person of perfect understanding is thought to be free of any form of grief or sorrow.

In order to make sense of this restriction, we have to think carefully about how the division by genus is meant to work. The distinction along the vertical axis should by now be clear enough; the 'present' versus 'prospective' distinction, though, still requires clarification. We have already noted that an 'object,' properly speaking, is really an event or state of affairs, expressible with a verb: what I desire is not the pizza but *to eat the pizza* (i.e., that I and no one else should eat it), and what I fear is not the lion but *to encounter the lion* (i.e., that I should encounter it). So 'present' in this discussion ought not to mean "in the room with me," as the pizza or the lion might be, but 'present' in the sense that a verb is present.

A simple way to understand it might be as a straightforward tense marker: 'present' would refer to something taking place right now, and 'prospective' would mean something that will take place in the future. But this interpretation saddles the Stoics with a strange asymmetry, for the future is of great extent while right now is only a moment. Also, there would be no category available for many emotions which Stoics certainly recognize; grief for someone who died last month, for example. If they saw no need for a third pair of genera relating to the past, it must be because the distinction that is intended is just a binary distinction between events or situations which *may* become real and those which *have* become real. The prospective object must be one seen as a live possibility for a future that is near enough to matter: parents fear that their children will die not when they reflect that they are mortal but when they learn of a dangerous epidemic.[40] Present objects are ones viewed as part of one's present situation; this does not mean that the significant event cannot already have occurred. The windfall or the bereavement is, in fact, in the past, in that it must have happened before it is viewed as a reality, but it is a past that one thinks of as recent enough to matter. As we cease to think of an event as being of recent occurrence, the emotion too fades away.[41]

With this in mind, we can see why one would want to claim that the person of perfect understanding has no genus of affective response for present evils. Having perfect understanding entails that one regards as evil only those things that really are evil; that is, integral evils such as personal failings, errors, and other events or situations whose causes lie within oneself. In order to believe that this sort of evil is present in the relevant sense, one would have to believe that a proposition concerning one's own shortcomings has just become true, something like "I act unjustly" or "I am ungenerous." But the person of perfect understanding is exempt by definition from everything of that kind. The situation simply never arises. One could, of course, be in the same room with the moral failings of other people; these, however, are evils not for oneself but only for the persons responsible, as the practical moralist Epictetus is careful to explain.[42] The wise person would respond to them as to any other object external to her sphere of control: as occasions for action, perhaps, but not as occasions for distress.

Classification by species

Both ordinary emotions and the *eupatheiai* are also further broken down into a number of species within each genus. The species of the former are very numerous, and no two surviving lists are quite alike in the number and names of the emotions included. In comparison with the orderly division by genus, classifications at this level are indeed markedly unsystematic. The awkwardness typical of these lists can easily be seen from figure 4, which is based primarily on the account in Stobaeus. No effort has been made to regularize the number of species in each genus: only three species are listed under delight, while distress is given ten species; other versions of the list have as many as fourteen. The genus directed at

Genus DELIGHT (*hēdonē*)	Genus DESIRE (*epithumia*)
Spite (*epichairekakia*): delight at another's evils	Anger (*orgē*): desire to punish a person who is thought to have harmed one unjustly
Glee (*asmenismos*): delight at what is unexpected	Heatedness (*thumos*): anger at its inception
Bewitchment (*goēteia*): delight through deceptive seeing	Bile (*cholos*): anger that wells up
	Hatred (*mēnis*): anger stored up to age
	Rancor (*kotos*): anger biding its time for revenge
	Exasperation (*pikria*): anger which breaks out suddenly
	Erotic love (*erōs*): desire for sexual intercourse
	Longing (*pothos*): desire through erotic love for one who is absent
	Yearning (*himeros*): desire for the company of a dear one who is absent
Genus DISTRESS (*lupē*)	**Genus FEAR (*phobos*)**
Envy (*phthonos*): distress at another's goods	Reluctance (*oknos*): fear of impending activity
Rivalry (*zēlos*): distress that another is getting what one desires for oneself but does not get	Trepidation (*agōnia*): fear of defeat
Jealousy (*zēlotupia*): distress that another is also getting what one has oneself	Consternation (*ekplēxis*): fear of an unfamiliar impression
Pity (*eleos*): distress that someone seems to be undergoing evils unjustly	Shame (*aischunē*): fear of disgrace
Grief (*penthos*): distress at an untimely death	Alarm (*thorubos*): fear which hastens with outcry
Anxiety (*achthos*): oppressive distress	Superstition (*deisidaimonia*): fear of gods or supernatural beings
Misery (*achos*): distress that produces speechlessness	Fright (*deos*): fear of what is terrible
Worry (*ania*): distress through calculation	Panic (*deima*): fear out of reason
Anguish (*odunē*): distress that settles deep inside	
Agony (*asē*): distress with thrashing	

Figure 4. Representative species-emotions.

prospective goods is dominated by forms of anger, which has taken on the status of a subgenus; the coherence of the category is maintained only by the fact that anger itself is identified as a species of desire. Comparison among the definitions shows considerable variety in the means of individuating single emotions: while each definition includes the genus term, some add to it a narrower identification of the intentional object, as when shame is defined as 'fear of disgrace'; others a description of the feeling involved, as when anxiety is defined as 'oppressive distress.' The result is a mélange of overlapping accounts (how is 'anger stored up to age' different from 'anger biding its time'?) and gaps: why do we hear about 'fear of defeat' but not fear of death? About 'delight through deceptive seeing,' but not delight through deceptive hearing?[43] Some irregularities are no doubt to be explained by vagaries of transmission.[44] No reasonable amount of emendation, however, would produce anything like the neat taxonomy that we find in all Stoic sources at the level of genus. It may be that the untidiness of the species-level classification reflects a deliberate philosophic choice made early in the history of the school. The point of offering such lists can only have been to demonstrate that the broad-brush classification by genus could be made fine-grained enough to capture the nuances of everyday emotional experience. That philosophical need is perhaps better served by a listing which includes a wide variety of terms and definitions from ordinary Greek usage than it could be by some neat and exhaustive classification which used terms other than those to which speakers of the language are accustomed. The genus-species arrangement thus serves as a kind of interface between top-down and bottom-up approaches to emotion. Each emotion term in common use can be assigned a place by genus in the four-part classification scheme and still given a definition matching linguistic expectations. Where ordinary Greek is well supplied with terms, as in the vocabulary of anger and of grief, the philosophical classification should be correspondingly rich; where previously existing definitions can be assimilated to the Stoic system, these will be favored.[45]

It is not surprising, then, to find that at least some definitions match those otherwise attested from the rhetorical tradition. The definition of pity, for instance, matches verbatim with that given in Aristotle's *Rhetoric*, as does the remark inserted at this point in Cicero's list, that "no one is moved to pity by the punishment of a parricide."[46] Only the overall status of pity has changed: while Aristotle regards pity with favor, the Stoics generally treat it as erroneous, although it should be noted that the tradition is not quite uniform on this point.[47] Evidence of reshaping can be seen also in the way the Stoic list treats Aristotle's trio of indignation (*nemesis*), envy, and rivalry in *Rhetoric* 2.9–11. For Aristotle, both indignation and rivalry are good emotions, such as are felt by good persons: indignation is distress at undeserved good fortune in others, rivalry distress which motivates us to obtain the goods others have. The Stoic list dispenses with indignation, reinterprets rivalry as a bad emotion, and introduces jealousy as yet a further bad emotion. This leaves the Stoics with three bad emotions concerned with good fortune in others, seemingly a superfluity. Yet all three are carefully distinguished: envy is when I am distressed at another's good fortune without reference to my own condition; rivalry is when I am distressed that another has obtained what I wanted for myself but did not get; jealousy is when I am distressed that another has obtained what I wanted even though I also have obtained it. The Stoic context has forced some hard thinking about linguistic usage; the distinction itself, though, has nothing distinctively Stoic about it.

Our few surviving accounts of the species-*eupatheiai* are more prescriptive, as befits the normative conception. Though full definitions appear only in a single late source (for Diogenes Laertius lists only the names),

Genus JOY	Genus WISH
enjoyment (*terpsis*): joy befitting the surrounding advantages cheerfulness (*euphrosunē*): joy in the sensible person's deeds good spirits (*euthumia*): joy in the management or self-sufficiency of the universe	good intent (*eunoia*): a wish for good things for another for that person's own sake goodwill (*eumeneia*): lingering good intent welcoming (*aspasmos*): continous good intent cherishing (*agapēsis*): [*definition missing*] *Here also belongs:* <erotic love (*erōs*): an effort to form a friendship, through perceived beauty.>
	Genus CAUTION moral shame (*aidōs*): caution against correct censure reverence (*hagneia*): caution against misdeeds concerning the gods

Figure 5. The species-*eupatheiai*.

their characteristically Stoic flavor suggests composition by philosophers rather than rhetoricians.[48] Care has been taken to specify the objects of these responses in such a way as to conform to expectations about wise belief. 'Cheerfulness,' for instance, is 'joy in the *sensible* person's deeds,' while 'moral shame' (*aidōs*) is 'caution against *correct* censure.'

It may be significant, then, that the genus concerned with prospective goods includes some affective responses that are directly concerned with the goods of other people. *Eunoia* or 'good intent' is 'a wish for good things for another for that person's own sake,' and *eumeneia* and *aspasmos*, 'good will' and 'welcoming,' are subspecies of this.[49] On the face of it, this would seem to contradict what was said above concerning the restriction of eupathic responses to objects belonging to one's own sphere of control. So, too, the eupathic version of erotic love, included here on firm evidence from Cicero and Diogenes Laertius, is not something a strictly solipsistic wise person could be expected to experience. An alternative account, also reported by Diogenes Laertius, indicates that the 'impression of beauty' could be spelled out further as 'an impression of a good natural endowment for virtue' in a young person.[50] As an object, this seems in keeping with 'correct censure' and 'the deeds of the sensible person.' One cannot help but conclude that the rich affective life of the wise is being said to include some concern for other human beings that goes beyond disinterested service to the level of genuine affective involvement.

Some remaining questions

Important questions remain unanswered. The material on eupathic responses raises an obvious and pressing concern about the relation of the person of perfect understanding to other human beings. The restriction of normative affect to one's own actions and states does not seem to leave much room for warm attachment, friendship, or the building of communities, all experiences that we might think important in an ideal life. The species-*eupatheiai* appear to tell a different story, but we have not yet seen how this can be. Also, a question arises about the responses of ordinary persons to those objects that are legitimately considered good or evil. Such responses could not count as *eupatheiai*, since they do not come out of an ideal epistemic condition; still, they seem importantly different from emotions directed at external events. Especially, we have to wonder about responses of ordinary persons to their own moral shortcomings. We have seen that the wise have no occasion to be distressed over any moral failings, but this leaves open the question whether remorse or regret might not be appropriate for the ordinary person. And such feelings are an important dimension of our emotional lives.

There is evidence of Stoic thought on all these points; however, I am not in a position to take up that material just yet. For I have not yet given any consideration to the one issue that was seen even in antiquity as the central difficulty in Stoic moral psychology. If emotions are to be defined as impulses, that is, as one kind of action, then we also bear responsibility for them as we do for any action. Must it not then be said that emotions are also a matter of one's own volition? But how can this be, given that our experience of emotion is frequently one of being carried away by it? This question must now take priority.

3

Vigor and Responsibility

There is a sense in which emotions have us under their control. Aristotle says—and it is hard not to agree with him—that a good person is one who not only acts rightly but feels rightly. Yet for ourselves it often seems as if we have no choice how to feel. A sense of passivity is expressed in the very word that became standard for emotion in Greek usage, for *pathos* is simply the noun form of *paschein*, to suffer or undergo. Nor is it only the reflex-like 'startle' and 'fight-or-flight' responses that seem to occur without our consent. It is, much more crucially, the core instances of emotion, responses that we not only feel but also express in our behavior. And emotional behavior is sometimes terrifying in its extremity. A mother finds herself driven to destroy the life of her innocent child, a child whom she loves and in calmer moments would not wish to harm. One does not have to condone her action to recognize that she was at that moment helpless in the grip of some very powerful feeling. Even our legal system admits emotion as a mitigating factor in some cases.

Surviving reports of Chrysippus's views indicate that he was quite aware of the difficulty people have in controlling their feelings. He mentions how Admetus, the husband of Alcestis in Euripides' play, feels himself 'compelled' to grieve for her sacrificial death, and how Achilles was 'conquered' by his anger at Troy. He also offers less exalted examples:

> For in disappointment we are 'outside of' or 'beside' ourselves and, in a word, blinded, so that sometimes, if we have a sponge or a bit

of wool in our hands, we pick it up and throw it, as if that would achieve something. And if we happened to be holding a dagger or some other weapon, we would do the same with that. . . . And often, through the same blindness, we bite keys, and beat at doors when they do not open quickly, and if we stumble over a stone we take revenge on it by breaking it or throwing it somewhere, and we say very odd things on all such occasions.[1]

Such behaviors, says Chrysippus, show something important about the nature of emotion. For emotions are 'irrational': while they are going on, we find ourselves 'blinded,' unable to prevent ourselves from doing things our calmer selves would not approve. It is, he says, "as if we had become different people from those who were previously conversing."

At the same time, in what seems a startling contradiction, Chrysippus also holds that emotions are in *our* power. His view of the causes of emotion is that of Zeno as reported by Cicero in the *Posterior Academics;* it is the standard Stoic position:

Whereas the ancients held that these emotions are natural and devoid of reason and placed desire in one part of the mind, reason in another, Zeno . . . did not agree; he thought that the emotions are volitional and are experienced through a judgment of opinion.[2]

The language is that of moral responsibility: emotions are *voluntarii* or volitional; they are, as other sources put it, 'up to us.' This language is not offered out of perversity or in ignorance of the recalcitrant nature of emotional experience. Chrysippus is actually quite pessimistic about the possibility of simply restraining oneself, for he holds that emotions tend to be unstoppable once they have begun. Nonetheless, he is prepared to assert that the recalcitrance of emotions can be explained satisfactorily within a moral psychology that counts affective responses as instances of voluntary action.

The position is in fact a coherent one. Chrysippus is able to make these bold claims because he has a clearly defined notion of what is required for something to be 'up to us' or voluntary and a strong case for why the core instances of emotion satisfy that requirement. His explanation of moral responsibility is developed in the first instance without reference to those special or "hot" impulses which count as *pathē*: it is a matter of very broad philosophical significance, meant to supply a basis for praise and blame which does not violate the principle of universal causal determinism. But Chrysippus and other Stoics were also prepared to apply that explanation to emotional outbursts and their moral significance, taking due note of those features of emotional impulses which differentiate them from one's other conscious actions. The result is a sophisticated affective volitional-ism which manages to combine intellectual seriousness, devoid of magical or mysterious elements, with sensitivity to the phenomena of our mental life. There are, to be sure, certain fairly obvious objections, based, as in similar modern discussions, on the nonsufficiency and/or nonnecessity of belief causes. But the Chrysippan analysis is able to resolve these objections without major modification.

The admission that morally significant responses can evade our control leaves us, as agents, in a difficult spot. We cannot prevent ourselves from doing certain things when we become upset, but all the same we cannot allege the strength of our emotions in order to excuse ourselves. This is a hard doctrine, yet if I read the evidence correctly, the Stoic founders were not inclined to soften it; rather, they issued it as a challenge. For helpless-ness is not the inevitable human condition, nor is it our natural condition; it is only the condition of persons who are not yet fully mature. To assume the full stature of our humanity would also be to enter a different realm of affective experience, one where strength of feeling does not have to mean loss of control. Although emotions as we presently experience them are not tame or easily managed, the affects of the wise carry them exactly where they wish to go. This is one reason why the attainment of wisdom is felt as liberation.

Rollability

As background to the arguments that will be applied specifically to those impulses which are emotions, it is helpful to keep in mind the reasoning by which actions in general are said by Stoics to be 'up to us' or volitional. It was noted in chapter 1 that an action, properly so called, is always de-scribable in intentional terms, as assent to an impression that there is some predicate one should fulfill just at this moment. It remains to consider what should be named as the cause or causes of that assent. If either all the causes, or all the important causes, rest with oneself, then the action is reasonably considered voluntary.[3]

Now, assent is necessarily preceded by an impression. One can hardly decide that some proposition is true or false unless one has that proposi-tion in mind. But Stoic thought does not consider the impulsory impres-sion to be the principal cause of an action. It is indeed a cause, but the real cause or reason for the assent is to be found in the agent's own mental character, where by 'mental character' is meant simply the structure and content of one's own belief set. There is nothing odd in this view. All that has to be assumed is that the things that seem plausible to a person are those that fit in easily with opinions that person already holds. Assent, that is, is a matter of recognizing a logical fit with existing mental contents, as when we say that something "falls into place" or "squares with" what one already knows. Whether assent is given on any particular occasion will thus depend on the nature of the existing mental contents and the sort of standard one uses for recognizing logical fit. But my mental contents—the beliefs I hold—are just me, my mind in a state of believing; they are not other than myself. It makes sense, then, to say that assent is caused by oneself more than anything else.

Chrysippus offers an analogy to the round shape or 'rollability' of some cylindrical object.[4] When given a push, a cylindrical object will roll forward; another shape will behave differently or not move at all. In trying to explain why the cylinder rolls while the other object does not, it hardly seems right to single out the pushing motion, since a very similar push does not yield anything like the same result in the other object. Chrysippus therefore finds it reasonable to designate the push a 'proximate' or 'accessory' cause and to claim that the *principal* cause of the movement is just the cylinder itself, by virtue of its rollable shape. In the same way, he argues, human action can depend on impressions and yet not be caused in this principal sense by anything other than the agent's own character. A similar impression occurring in someone whose character was different could produce a very different impulse, or no impulse at all.

The mechanistic nature of the analogy suggests explanation at the physical level. In theory, there should be such an explanation. Stoic physics requires that causes be material things—bodies—and the causes of mental events are no exception.[5] One could, in fact, restate the above explanation in material terms, saying something like this: whereas impression is brought about by the external world and by the sensitive, motile nature of animate *pneuma* generally, assent is constrained only by the internal tension of one's own stretch of *pneuma*. One degree of tension will allow certain short-term modifications of *pneuma* to be converted into the more stable configurations that constitute belief, and another degree will not.

But this sort of explanation is vacuous unless appeal is also made to intentional characteristics. Just as the imprint is not reducible to the wax that constitutes it, so the causes of mental events should operate by virtue of their intentional properties. For instance, Kleon's entry into political life is describable as a judgment (at least implicit) on Kleon's part that presenting himself as a candidate is the thing to do just at that time. The causes of his making this judgment are his own beliefs, considered for their content: he believes that holding office will help his family, that he will have extra support this year, and so forth. These beliefs are material things, configurations of *pneuma*. But their efficacy as causes would not be stated by giving a nonintentional account of them: each can be considered a cause of the judgment only in virtue of being a configuration that corresponds to precisely *this* intentional object. If it were otherwise—if the causal account could be satisfactory without reference to any propositional content—it might be doubted whether the event explained was really a judgment at all.

A number of texts express the notion of determination by character simply by speaking of assent as either 'strong' or 'weak.' 'Weak' in this usage does not connote lack of enthusiasm: it is interchangeable with 'hasty' or 'precipitate,' and refers to the character of mind that is too ready to accept impressions that lack proper justification.[6] Conversely, a 'strong' assent is the assent of a strong mind; it may also be called 'nonprecipitate.' The usage is related to that in which knowledge (the epistemic condition of the wise) is linked to high levels of 'tension' or 'tensile strength' in the *pneuma*.[7] A tight internal structure, with many correct beliefs linked to each other in coherent logical relations, is proof against the most plausible-seeming falsehood. A close paraphrase of Chrysippus in the Latin author Aulus Gellius draws the contrast between strong and weak assent in terms that sound almost architectural. Minds which are "constructed by nature" in a healthy way are able to let a misleading impression pass through them without being damaged, but those minds that are "rough, unlearned, crude, and not shored up by the supports of education" offer "obstruction" to the impression, rather like loose boards to a gale. Thus they are liable to "collapse," and when they do so the fault will rest with "their own crookedness and voluntary impulse."[8]

We can see, then, what it has to mean for a Stoic to assert that emotions, like other *hormai*, are volitional or in our power. The assertion of Zeno, reported by Cicero in Latin translation, that emotions are voluntary (*perturbationes voluntarias esse*) is equivalent to saying that emotion events are in our power precisely because they are also assents, judgments with a certain content. As Zeno also says, they are 'experienced through a judgment of opinion' (*opinionis iudicio suscipi*).[9] For assent is regulated by characteristics of persons, above all by prior beliefs a person holds. The Zenonian expression is repeated many times in later sources, often paired with 'through judgment' or 'through opinion.'[10]

A not uninteresting question for the history of volitionalism concerns the Greek expression Cicero is rendering by the Latin word *voluntarias*. The early Stoics knew and used the 'up to us' formula favored by Aristotle (*eph' hēmin*), and Latin *voluntarius* could be used in an equivalent sense. I am inclined to think, though, that *voluntarius* here and in similar contexts in both Cicero and Seneca actually represents *prohairetikos* in early Stoic texts, just as it does in Cicero's translations from Aristotle. It has often been claimed that *prohairetikos* is not attested in the early Stoa, though it is used frequently by Epictetus in the later period.[11] But there are traces of a Stoic usage both in the Herculaneum papyri and in verbatim reports by Origen.[12] In attaching this term to the *pathē*, the Stoics were making the most explicit claim they could make about responsibility for emotional experience.

Because of the Stobaean report and parallel texts, we are actually in a better position to understand the causation of emotional impulses in Stoicism than we are for other species of behavior. For these tell us explicitly the causes of emotions in each of the four genera. Grief, for instance, is "a contraction of mind which is disobedient to reason, and its cause is a fresh believing that an evil is present toward which it is appropriate to contract."[13] Thus not only do we know that the principal causes consist entirely in one's own beliefs, but we can even spell out the content of those beliefs. They will consist, always though not necessarily exclusively, in suitably particularized versions of the evaluation and appropriateness premises of the pathetic syllogism. Without these, no affective response would occur.

To be sure, the model is still highly schematized: in real situations, there might be a much larger number of background beliefs that figure in the processing of the impulse. The exact sequence of practical reasoning that takes place in any given instance might be quite complicated, with many interrelated beliefs coming into play. So we might never be able to offer a precise listing of belief-causes for a real emotion event, or indeed for any action. The Stoic claim, though, is that all the principal causes are of the same kind. There need not be any causes that are *not* beliefs.

Overriding impulses

The causes of emotion, then, are exactly like the causes of other sorts of impulse. But one does not therefore have to say that all impulses are alike. Introspection insists that anger, fear, grief, and desire have a "hot" or vehement quality to them that sets them apart from run-of-the-mill actions like walking or brushing one's teeth. It is in this that emotions seem to run roughshod over our better judgment, compromising our sense of agency and self-management. That special feature is picked out by the early Stoic terminology of *pleonasmos* or 'excessiveness.' Already in the writings of Zeno of Citium, an emotion is defined as an excessive impulse, a *hormē pleonazousa*.[14] Or it may be characterized as 'disobedient to reason' or 'turned away from reason'; these expressions, too, are probably Zenonian in origin.[15]

Our word "excessive" is not an entirely satisfactory translation for Zeno's term *pleonazousa*. Built on a root meaning 'more' (*pleon*), the Greek word is in its grammatical form a present participle of the verb *pleonazō*, meaning 'be more' or 'exceed' or 'go beyond bounds.' Hence it is 'exceeding' rather than 'excessive.' The difference of inflection could easily be felt by a Greek speaker. The unnamed Stoic source quoted by Stobaeus comments on Zeno's preference for the verb over the related adjective *pleonastikē*.

> He [Zeno] does not say 'an impulse whose nature it is to exceed,' but 'one that is in fact exceeding.' For it is not a matter of the capacity but of the activity.[16]

This interprets Zeno to have said that the excessiveness which characterizes emotional impulses is not some inherent attribute belonging to them by nature. It is just what such impulses regularly do in human beings as we know them: they exceed something. What they exceed, and how, is not stated here, but an answer is ready to hand: they exceed other impulses which the same agents might form, and sometimes do form, in accordance with correct reason.

Such is the account of excessiveness that was worked out by Chrysippus in his own comments on Zeno's definition. In his treatise, Chrysippus associates terms like 'excessive' and 'disobedient to reason' not only with normative conceptions of correct behavior but also with the psychological phenomenon referred to in ordinary-language expressions like "being carried away." They do not mean only "that the person is proceeding in error, perceiving something wrongly through reason"; they also refer to one's being "pushed in excess" (*ōthoumenon epi pleion*). He continues,

> It is in reference to this that we speak of the 'excessiveness' of the impulse, because it oversteps that measure in impulses which is natural and is through oneself. What I mean would be more comprehensible through

the following. When one walks through impulse, the movement of the legs is not excessive, but is to some extent fitted to the impulse, so that if the person wishes to stop or make a change, he can do so. But when people run through impulse, this is no longer the case: the movement of the legs is excessive and contrary to the impulse, so that they are carried away and [the legs] do not obediently make a change right when one initiates it, as in the previous case. I think that something very similar happens also in the impulses [involved in emotion], because of overstepping the measure that is in accordance with reason, so that when one has an impulse [of this kind] one is not being obedient to reason.[17]

In stating his analogy Chrysippus is careful to indicate that running, like walking, comes about 'through impulse.' Running differs from walking not in the sort of mental event which initiates it but in the kind of action it is, the way it propels the body forward or, as we would say, its momentum. The sense of being carried forward even contrary to one's wishes is not, in fact, a feature of the initial impulse to run; rather, it comes in at some later point when one forms a second impulse telling oneself to stop. It is then that one finds oneself unable, for the moment, to act as one thinks appropriate, as the running impulse 'oversteps,' or overrides, the subsequent impulse to the contrary. So also with those impulses which are emotions: they are initiated in the same way as other impulses, and yet there is a kind of momentum to them that carries a person forward in time.

Chrysippus' treatment asks us to consider an episode of emotion over its whole history, including the evaluative and other beliefs that give rise to it in the first place. If we will do this, he confidently asserts, we will see that these causes are similar in kind to those that generate any action. Human beings are rational creatures, in the descriptive though not always the normative sense of the word rational—and thus every impulse we form is formed in the way characteristic of rational creatures, through a judgment of what is to be done. But even so there will be some moments when an impulse *seems* involuntary and when considerations of one's own best interests are helpless before it. If we consider a person's inner experience just at that moment when, being in the grip of strong feeling, she attempts to restrain herself from doing or saying something regrettable, then the emotion may well be disobedient to reason in that moment. For the other impulse, the impulse to cease feeling that way and to stop doing the things the emotion is driving one to do, is a reasoned impulse which cannot take effect. It is as if the rational mind has lost the ability to execute its own commands.

The runner analogy offers a promising way to understand the phenomenon of mental conflict, in which, according to the vernacular conception, a person's "heart" is at odds with her "head" or one "part" of the self argues against another "part." The sense of inner struggle can be accommodated within Chrysippus's account, for his description of one's inability to stop having an emotion is also a description of conflict between emotion and reason. But the warring parties are not here conceived as distinct centers or motivation-generating mechanisms within the psyche. Instead, they are motivations of different sorts generated at successive moments by one and the same motivational center. The mind is unitary in that all its action tendencies come about in the same way, through the exercise of its capacities for impression and assent. It is nonetheless subject to mental conflict insofar as there may be logical contradictions between one and another of the propositions to which it assents.

Implicit in this interpretation of the phenomena is a deep strain of pessimism about the ability of humans simply to restrict or subjugate feelings that run contrary to their perceived best interests. In contrast to that assumption by which "stoical" in modern English has come to mean "self-controlled," Chrysippus actually holds that our resources for controlling emotions after they begin are extremely limited. What is active in the emotional person is not a pair of faculties but a single faculty, the reasoning faculty, which is susceptible to more than one sort of modification. The emotive faculty simply is the reasoning faculty, taking on a different role: in episodes of strong emotion, the "head," as it were, actually becomes the "heart."[18] There is, then, no separate faculty in a human being which will necessarily be able to assert control over an emotion. The point is vividly expressed by Cicero, in an image that extends Chrysippus's comparison but does not alter its import:

> Emotions stand on slippery ground. One push, and they slide right down the slope. There is no way to stop them.[19]

Seneca, too, grasps Chrysippus's point exactly:

> For once the mind is stirred into motion, it is a slave to that which is driving it. With some things, the beginnings are in our power, but after that they carry us on by their own force, not allowing a return. Bodies allowed to fall from a height have no control of themselves: they cannot resist or delay their downward course, for the irrevocable fall has cut off all deliberation, all repentance; they cannot help but arrive where they are going, though

they could have avoided going there at all. Even so the mind, once it propels itself into anger, love, and other emotions, is not permitted to check its
impulse. Its own weight must carry it to the bottom.[20]

Given time and improvement of character, one could perhaps find a new
mode of existence in which emotions, in the ordinary and depraved sense,
will not occur. Until then, we are all at risk.

Medea and Odysseus

Armed with this understanding of emotion's disobedience to reason, Chrysippus is ready to take on the most egregious representations of mental
conflict in Greek literature. Medea, in Euripides' play, is both highly emotional and highly intelligent, one of the most articulate of all characters
in tragedy concerning her own inner experience. She resolves early in the
play to take revenge on Jason by murdering the sons they have had together; this, however, will cause pain to herself as well, and the thought
of her own loss causes her to hesitate and eventually to put her sense of
internal division into words:

> I understand what evils I am about to do,
> but anger is more powerful than my counsels.[21]

Chrysippus quotes these lines in illustration of his own view, as a way
of bringing vividly to mind the force that emotions may exert even contrary to one's perceived best interests. The exact context is not preserved;
however, we can gain a fair idea of Chrysippus's intent from what he says
about a similar example taken from another Euripidean tragedy, *Andromache*. In that play Menelaus encounters Helen during the sack of Troy and
raises his hand to strike her down, but then drops the sword and allows
her to kiss him. In this instance it is the prior resolve that is based on considerations of policy; emotion comes second and wipes out a decision the
audience is likely to regard as reasonable and just.

> One person gives up when dangers ensue, another is undone and yields
> when a reward or punishment is brought to bear, and others for numerous
> similar reasons. For all such things subdue and enslave us, so that yielding
> to them we betray our friends or our cities, and give ourselves over to many
> shameful acts because our previous effort has been given up. An example
> is Menelaus as depicted by Euripides. Drawing his sword, he moves toward

Helen to slay her, but then, struck by the sight of her beauty, he casts away his sword and is no longer able to control even that. Hence this reproach is spoken to him:

> You, when you saw her breast, cast down your blade
> and took her kiss, fondling the traitor dog.[22]

Menelaus is more than an example; he is a graphic illustration of the condition of *psuchē* that prevails among ordinary persons. The accompanying discussion makes this clear. The 'lack of sinew' (*atonia*) that lets the sword slip from his grasp only makes manifest the lack of psychic tension (again, *atonia*) that fails to establish a clear logical relation between one judgment and the next. In a sense, his passivity as he accepts the woman's embrace displays a weakness of reason. However, this is not a weakness before some unreasoning force, but a weakness within the reasoning mind, a structural weakness in the belief system.

By this standard Medea, too, is weak, however imposing she may appear on the stage, for she too endorses contradictory impressions as to what she should do. Her case differs from that of Menelaus in that its sequence of presumed mental events matches that of the runner analogy, with the vigorous emotion impulse preceding the more reasonable decision. But this difference is less significant than it might seem, for the essential point is not which judgment comes first, but that there is a change from one judgment to another.

Medea may not recognize that she has changed her mind. Although she is certainly aware of holding more than one view of her situation, the moment in which she moved from one to the other may have gone by very quickly. The lines quoted above are only the culmination of a longer monologue in which her intentions change several times; each time, it is the intention itself that fills her consciousness, not her own inconsistency. Her inner experience as Euripides represents it accords well with the account of mental conflict in a Stoic source known to Plutarch, which speaks of "a switching of reason, being one, to both sides, which escapes our notice because of the suddenness and speed of the change."[23] Menelaus, too, may be thought of as vacillating. In his abashed stillness before Helen we are perhaps to imagine a renewal of his intention to exact vengeance, which then goes unheeded owing to the force of his emotion.

A more encouraging example is cited by Chrysippus from book 20 of the *Odyssey*.[24] Odysseus has returned in disguise to his home in Ithaka and witnesses unobserved the treachery of his maidservants who sleep with Penelope's suitors. His gorge rises, but to take action now would ruin his planned retribution and perhaps cost him his life. Striking his breast, he addresses his own heart, telling it to tolerate the offense for the time being, and so holds his peace. In his case the emotional impulse does not, after all, result in action; considerations of expediency—very urgent ones, as it happens—overrule it. Again, the full discussion does not survive; however, the fact that Chrysippus invoked this passage is highly significant in itself. Because of Chrysippus's emphasis on the phenomenon of overriding, one might well be inclined to assume that on his theory, no ordinary person can ever act contrary to the promptings of emotion. By including the Odysseus example, Chrysippus shows that this is not the case. It should be remembered that in specific situations, the process of practical reasoning may be extremely complex, with many interrelated beliefs and impressions coming into play.[25] To explain what happens in Odysseus, Chrysippus perhaps made use of that more complex model, arguing that even though the emotional impulse overrides most competing considerations, there will also be cases in which some highly salient nonemotive concern takes priority.

Plato and Platonists

In choosing Odysseus's self-admonishment to illustrate his position on mental conflict, Chrysippus can hardly have been unaware that the same example had been mentioned already by Plato in the fourth book of the *Republic*. Like Chrysippus, Plato takes the phenomenon of mental conflict as a given; for him, it serves as a premise in a larger argument about the nature of justice. If someone is doing contradictory things at the same time, says Socrates, he must be doing them with different parts of himself, just as a man might be standing still with his legs and torso but moving with his hands and head. Since Odysseus is both wanting and not wanting to act against the servants, he must be using different parts of his mind, namely, 'reason' and 'spirit' (or 'anger'; *thumos* has both meanings in Greek). When both spirit and a third part, termed the 'desiring' part, cooperate with reason, the result is an inherently beneficial condition of the person. This is the condition of persons which Socrates terms 'justice.'[26]

Chrysippus's allusion suggests that he perceives some continuity between his own moral psychology and that of the *Republic*. The impression would not be unjustified.[27] Plato's principal psychological claim in that work is that human beings cannot truly be well off until all their motivations to act are made to work together under the guidance of reason, where 'reason' is understood normatively as a correct perception of what is good. If this happens, then those motivations share in the excellence of the whole: motivations to fight and even sexual urges will be, in their own way, just. In keeping with this larger theme, Plato also indicates, both in the *Republic* and in a related section of the *Phaedrus,* that the group of motivations identifiable as emotions is of such a nature as to be modified by discursive reasoning. Hunger, thirst, and raw sexual urges are less tractable, but anger, erotic love, and similar motivational elements are heedful of reasoned considerations, just as the auxiliary guardians of the ideal republic heed their rulers and the white horse of the *Phaedrus* myth cooperates with the driver. There is, certainly, a difference of kind between the motives of the *thumos* and those of the reasoning element, but it could hardly be alleged that Plato regards the former as independent of belief and thus inaccessible to persuasion.

Chrysippus can even agree with Plato that the contradiction within Odysseus suggests multiple elements in the soul. For he too holds that the psyche has parts. Evidence on this point comes from another context, a discussion of what it means for minds to be called "beautiful" or "ugly." There Chrysippus remarks that the *psychē* "has parts (*merē*), of which its reason and its condition in reason are composed," and that these parts may have "proportion or lack of proportion" among themselves.[28] But the sort of parts which could be components of the mind's 'condition in reason' must be elements that have some propositional content. That is, they must be various judgments a person has made, perhaps to be conceived as successive activities of the central directive faculty.[29] Like Plato, Chrysippus is strongly interested in ideas of harmony in multiplicity as a model of psychic excellence. It is understandable that he would seek to present this position as a development of the mainline philosophical tradition—though he would wish to be careful to specify what he means by the terms he uses.

For some ancient readers of Plato, this was not enough. Both Galen and Plutarch, writing in the first and second centuries C.E., consider themselves Platonists, as does the handbook writer Alcinous, who seems to belong to the same time period.[30] All three of these authors object quite strongly to the Stoic habit of locating all psychic functions in a single command center. For Plutarch, it is as though Chrysippus and other early Stoics somehow "failed to notice" that the psyche is a composite of rational and irrational elements, even though this composition is in his own view "quite obvious."[31] Galen, who criticizes Chrysippus's views at great length, is even more sharp. Plato, he says, speaks very properly when he uses Odysseus as an example, for the lines from *Odyssey* 20 give an obvious illustration of competition between emotion and reason. Chrysippus's use of the same lines is another matter.

> Sometimes neither of the two is strong enough to pull the other in its direction right away, but there is opposition and conflict between them until in time one defeats the other—reason in the case of Odysseus, anger in the case of Medea. For they are two parts of the psyche or, if not parts, at least capacities. But Chrysippus, even though he does not acknowledge that these are parts of the psyche, or that there are any irrational powers which are different from reason, nonetheless does not hesitate to recall the words of Odysseus and Medea, though these quite obviously refute his own view.[32]

As far as Galen is concerned, the views of Chrysippus and of Plato are diametrically opposed, and the phenomena of emotional experience—which after all are what literary examples are meant to recall—come out squarely in support of Plato. Yet Chrysippus fails to acknowledge this and even quotes the very passages that refute him. Sheer perversity is the only possible explanation.

Underlying these second-century objections to Stoic psychology is a particular reading of the relevant Platonic passages. This reading attributes to Plato a 'distributed' psychology in which the 'parts' referred to in *Republic* 4 and related passages are spatially distinct motivation generators within a person. One's behavior is determined by a kind of negotiation among these motivation generators. Ideally, drives such as hunger and emotions such as anger and fear will be guided by rational preferences for the good, but at times there may be an outright power struggle, in which reason may be overwhelmed by the other parts seeking to impose their own preferences. The image of a horse which takes the bit in its teeth and runs away with the driver strikes these Platonists as particularly apposite to the loss of rational control in times of strong emotion. The emphasis of the *Phaedrus* myth falls for them on the contrast between a reasoning self and a "beast within," rather than on that between the refractory black horse and the reliably obedient white horse.[33]

Also very important to these Platonists is a passage in the *Timaeus* cosmogony which places the immortal *psuchē* in the head, the 'ambitious' or spirited part in the chest, and the appetitive part in the lower abdomen.[34] There is some question whether Plato means the *Timaeus* physiology to be taken seriously: he presents it as only a "likely story," a speculative framework within which to explore certain moral and psychological ideas. But for the later Platonic tradition it is much more than that. Indeed, in the medical writer Galen, the literal reading of *Timaeus* cosmogony bears the full burden of anatomical precision. For Galen, the different determinants of behavior actually reside in different bodily organs, judgment and volition being localized in the brain, emotions in the heart, and desires in the liver. Thus the brain and heart are quite literally in competition for control of the organism as a whole. His own anatomical knowledge, derived from cadaver dissection and from records of vivisections performed at Alexandria, seems to him to corroborate what Plato established by behavioral observation and argument.[35] For instance, he places great emphasis on the size of the vena cava leading from the liver, believing this sufficient proof that the liver, not the brain or heart, is the origin of the venous system which distributes both nutriment and appetition.[36]

Galen complains that Chrysippus has not even bothered to read the passages of Plato that deal with mental conflict. The charge is implausible. What seems more likely is that Galen and his contemporaries did not stop to reflect that their own interpretation of Plato might not be the only viable reading. In fact, theirs is a partial and overliteral reading, and one that exacerbates the tensions within Plato's account. Modern readers of Plato have complained that his way of explaining mental conflict comes near to creating multiple "little persons" within each person. The Platonic *thumos* seems to have its own capacity to form judgments, since it has a way to disagree with the decisions of the reasoning part. Meanwhile reason has motivations as well as theoretical understanding, and even appetite is able on its own to identify objects and choose a course of action in relation to them.[37] Chrysippus's approach to mental conflict avoids these difficulties while preserving Plato's central insights about the importance of moral reflection and inner harmony.

The Posidonian objections

For a more astute response to the Stoic position, we now turn to another treatise *On Emotions,* one written much closer to Chrysippus's own time. The author is Posidonius of Apamea and Rhodes, who was himself a committed Stoic and a respected intellectual leader in the early first century B.C.E. Posidonius's work does not survive in full, but extensive paragraphs quoted by Galen give an idea of the contents. Examining Galen's direct quotations from this author, we can see that Posidonius, too, was interested in the causal history of emotional response. In his work he seems to have raised for discussion a series of possible objections to Chrysippus's account of that causal history.

Some of Posidonius's questions have to do with feelings that occur independently of the expected judgment. Posidonius wonders about tears that spring unbidden and about emotional responses to instrumental music, where there are no words that might work upon the belief structure. Also, he is troubled about the feelings that evidently occur in animals and in very young children. If, as Stoic psychology holds, these two groups of agents are not capable of rational assent, then what is it that causes their versions of affect?[38] Others of his points have to do with cases in which people fail to experience emotions at times when, given Chrysippus's causal account, it looks as though they should. The basis is empirical. If, as the Stoics claim, the emotion of grief is caused by the belief that a bad thing, namely, the loss of a loved one, has occurred, then it looks as though people should continue grieving for as long as they believe this. But this is not what we observe; rather, the grief diminishes gradually with the passage of time, even though the beliefs that are supposed to have caused it remain unchanged.[39] Similarly, there is a question about why people find their distress lessened when they have prepared themselves mentally through the method of prerehearsal or dwelling in advance on one's misfortunes.[40] Another possible objection concerns cases in which people accept the truth of reports that some terrible or threatening event has taken place but remain unmoved by it owing to a failure of imagination. Only when people visualize the event in their minds, says Posidonius, does the emotional response occur.[41]

There is much that we do not know about Posidonius's book, for Galen's quotations are selective, and no other ancient author provides us with anything definite. Probably the work was little known in antiquity. We cannot even be sure of his philosophical motives in raising these objections. We have, it is true, the interpretations of Galen, who is quite certain that Posidonius meant to refute Chrysippus's view and reinstate a tripartite psychology along the very lines that Galen himself would prefer. There is some question, though, whether in that case Posidonius could have been generally regarded as a major representative of Stoic ethics, as he surely was. Hence some recent interpreters have preferred to believe that his purpose was merely to review some test cases and provide more thorough explanations of them than Chrysippus had done.[42] In the absence of definitive evidence, I think it best to reserve judgment as to the stand Posidonius actually took in relation to his Stoic predecessor.

The Posidonian objections are still of great interest in their own right, not least because some bear a striking resemblance to points raised by modern theorists of emotion against the cognitivist analyses of Richard Lazarus and others.[43] The claim about animals and children is, of course, fundamental to most current cross-species research; it is what R. B. Zajonc means when he insists that affect is ontogenetically and phylogenetically prior to cognition. Patricia Greenspan, Michael Stocker, and others have claimed that the sort of judgments that seem most relevant to emotion can also be made without one's having any affective response.[44] Like Posidonius, though typically without being familiar with his claims, these philosophers insist that one can believe oneself wronged without feeling angry, believe a terrorist attack is likely without being afraid, believe a joke is funny without being inclined to laugh, and so forth.

My point in mentioning these similarities is that objections of the kind and even of the content Posidonius lays out would be likely to arise in any case, whether or not his treatise ever became known. They are points that any thoroughgoing cognitivist analysis has to deal with sooner or later. If they are overlooked or allowed to stand, then the causal history offered by Chrysippus is seriously deficient, having failed to mention an additional cause or group of causes independent of belief. Such additional causes are what Galen has in mind when he refers to an emotional 'pull' (perhaps thinking again of the horse), and they may be what Posidonius is thinking of as well when he speaks of a 'movement of the emotive capacity' as distinct from impulse.[45] To maintain a consistent moral psychology, a Stoic philosopher must be able to counter such claims. For as we have seen, the claim that the causes of emotion consist solely in beliefs is central to Stoic volitionalism. Once that claim is set aside, then the foundation is removed from Chrysippus's larger view.

It will help to clarify the import of Chrysippus's position, then, if we pause to consider how a philosopher of his commitments might reply to the objections raised by Posidonius. This is more than a thought exercise, for on several points there is evidence suggesting that the older philosopher had already advanced at least the beginnings of a position, and on others we know how later admirers of Chrysippus handled similar problems. Even where evidence is lacking, however, it is fair to consider what argumentative resources were available to serious Stoics for dealing with the questions Posidonius raises. At the very least we should seek to understand why this group of objections did not appear devastating to later proponents of the cognitive view.

In the first place, Chrysippan philosophy does not need to deny that feelings sometimes occur in the absence of judgment. It is, in fact, a point of Stoic doctrine that animals and young children exhibit behaviors quite similar to the affective responses of human adults, and there is no reason not to concede that these nonrational responses might resemble emotions at the level of feeling. It can be true that rational creatures regularly sense certain physiological changes in themselves when making a judgment of the relevant sort, and also true that nonrational creatures experience the same kinds of changes without making any judgment at all. What cannot be conceded is that a psychophysical change produced in the absence of judgment can ever count as an emotional response. The absence of a capacity for rational assent is of such psychological and ethical significance as to justify using some different term for animal and infant responses: they would be *pathos* analogues rather than *pathē*.

What about feelings that occur without judgment in persons who are fully capable of judgment? Such are the unbidden tears Posidonius mentions, and also the feelings engendered by instrumental music. Here again it is within Stoic resources to argue that the phenomena in question are not genuine affective responses. It will be argued in chapter 4 that a category of inconsequential feelings not dependent on assent was identified quite early in the Hellenistic school, perhaps under the term 'pre-emotions' (*propatheiai*). Tears and reactions to music are among the examples given in that context. As Posidonius seems to regard his examples as posing a significant difficulty for Chrysippus, he evidently believes that they are instances of actual emotion; perhaps, then, he was unfamiliar with the point about pre-emotions, or had rejected it. Other Stoics, though, might simply disallow his interpretation of the phenomena.

There remains an important group of cases in which judgments of the expected type are said to have occurred, but no affective response ensues. These call for a different approach. The defender of Chrysippus will not, I think, be very troubled by the objection that grief diminishes over time. The gradual evanescence of the feeling can easily be accommodated within an account that cites as the principal cause of grief the belief that "a bad thing is now present to me." For the belief that something is present is equivalent to a belief that something has *recently* become the case. The word 'fresh' (*prosphaton*) in the Zenonian definition could be understood in this way, to mean that one's judgment necessarily has a recentness component.[46] In other words, part of what one believes about the triggering event is that it has *recently* come to pass. This is not the same as saying that the event must really be of recent occurrence. It is the agent's perspective on time that matters. In the usual course of life, grief fades as one alters one's assessment of the recentness of one's misfortune, but it could happen that a person whose circumstances were unusual might fail to make this adjustment and so become locked into the emotion for a long time. Cicero, speaking on behalf of the Stoic view as he knows it, gives as an example the perpetual grief of Artemisia, who continued mourning for her deceased husband for the remainder of her life.[47]

The diminishment of grief might also be accounted for by other belief-based explanations. Martha Nussbaum has developed a complex account drawing on several dimensions of cognitive experience. She argues that there are at least three reasons why grief might subside, even where the belief responsible for it persists. It could be that that particular belief is not foregrounded in concrete situations, or that one's other beliefs have been adjusted to accord with it, so that fewer expectations are frustrated. Or it might be because of loss of salience, as the belief begins to seem less significant for one's own flourishing in relation to other beliefs one also holds.[48] This third explanation, the one based on the salience of various beliefs within practical reasoning, has an ancient correlate in Cicero's presentation of the prerehearsal issue. Cicero is not, it seems, responding directly to Posidonius but rather expanding upon what had already been said on this point by Chrysippus. Noting the claim of some philosophers that grief is alleviated by pondering possible calamities before the fact, he offers an explanation based on considerations of relative importance.

> Chrysippus is of the same view, I know: what is unforeseen strikes us with greater force. But there is more to it than that. It is true that a sudden assault of the enemy creates rather more confusion than an expected one, and that a sudden storm at sea strikes more fear into those on shipboard than if they saw it coming, and there are many similar cases. But if you were to study such events carefully and scientifically, what you would find, quite simply, is that when things happen suddenly, they invariably seem more serious than they otherwise would. . . . Thus the cause of distress is not solely that the events are unexpected. . . . The reason is rather that the event is fresh in one's mind.[49]

A similar point might be made about the lack of emotional response in those who, for whatever reason, are unable to visualize the circumstance reported to them. When we visualize a distant event, we invest it with salience for ourselves: we bring it before the mind's eye and so lend it some of the large share of practical significance that we usually accord to objects in our immediate environs. Posidonius is not entitled to claim that such visualization is clearly distinguishable from belief: belief is deeply implicated here. To be unable to imagine a thing is to be less than half convinced of its existence.[50]

The thesis that all causes of emotion are describable in terms of belief proves to have a great deal of elasticity. Whether the objections are the specific ones raised by Posidonius or others constructed along the same lines, a determined Chrysippan approach will inevitably be able to devise an explanation for the apparent nonsufficiency of the beliefs listed in the pathetic syllogism by pointing out the relevance of subsidiary beliefs not mentioned in that admittedly schematized account. One does not have to rely on the notorious vagueness of the term 'cognition' to make the case. The appeal is rather to the complexity of practical reasoning in many real cases, cases of calm action as well as of emotion. The pathetic syllogism is a schematized general account, meant to capture the most salient belief-causes of most typical instances of emotion; it is not to be expected that any general account would be able to capture every belief that is ever operative. Objections of Posidonius's nonsufficiency type are not likely, then, to make any serious dent in Chrysippus's causal account or in the affective volitionalism that depends on it. The effect of posing them will be to produce a more subtle and complex account along the same lines as before.

The point made by Paul Griffiths may still be valid, that so-called pure cognitivist approaches to emotion operate on an a priori basis, restricting their definition of the explanandum to the phenomena that their theory is suited to explain.[51] To urge this point against Chrysippus, though, would be to miss the entire motivation of Stoic affective theory and the reason for its structure. A description of all psychic events that can be called affective was never Chrysippus's aim. His concern is rather to produce a psychological account which will allow the fundamental principles of his ethics to retain their grip. Hence he is not satisfied with a single category for all instances of psychophysical change but instead structures his account around responses that, by reason of their behavioral expression, are arguably treated as evidence of underlying beliefs. These, he feels, encompass such core instances of anger, sorrow, tenderness, and delight as can easily be exampled from Greek literature, not excluding those that drive their subjects to violent or craven acts against their own best judgment.

It is for responses of this status that Chrysippus and other Stoics demand we accept responsibility. The ethical imperative to which they answer is not unlike the exhortation of Robert Solomon at the close of his essay "On the Passivity of the Passions":

> The truth is, we are adults. We must take responsibility for what we do and what we feel. . . . Arguing as I have amounts to nothing less than insisting that we think of ourselves as adults instead of children, who are indeed the passive victims of their passions.[52]

Solomon is at odds with the views of Zeno and Chrysippus only in that he says unequivocally that we are adults. In classic Stoic thought everyone past age fourteen bears the responsibilities of an adult, including responsibility for emotion. On the same school's realistic understanding of ordinary mental capacities, however, it would be truer to say we are in the process of becoming adults: our intellectual and moral characteristics are always to be compared with that normative conception of human nature which is the endpoint of personal growth and development. The sense of helplessness or being the "passive victim" of one's passions is from this perspective a lingering vestige of childhood.

Freedom

The principle that is at stake can also be expressed in terms of human freedom. The word 'freedom' is used in modern and some ancient discussions in conjunction with will or choice, to assert that our actions are self-determined. Stoic usage is different: while autonomy or self-determination is certainly a characteristic of human action, the word 'free' (eleutheros) does not occur in this context.[53] When Stoics speak of freedom it is on analogy with the social stratification that was a familiar part of life in the ancient Mediterranean. Being free means not being a slave; that is, doing what you want, and not having to do what you do not want. Among the paradoxes or counterintuitive teachings characteristic of the school is a claim that "only the wise person is free." As Susanne Bobzien observes, the Stoics certainly did not mean by this that the actions of the wise are autonomous while those of ordinary persons are not! The point is rather that the person of perfect understanding does exactly what he or she wishes to do. The ordinary person has not yet achieved such self-command but can and should aspire to it.

In this chapter we have seen one important way the ordinary person is not free: we are liable to be carried away by our own affective responses, so that we sometimes act contrary to what we otherwise mean to do. The assertion that the ideal human life is a life of freedom therefore raises a question about the nature of those 'eupathic' responses that constitute the Stoic ideal for human affectivity. Are these responses, too, of such a vigorous nature that they override other judgments the wise person might form? Is being "carried away" a feature of the normative experience of affect, or only of the perversion of affect?

The uncompromising nature of emotional impulses must be directly related to their being caused by ascriptions of genuine value. This feature is shared by the *eupatheiai*. The wise do not believe that externals have genuine value, but they do believe that human conditions and activities have that sort of value, and it is toward these that normative affect is directed. Thus we have every reason to think that the Stoics' wise person can experience very powerful feelings when the occasion calls for them. An awareness of having done the right thing should evoke not just a mild satisfaction but real, deep joy. The thought of abusing a child should be met with more than unwillingness: aversion should go off like an air-raid siren that arrests one's very being. The principle is recognized by Lawrence Becker, writing as a modern-day Stoic in response to yet another point raised by Posidonius. Posidonius inquired why it is that the wise, who recognize 'all things honorable' as unsurpassable goods, do not also find themselves deeply moved by those things. The Stoic response, argues Becker, is that they do. Those who perceive virtue to be surpassingly valuable should in fact be surpassingly passionate about it.[54]

Powerful as such responses must be, however, it is quite certain that no judgment formed by the person of perfect understanding could be said to 'override' subsequent judgments in the way Chrysippus describes. Overriding is a matter of conflict among a person's judgments; it requires changing one's mind from one moment to the next about what kind or level of response is appropriate to the situation. And knowledge, as Stoics understand it, is a state in which there is no occasion to reverse one's view. The wise are 'nonprecipitate in assent': for them to form a judgment, all relevant considerations must already have been brought to bear.[55] Thus the wise get their affective responses right in the first place; they do not alter their view as to what response is appropriate. Consequently they may experience very strong feelings and yet never have the sense that their feelings are running away with them. Any eupathic response will be a wholehearted one, with no second thoughts.

In saying this much about the *eupatheiai*, I have had to extrapolate from the surviving texts; there is no extant source that spells out the implications in the way I have done. Yet I think we can be confident of the point, and it is an important point. For like every statement about the wise and their experiences, it has application in the way we understand the nature and experience of ordinary humans. It tells us that the loss of control that we know as a regular part of our emotional lives is not, for Stoics, something that belongs to the very nature of affective response. It is something that happens, but not something that has to happen. Thus when we specify the adaptive function such responses have—or, in the Stoics' own way of speaking, when we list the capacities which human beings have *by nature,* the 'overriding' feature of emotions does not have to be included. It is in our nature to respond affectively, but it is not in our nature to be overpowered by our own affective responses. We are unfree only because we are at variance with ourselves.

4

Feelings without Assent

The anthologist Aulus Gellius tells a story purporting to be from his own experience aboard a ship at sea. A storm arises; the passengers on deck are facing imminent destruction. One passenger, however, is known to be a Stoic philosopher, and the inquisitive Gellius finds himself watching this man in spite of his own extremity. The philosopher does not scream or cry out as others are doing, yet his appearance is hardly unmoved: his complexion is pale, his hands tremble, and his expression is one of alarm. After the storm passes, Gellius seeks an explanation. Should not philosophy have guarded against such feelings?

The philosopher is not the least bit embarrassed. "Since you wish to know," he replies, "hear what our forebears, the founders of the Stoic sect, believed concerning that alarm which is brief, but necessary and natural. Better yet, read it, for reading will make it easier to believe and also to remember." He then produces from his satchel a volume of Epictetus's *Discourses* and points out the following words:

> Mental 'impressions,' through which a person's mind is struck by the initial aspect of some circumstance impinging on the mind, are not voluntary or a matter of choice, but force themselves upon one's awareness by a kind of power of their own. But the 'assents' through which those same impressions are cognized are voluntary and happen by one's own choice. That is why, when some terrifying sound occurs, either from the sky or from the collapse of a building or as the sudden herald of some danger, even the wise person's

mind necessarily responds and is contracted and grows pale for a little while, not because he opines that something evil is at hand, but by certain rapid and unplanned movements antecedent to the office of intellect and reason. Shortly, however, the wise person in that situation 'withholds assent' from those terrifying mental impressions; he spurns and rejects them and does not think that there is anything in them which he should fear.

And they say that between the mind of the wise person and that of the nonwise there is this difference, that the nonwise person thinks that the kinds of things which when they first struck his mind impressed him as scary or harsh really are that way, and 'adds belief,' endorsing those same beginnings as things rightly to be feared; but the wise person, although he experiences a brief and superficial response in color and expression, does not 'assent,' but maintains the state and strength of his opinion which he has always had about impressions of that kind, namely, that they are not at all to be feared but alarm us by false appearance and empty fright.[1]

Gellius declares himself satisfied that the passage he has thus translated accords fully with the writings of Zeno and Chrysippus. In his judgment, then, the philosopher's excuse is textbook Stoicism. Fear, like every emotion, is to be eliminated—but what the pale and trembling passenger experienced was not an instance of fear.

In the passage thus recorded, Epictetus examines the process by which emotions are generated, using as his paradigm the emotion of fear. That process begins involuntarily, with a mental impression (*phantasia*) in which some circumstance—say, the rumble of a building which is about to collapse—strikes the mind as an impending evil meriting fear. When such impressions occur, says Epictetus, one necessarily experiences certain sensations, even if one is wise. The terms used to refer to these sensations alternate between inner experience and visible physiological changes: the mind itself "is contracted and grows pale," and there is also a change in "color and expression." However, the morally significant question is not what these sensations are, but whether one assents to the view that has presented itself, that the thing that seems about to happen really is "scary or harsh." One who is wise will not assent and thus remains free of fear; in his case, there is only a "brief and superficial response."

The concession Epictetus makes here has two far-reaching implications for his presentation of Stoic views on emotion. First, it implies that the concept of 'emotion' (*pathos*), as understood by Stoics, is delimited by something other than changes of color, expression, and other observable signs of arousal. A person could undergo some verifiable physiological alteration, in the presence of the kinds of stimuli that frequently trigger emotion, and yet not have the emotion, if he or she does not also believe certain things. The Stoic claims about the voluntariness of the *pathē* would then not apply to all phenomena that might loosely be called affective, but only to a subset of them. This clarification can make a great difference in how the school's position on the *pathē* is mapped onto lived experience. I feel a flash of irritation at my spouse who has eaten the last plum: is this anger? According to this fragment of Epictetus, a Stoic can say that unless further conditions are met, what I feel is not anger at all. It is not even a trivial case of emotion, and the claims made about emotion do not apply to it.

A second, and related, implication concerns the Stoics' normative conception of a life in which emotions, properly so called, have ceased to occur. We have seen that the *apatheia* or 'impassivity' which comes with wisdom does not exclude what the Stoics called *eupatheiai*, 'well-reasoned' upliftings, reachings, or withdrawings of the psyche in relation to perceived goods and evils. But eupathic response, in that it is well reasoned, is concerned always with integral goods and evils; that is, with a person's own character and actions. For external objects the normative human being does not have any affective response at all, since he or she does not recognize these as either good or evil. We now learn, however, that the wise person does still feel *something* in connection with kinds of things that are the usual objects of the *pathē*. The normative human condition does not preclude having an impression that the crash of thunder or the crumbling plaster indicates an evil in prospect. That the wise person still has such impressions, and with them some trembling, pallor, or 'contraction,' implies that he or she still has the capacity to respond to external objects just as the ordinary person does. It is just that that capacity is no longer exercised.

Epictetus is not alone in taking this view of Stoic doctrine. Seneca makes the same assertion a number of times in his works and draws out the implications at some length, as we shall see. Plutarch, too, alludes to it as a Stoic claim, though he does not endorse it himself. A similar claim appears already in a Stoicizing context in Cicero nearly a century earlier. Moreover, while Epictetus does not assign any particular term to the response he describes, what he says about it matches well with what Stoic-influenced authors in Alexandria call the *propatheia* or 'pre-emotion': an involuntary feeling which is not counted as emotion because assent is not given to the relevant impression. The most influential of the Alexandrian formulations is by Origen, whose authority as an interpreter of Scripture guaranteed that the concept would continue to figure in exegetical writing for many years to come.

But what about the earlier period of Stoicism? Should we accept the claim made by Aulus Gellius, that the view expressed in the Epictetus fragment was also that of Zeno and Chrysippus? Or should we assume, instead, that the doctrine of involuntary feelings or pre-emotions represents a later innovation not integral to the Stoic system? I will argue here that a close scrutiny of surviving texts does tend to corroborate Gellius's historical intuition. Not only is Epictetus's assertion consistent with early Stoic thought on emotion, but it is an assertion that must actually have been made in works by the Stoic founders. Furthermore, even if we did not have any direct evidence for the Hellenistic period, we would still have reason to suspect that a feeling occurring without assent was part of the Stoic theory from a relatively early date, because of the wide geographical distribution of later authors who seem to have independent knowledge of it. The *propatheia* tradition at Alexandria makes its appearance quite early, in the commentaries of the Jewish scholar Philo; it cánnot merely reflect the influence of Seneca, as Richard Sorabji claims.[2] The points of similarity that we will explore in this chapter, between authors working in and around Rome and Philo and Origen in Alexandria, are best explained on the assumption that all those later authors found material on feelings occurring without assent in earlier Stoic works.[3] The original formulations have been lost, but their influence can still be seen.

Our own understanding of Stoic thought should be framed accordingly. The implications stated above, concerning (a) the extension of the word 'emotion' and (b) the affective capacities of the wise, should be accepted as belonging to the period of the founders. The role of innovation, and creative adaptation, too, should not be discounted; there are new departures both in Seneca and in Alexandrian exegesis. However, the basic meaning of the doctrine remains constant. There is no need for us to posit an original Stoicism in which feelings directed at externals were uniformly regarded as culpable and subject to modification.

Beginnings and 'bitings' at Athens

As background, it is helpful to keep in mind that at least one Greek philosopher had already developed views on the connection between thought and involuntary physiological response well before Zeno came on the scene. In his treatise *On the Soul* and again in *On the Movement of Animals,* Aristotle notes that while both action and emotion involve full-scale belief, there are also involuntary movements which respond merely to impressions. He is referring especially to changes in heart rate and to sexual arousal.

> What brings about movement is not the reasoning faculty. . . . For the theorizing faculty does not theorize any action to be taken, nor does it say anything is to be pursued or avoided, whereas movement is always of one pursuing or avoiding something. Not even when it theorizes that something is of such and such a kind does it at that moment command pursuit or avoidance. For instance, it often thinks of something as fearsome or pleasant but does not command fear. The heart, though, is moved, or, in the case of what is thought of as pleasant, another part of the body.

> Some parts of the body also experience involuntary movements, and most experience movements which are not voluntary. By 'involuntary' I mean such movements as those of the heart and of the private part. For often these are moved when one has some impression, even though the intellect does not command it. By 'not voluntary,' I mean such as sleep and wakening and breathing and other things of that sort, for neither impression nor desire is in control of any of these.[4]

In both passages, the feelings of sexual arousal or a rapidly beating heart are distinguished on the one hand from actual pursuit or avoidance—for which one has to believe that the object of the feeling really is pleasant or fearsome—and on the other hand from automatic movements like breathing. It is reasonable to infer that Aristotle finds these 'involuntary' sensations philosophically interesting largely because of their association with impressions. Sexual arousal, for instance, does not depend on conscious decision in the same way as walking or buying a coat does, and yet it still requires an impression, since typical instances involve thoughts or mental images of sexual acts or desirable partners. What Aristotle means by an 'impression' may not be quite the same as what Zeno or Chrysippus calls by that name, and the sentences given here are by no means the only things he has to say about the role of impressions in voluntary movement.[5] But his remarks are still of interest to us in that they show that the causes of various intermediate psychophysical events were already being discussed at Athens by the latter part of the fourth century.

A similar interest in involuntary reactions can be traced in a fragment of Chrysippus preserved by Galen. In this fragment, Chrysippus concerns himself with cases of involuntary weeping and, in a similar vein, of cessations of weeping; also, he mentions an explanation given elsewhere for laughter.

> People who are weeping stop, and people weep when they do not want to, when the impressions created by underlying facts are similar, and there is either some impediment or no impediment. For it is reasonable that in such cases [i.e., those of involuntary weeping] something happens similar to the way that the cessation of weeping and lamentation come to pass, but rather in the beginnings of the circumstances bringing about the movement. It is just as I said in the case of the circumstances that bring about laughter and other similar cases.[6]

What Chrysippus says here should not, I think, be assimilated either to the discussion we encountered in chapter 3 of how one is carried away by emotion, or to his explanation (which immediately precedes) of how grief diminishes over time. He does not attribute this weeping to assent or impulse and does not mention the runner analogy which supplies his usual explanation for the recalcitrance of emotions.[7] Neither is he now concerned with beliefs which persist but cease to be 'fresh.' Instead, the explanation remains at the level of impressions, with some appeal—the import of which is not immediately clear—to "impediments" and to "the beginnings of the circumstances bringing about the movement." The reason for this difference is that the cases with which he is now concerned are ones which he himself recognizes as involuntary. We should be thinking of tears which spring up when one is not really grieving or, conversely, of people who stop weeping when merely disturbed from their grief for a short period.

Further interpretation is at best conjectural, for Chrysippus's language is vague and the original context unrecoverable. The most we can say with certainty is that Chrysippus believed such phenomena could be explained without disruption to his principal contentions about affective response. Nonetheless, in order to have at least a tentative sense of Chrysippus's intended explanation, I venture the following suggestion. Suppose that what Chrysippus means by an 'impediment' is a sharp contradiction between one's overall view of one's circumstances and another impression which presents itself. Person A is in neutral circumstances, with no particular reason either to weep or to be glad. Tears will come to her eyes, however, if she hears a mournful tale. This is a case in which there is no impediment. Meanwhile person B is genuinely grieving a bereavement but is beguiled by a child's antics. The new impression creates an impediment to tears that would otherwise flow, by absorbing B's attention. In both cases the person's real assessment of her situation, and consequently the real emotional state, is contrary to what is indicated by the tears or lack thereof. There has been a momentary interruption, but it will soon be reversed. For this reason Chrysippus refers to "the beginnings of the circumstances bringing about the movement." Had there been a complete psychological process of impression and assent, he would have said that the agent wanted to weep or to stop weeping.

In addition to this fragment of Chrysippus there is also a small group of texts concerned with the inner experience of the wise. An aphorism attributed to Zeno has application here. As quoted by Seneca in book 1 of On Anger, Zeno remarked, "In the sage's mind also there remains a scar even after the wound is healed." In this the 'wound' must be some painful condition of mind, and the scar a painless indication that such a condition existed in the past. That the 'wound' must be specifically a capacity for emotion is not made clear by the fragment itself but is strongly suggested by the context. Seneca is speaking of the judge who must determine penalties for a convicted felon. He writes,

> When the sage is in such circumstances, will not his mind be touched? Will he not be more than usually upset? I admit it: he will feel a slight and superficial affect, for, as Zeno says, "In the sage's mind also there remains a scar even after the wound is healed." Thus he will feel certain suspicions and shadows of the emotions but will lack the emotions themselves.[8]

Assuming the Senecan context is not completely unrelated to Zeno's intentions, we can find in the scar aphorism a view as to the causation of this "slight and superficial affect." Just as a scar is an indication of what has happened in the past, so, perhaps, the wise person's inconsequential reactions are indications of his having once held the same mistaken evaluation of externals as disposes the imperfect mind to emotion.

A complaint made by Plutarch may refer to the same view of Zeno or to related material in Chrysippus. Plutarch writes as though his Stoic opponents are themselves claiming to be wise: this claim, he says, is refuted according to their own canons by the fact that they continue to have emotions. As far as he is concerned, the language of eupathic responses is just philosophical sleight of hand: fear is still the same feeling and still counts as an emotion, even if one chooses to call it 'caution.' Moreover the same can be said for another group of feelings which do not appear to be eupatheiai:

> Refuted by their tears and tremblings and changes of color, they say, instead
> of grief and fear, 'bitings' and 'troublings,' and use 'eagernesses' as a euphe-
> mism for desires.[9]

What Stoics are these who say that "tremblings and changes of color"
need not be indications of fear and who claim that tears may be evidence
not of grief but only of a 'biting'? Although Plutarch does not name a
specific source for the terms he finds offensive, there can be little doubt
that the objects of his attack are the most authoritative Stoics, Zeno and
Chrysippus themselves. For opinionated as he may be, Plutarch is also a
serious scholar who makes extensive use of primary sources. In the treatise quoted, as in others of his writings, he not only names Zeno and
Chrysippus but actually quotes a discussion of mental conflict from one
of Chrysippus's treatises.[10] And in the very paragraph with which we are
concerned he describes as an admission of 'these same persons' (*kai autoi*)
a point which we know to have been discussed at length in Chrysippus's
treatise *On Emotions*. We should therefore credit the Stoic founders with
having devised nonprejudicial terms like 'bitings' and 'troublings' for responses which do not have the moral significance of genuine emotions.

A specialized psychological sense for the word 'biting' seems also to
have been known to Posidonius, who included it along with impressions
in a list of events he calls "corporeal in association with the mind."[11] This
is as opposed to "purely mental" events such as judgments and emotions
and is distinguished also from the corporeal manifestations of the emotions proper, called "mental in association with the body" and including
"tremblings, paleness, and changes of expression due to fear or grief." Not
much can be learned from this, for the Posidonius fragment does not spell
out the philosophical implications of the classification. It may be significant, however, that 'bitings' are here assigned to the same category as
impressions. As noted in chapter 1, 'biting' is a term sometimes used by
both Zeno and Chrysippus to refer to the psychophysical event which constitutes grief itself; that is, to the feeling of grief as opposed to its cognitive content. Here, by contrast, 'biting' is counted among psychophysical
events which do not meet the assent criterion.

For the role of unassented 'biting' in normative experience we can turn
to a further bit of evidence gleaned from Cicero's account of Stoic views
on grief in the third Tusculan Disputation. This account is drawn not from
Posidonius but from Chrysippus's *On Emotions* and other early works.[12]
Throughout the third disputation, Cicero explains why he believes, following the Stoics, that the wise person is not susceptible to grief. Near the end

he recapitulates the main points in support of this thesis: grief is 'empty,' serves no good purpose, and is not in accordance with nature but is rather caused by false beliefs. At the same time, however, he allows that a lesser response, which he calls "a bite and a small contraction," is natural even in the wise:

> Distress of any kind is far removed from the wise person, because it is an empty thing, because it serves no purpose, because it has its origin not in nature but in judgment and opinion and in a kind of invitation that is issued when we decide that grief is appropriate. Once this entirely voluntary belief is removed, distress will be eliminated—the real, unhappy distress, that is, but the mind will still feel a bite and a small contraction from time to time. This last they may indeed call 'natural,' provided they do not use the name 'distress.' For that is a grim and deadly name, which cannot by any means coexist or, as it were, dwell together with wisdom.[13]

Cicero's way of stating the matter is of interest particularly because of its emphasis on assent and its interest in the inner experience of the wise. What is properly called distress is dependent on judgment and is therefore volitional; the 'bite and small contraction' is nonvolitional but by the same token is not counted as full-scale distress. The passage thus bears comparison with what we have seen in Epictetus, but at a much earlier date. Like Epictetus, Cicero uses the technical Stoic vocabulary of 'contraction'; here, however, 'contraction' is paired with 'biting' and is associated with distress, as would be expected from the usual role of 'contraction' in Stoic theory, rather than with fear. In addition, Cicero indicates that 'biting and contraction' occur with some regularity in the wise person's experience. He does not, like Epictetus, say that such feelings occur 'necessarily,' but he does say that they will occur from time to time and may be considered natural.

The Senecan account

The view that feelings sometimes occur in the absence of assent is developed to its fullest extent in the works of Seneca. From what we have seen, it is clear that Seneca's position on the subject is not entirely new. The main assertions, together with their far-reaching implications, belong already to the earlier period of Stoicism. But his way of explaining those assertions is his own: many of the examples he gives, and some at least of the doctrinal formulations, represent his independent contribution to the subject. In studying his work we should understand that we are seeing a reformulation of Stoic doctrine, rather than a new departure. At the same time, we should expect that he will sometimes exploit opportunities for embellishment and innovation, when he feels that doing so will not distort the doctrine he has inherited.

The most extensive discussion is contained in the early treatise *On Anger*. Book 2 of that work begins by offering to delve into the theoretical issue which is the "bones and sinews" of the treatise as a whole: the psychological process by which anger is generated in us. Does anger come about "of one's own will," or does the emotion come into being "like many things which happen in us without our knowledge"?[14] Seneca lays out succinctly what he understands to be the Stoic view: anger is a high-level response requiring not only an impression of injury received but also assent to that impression. The latter, but not the former, involves complex cognitive processing.

> That anger is stimulated by the impression of injury received is not in doubt; what we are asking is whether it follows immediately upon the impression itself, rushing forth without the mind's agreement, or whether it is generated when the mind assents. We hold that anger dares nothing on its own; rather, it comes about with the mind giving its approval. For to gain an impression of injury received, and conceive a desire for revenge, and to link together the two ideas that one ought not to have been wronged and that one ought to take revenge—none of this is characteristic of that impulse that is stirred involuntarily. The one is simple (*simplex*), the other complex, made up of many things: it understands something, thinks it wrong, condemns it, and punishes it. These things cannot happen unless the mind assents to that which impinges upon it.[15]

Anger, properly so called, is psychologically complex; its complexity is in fact what marks it as a rational and therefore voluntary response. But Seneca also speaks of an involuntary 'impulse,' one which rushes forth "without the mind's agreement," following immediately upon the impression itself. This prior event does not require us to link together multiple propositions in the way anger does; it is not "made up of many things" but is rather *simplex*, a 'simple' psychic event.[16]

What is this *simplex* event? Certainly it is not an impulse in the usual Stoic sense of that word, for impulses normally require assent, and this event is specifically said to take place without assent. But neither does it take place without any engagement of the cognitive faculties at all. For even this event requires some conceptualization of the raw sense experience: whatever it is, it already has the content *that an injury has been received*. One cannot see someone's behavior as an injury to oneself without drawing on a sophisticated array of concepts, for the very notion of injury is put together out of ideas of personhood, intention, fairness, and what is due to oneself as an individual. We should therefore assume on a provisional basis that the *simplex* event is one which requires the capacity for rational impression. Either it is just the same event as the impression itself, considered as feeling rather than as the bearer of content, or it is some kind of concomitant or effect of that impression.[17]

This initial assessment is partially confirmed when Seneca begins giving examples, for a number of the examples chosen require the application of concepts and even some linguistic processing. However, there is little consistency on this point: others, which are also supposed to illustrate Seneca's point, suggest subrational movements or reflexes which take place automatically. In the selection that follows, examples are numbered for ease of reference:

"What is the point of this inquiry?" you ask. For us to understand what anger is. For if it comes about against our will, it will never yield to argument. For all responses which do not come about through our own volition are intransigent and irresistible; for instance, [1] goosebumps when one is sprinkled with cold water, [2] recoiling from certain kinds of touch, [3] the hair rising at bad news, [4] blushing at bad language, and [5] vertigo when one looks over a cliff. Since none of these things is in our power, no reasoning can persuade them not to happen. Anger is dispelled by teaching, for it is a voluntary fault of the mind, not one of those things which come about through some requirement of the human condition and which, for that reason, befall even the wisest persons. It is among these that we should place that initial impact on the mind which stirs us after we believe we have been wronged.

This latter arises also [6] during comic stage shows and [7] while reading of past events. Often we appear to become angry at Clodius when he drives Cicero into exile and at Antony when he kills him. Who does not get stirred up against Marius's taking up arms, against Sulla's proscriptions? . . . [8] Singing sometimes excites us, and quick tempi and the warlike sound of trumpets. Our minds are moved [9] by gruesome paintings and [10] by the terrible sight of the most just executions. It is thus that [11] we laugh along when others are laughing, and [12] a crowd of mourners depresses us, and [13] we boil up when others are fighting. These things are not anger, any more than it is grief [14] that makes one grimace at the sight of a staged shipwreck, or fear [15] that runs through the minds of readers when Hannibal lays siege to the city after the battle of Cannae. Rather, all these things are movements of minds which do not will to be moved, and are not emotions but beginnings preliminary to emotion.

It is thus that [16] a trumpet pricks up the ears of the military man, though he be dressed as a civilian in time of peace, and thus that [17] warhorses are roused by the rattle of arms. . . . None of these things which strike the mind by chance ought to be called emotions; the mind undergoes them, as it were, more than it performs them. Emotion, then, is not when one is moved upon receiving impressions of things, but when one entrusts oneself to them and follows up this chance movement. For if anyone thinks that [18] paleness, [19] tears welling up, [20] the arousal of the sexual fluid, [21] a deep sigh, [22] a sudden brightening of the eyes, and other things like that are an indication of emotion and a signal of the mind, he is deceived and does not understand that these are impacts on the body. Hence [23] even the man who is generally very brave grows pale when putting on his armor; [24] the fiercest of soldiers is weak at the knees when the signal to engage is given; [25] a great general's heart pounds before the lines of battle meet; [26] the most eloquent orator's scalp tightens as he prepares to speak.[18]

With the full force of his rhetorical training behind it, Seneca's list is dazzling, but it is also baffling. In itself, it defeats analysis. What would appear to be the crudest of reflex actions in 1 and 2 are thrown casually together with 3 and 4, both of which require one to interpret information presented verbally. Aesthetic responses to drama, music, and literature (6–9, 14, 15) are not differentiated in any way from sympathy responses to the infectious emotions of others (11–13), or from the conditioned reflexes of the trained military man (16), and even the trained military horse (17). Some items are described strictly as corporeal changes (18–22) and called "impacts on the body," yet from these Seneca proceeds seamlessly to 23–26, all of which depend on inferences that the body, as distinct from the mind, could hardly be expected to make.

In order to make sense of what Seneca is saying about unassented feelings we have to keep in view the purpose he has stated for the entire discussion. He has not offered to provide a single coherent explanation for all the sorts of feelings he is now using as examples. His purpose, rather, is to convey to the reader "what anger is." That is, he seeks to refine the

Stoic claims as to what constitutes a genuine emotion by fixing more precisely the point at which one must be said to have assented to the relevant proposition. To this end it is of value to him to mark out a broad spectrum of psychophysical events which stop short of that divide. By grouping some relatively sophisticated responses together with other sorts of feeling which ordinary intuition recognizes as involuntary, he invites his readers to see what all such cases have in common: all occur without one's having made any commitment to the truth of the occurrent impression. Anything and everything that takes place without such commitment is eligible to be listed here.

Because of the variety among Seneca's examples, I think we should resist the effort of Richard Sorabji to assimilate the Stoics' unassented feelings to the rapid-process amygdala response identified by contemporary neuroscience.[19] A preconscious alarm processed in milliseconds—the rabbit startled by a shadow—could find a place in Seneca's list, but so also do many instances in which the stimulus has been fully conceptualized. The examples involving information presented verbally—dirty jokes, stage plays, and stories in books—indicate that even fully articulate thoughts can occur in us without meeting the requirement for voluntariness. Being stirred up against Sulla for his proscriptions requires, at the least, comprehending a written history and forming a moral assessment based on that information. Still it is not an emotion, any more than gooseflesh or vertigo is an emotion. Until and unless one judges that a certain response—in this case, seeking revenge—is appropriate for oneself at this time, no actual emotion has occurred.

So also in a generalized case of anger, Seneca pushes his account as far toward emotion as it can possibly go without reaching anger itself. This is where all the preceding examples have been leading:

> Anger has to rush out, not merely be moved. For it is an impulse, and there is never an impulse without the mind's assent, nor can it happen that someone takes action in the matter of revenge and punishment with mind unaware. A person thinks himself harmed, wants to take revenge, but some reason tells against it and he immediately settles down. This I do not call anger, this movement of the mind in obedience to reason; no, anger is that movement which overleaps reason and drags reason along with it. Thus that first agitation of the mind which the impression of injury inflicts is no more anger than is the impression of injury itself; the impulse that follows, though, which not only receives but endorses the impression of injury, is

indeed anger, the excitement of a mind which is pressing on toward revenge through a voluntary judgment.[20]

Ordinary intuition might be inclined to say that the person who "immediately settles down" has already experienced anger but has suppressed
it. Seneca's analysis is different. On his view, this agent has indeed had
the impression of injury ("thinks himself harmed") and even wants revenge—that is, he has had the further impression that seeking revenge is
appropriate to him at this time.[21] But thought has not been converted into
belief: he has not endorsed that impulsory impression, because of some
competing consideration which enters into his process of practical reasoning and leads him to the opposite conclusion.[22] Whatever feeling may have
accompanied his impressions thus remains "in obedience to reason." He
has come right to the verge of a judgment which, if made, will override
any subsequent effort to be reasonable. But he has not made that step; he
has not gone over the cliff.

Considering the kinds of phenomena mentioned as examples, one may
find it slightly odd that Seneca chooses the expression 'beginnings preliminary to emotion' (*principia proludentia adfectibus*). Most of the examples
given are not in fact preliminaries to anything. One does not go on from
a conditioned reflex, a sympathy response, or an aesthetic response to experience emotion for real: in these cases, the 'beginning' is the entirety of
what occurs. Again, though, the choice of expressions is comprehensible
if one bears in mind that the purpose of the entire discussion is to give the
closest possible analysis of the process by which anger, real anger, is generated. Foremost in Seneca's mind is the distinction between two events:
first, the feeling which may accompany a fully conceptualized impression
that taking revenge is now appropriate; and second, the endorsing of that
impression, in which, consequent upon opportunity, revenge taking actually begins. Since the endorsing, if it takes place at all, must have been preceded by the impression, it is reasonable to describe the feeling connected
with the impression alone as 'preliminary,' even though there will be cases
in which no assent is ever given. We do not have to assume that Seneca
was familiar with the term 'pre-emotion' (*propatheia*), which we know to
have been used at Alexandria. More important is that he has in mind the
same notion as must have suggested that term: that whether or not the unassented feeling will ever become an emotion, it certainly is not one yet.

From the standpoint of Stoic theory the least satisfactory part of Seneca's explanation is his appeal to the body following examples 18–22. We
saw in chapter 1 that although the *psuchē* is itself corporeal, a Stoic account

can reasonably draw a distinction between body and mind where the point is to contrast functions like impression, assent, and impulse with whatever else in a person either enables or constrains those functions. But that is not quite the distinction Seneca intends here. The five examples from 18 to 22 cannot be set apart from what is said elsewhere in the passage about 'impacts on the mind,' and about things that 'strike' or 'move' or 'run through' the mind. On the contrary, the connective particles 'for' (*nam*) and 'hence' (*itaque*) establish a logical structure for the paragraph in which paleness, tears, and so on must be similar in kind to the earlier and later examples. That is, the paleness in 18 is not just any paleness—not that caused by a fever, for instance—but a quasi-emotional paleness like that of the brave soldier in 23, and so with the other items. In all of these, the response is nonmental just insofar as it is not an indication of assent. The distinction that is needed is the distinction between the rational mind's most distinctive function, that of assent, and a basic function we share with animals, that of impression. In an effort to emphasize the crucial role of volition, Seneca slips into a habit of referring to the latter as a function of the body, implicitly restricting 'mind' to the region of assent. But it would be more usual for a Stoic author to assign both functions to the mind, and Seneca himself moves back and forth between the two, as again in *On Anger* 2.4.2, where the preliminary to emotion, now called an 'impact on the mind,' is likened to "those things which, as I said, happen to the body." Further examples given there are "being stimulated [to yawn] by another's yawning" and "blinking when fingers are thrust suddenly in one's face," reactions hardly different from 1 and 2 above.

"A requirement of the human condition"

The discussion in *On Anger* makes it clear that because the feelings of which Seneca speaks do not depend on assent, they are nonculpable, and there is no reason why the person of perfect understanding should not experience them just like anyone else. Indeed it says more than that, for Seneca's position is not only that "the wisest persons" *may* experience unassented feelings but that they *must*: such experiences come about "through some requirement of the human condition." For Seneca, then, the 'preliminaries to emotion' manifest a capacity which is always present in human beings, something that is part of what it is to be human. This is a note sounded already by Cicero, when he says that the 'bite and small contraction' which is compatible with wisdom may also be called 'natural.' It is comparable, too, to a point made in the Epictetus fragment, that the mind of the wise person 'necessarily' responds and is contracted when recognizing certain kinds of objects.

The involuntary affects of the wise figure prominently in several of Seneca's Moral Epistles. In the eleventh letter, Seneca describes a meeting with a young student who blushes at being questioned. Reflecting on the conversation, he writes:

> I suspect he is one who will retain the tendency to blush even when he attains his maturity and rids himself of every fault—even when he is wise. For natural faults of body or mind (*naturalia corporis aut animi uitia*) are not removed by any amount of wisdom: what is innate and implanted may be mitigated by treatment, but not overcome. . . . Even if people are able to stand up to an unfamiliar situation, it does affect them, if their body's natural disposition gives them a tendency to blush. For some people have lively, energetic blood that rises swiftly to their faces. This is not cast out by any amount of wisdom; if it were, if wisdom could erase all a person's faults, then wisdom would have nature itself in charge.

His concerns in the fifty-seventh letter are similar. Again, he writes about a personal experience: he has recently become apprehensive while passing through a dust-filled tunnel between Baiae and Naples.

> I felt a kind of impact on my mind and, though without fear, a change, brought about by the newness and unpleasantness of the unfamiliar circumstance. And now I am not speaking about myself alone (for I am far from being even a tolerable human being, let alone a perfect one) but about that person over whom fortune no longer holds sway. His mind, too, will be struck; his color will change. For there are some things, dear Lucilius, that no amount of virtue can escape: nature gives the virtuous a reminder of their own mortality. So they will change expression at sad events, and shudder at sudden events, and grow dizzy when looking down from a great height. This is not fear, but a natural affect which cannot be assailed by reason. . . . What I felt, then, was, as I said, not an emotion, and yet it was a change.

By the seventy-first letter the topic is familiar:

> I come now to the point you are expecting from me. Lest it should seem that what we call virtue strays outside the natural order, the wise person

will tremble and feel pain and grow pale, for all these things are feelings of the body.[23]

Not coincidentally, all three passages include an appeal to what is 'natural' to a human being. In the epistle 11, a tendency to blush is among "natural faults of body or mind." In epistle 57, we read of 'nature' giving a reminder of mortality and of "a natural affect which cannot be assailed by reason." In epistle 71, the unassented feelings, now simply called feelings 'of the body,' are retained in the account "lest it should seem that what we call virtue strays outside the natural order."

In a Stoic context the inclusion of the word 'natural' cannot but be significant. Seneca, like other Stoic authors, is deeply committed to the idea that norms for human conduct should reflect nature's intentions for the species, as revealed in those features which cannot be omitted from a careful description of human psychology. The fleeting reactions of the wise are an important topic for him in part because they remind his reader of this naturalistic strain in Stoic ethics. One should not imagine the Stoics' wise person to be some kind of monster whose affective equipment has somehow been radically altered. The attainment of tranquility does mean that emotions, as defined by improper assent, cease to occur; it does not mean that any psychic capacity has been removed.

Pursuing this theme, Seneca gives considerable scope and elaboration to 'natural' affect. In the *Consolation to Marcia,* for instance, he admits that missing a family member is natural not only in bereavement but even in separation and says that it is "necessary" that there be "a biting and a contraction of even the firmest minds."[24] Animals utter loud cries for a day or two over their missing young and search about, but only human beings grieve consciously, willfully, and at length. This suggests that in humans, too, noisy weeping and other such reactions might continue for a period of days and still be excused as mere preliminaries to emotion. Even more remarkable is a discussion of the wise person's tears in Moral Epistle 99. The wise person weeps both involuntarily, as at a funeral with sobs shaking his whole body, and voluntarily, when remembering the loved one's kind deeds and cheerful companionship. The involuntary tears are forced out by a certain 'requirement of nature' (*naturalis necessitas*) and are an indication of 'humanness' (*humanitas*). The other, voluntary tears can only be eupathic; they have some admixture of joy and are not uncontrollable.[25] This is the only text known to me in which a eupathic response gives rise to weeping.

Alexandrian *Propatheiai*

We noted earlier that traces of Stoic material on unassented feelings are to be found in Philo of Alexandria, the Jewish scholar whose works belong to the first decades of the first century c.e. It remains to be seen what specific use Philo makes of this element in Stoic thought, and likewise what is said about the *propatheia* or 'pre-emotion' in the exegetical writings of Origen and his successors. For both Philo and Origen were familiar with the same Stoic authors as were read by Cicero, Seneca, and Epictetus, and in several ways their 'pre-emotions' are similar to the 'bitings,' 'preliminaries,' and 'unplanned movements' we have seen in those authors. The points of similarity undoubtedly reflect the emphases of some authoritative account from the earlier Stoa, whether the account was Chrysippus's own or that of some other influential Stoic. And among them are the most philosophically significant points we have seen: the involuntary nature of such feelings, their dependence on rational impression, and their continued occurrence in the wise.

Meanwhile it is instructive to see how useful the Alexandrians found this Stoic concept to be in their own work of scriptural exegesis. The task was challenging: readings had to be discovered which not only had plausible textual support but could accord with the prior theological commitments of the exegete and serve the purposes of religious instruction. In the Christian writers, there was a need also for Scripture passages to be interpreted in such a way as to support a position in the Christological controversies of the day. With much at stake, the exegetes were philosophical opportunists, ready to lay hands on any philosophical tool they found sharp enough to carve a fine psychological distinction and robust enough to maintain that distinction under dialectical pressure. Consistency by the canons of Greek philosophical debate was not a major concern: concepts taken from Platonist philosophy, including the Platonist standard of moderation in emotion (*metriopatheia*), could be deployed alongside or even combined with Stoic ideas. However, Philo, Origen, and other authors in this tradition did share certain broad presuppositions with the Stoics in matters of ethics. Anger, fear, grief, and the like, because of their commitment to the value of externals, are considered in their works to be unnatural and improper, not compatible with virtue or wisdom and by the same token not attributable to the divinity. Further, all these authors share with the Stoics a strong interest in describing the perfection of human nature. In Philo, the exemplar of virtue is found especially in Abraham; in the Christian authors, in the incarnate Christ. Scripture passages which appear to validate ordinary emotions or to attribute them to God, to Abraham, or to Jesus Christ were therefore of particular concern. The involuntary 'pre-emotion' could sometimes be called upon to resolve the difficulty.

Philo's commentary on Genesis and Exodus supplies evidence that he recognized some emotion-like feelings which are involuntary and thus do not compromise the passionless condition of the virtuous. The clearest instance is to be found in his comment on Genesis 25:2, the words "Abraham came to bewail Sarah and to mourn." The passage is problematic for Philo because Abraham figures in his exegetical system as the exemplar of human excellence and ought, therefore, to be untouched by grief. To solve the problem, Philo notes that Scripture represents Abraham not as actually mourning Sarah but only as "coming there to mourn." This language, he says, fitly represents one response which is possible, and indeed necessary, in the virtuous person.

> But excellently and carefully does [Scripture] show that the virtuous man did not resort to wailing or mourning but only came there for some such thing. For things that unexpectedly and against his will strike the pusillanimous man weaken, crush and overthrow him, whereas everywhere they merely bow down the man of constancy when they direct their blows against him, and not in such a way as to bring [their work] to completion, since they are strongly repelled by the guiding reason, and retreat.[26]

There is some uncertainty as to the terminology Philo is using, for the commentary on Genesis is preserved in full only in a sixth-century Armenian translation. (The English translation given here is by Ralph Marcus [1953].) Even so it is possible to discern how Philo makes use of the Stoic concepts of impression and assent in his interpretation. Anyone, wise or foolish, may be "struck" unexpectedly and against his will, by "things"— that is, by impressions that represent his circumstances as evil. Grief does not occur, however, unless these things "bring their work to completion" in a further mental event described, with metaphorical violence, as if it were the knockout in a psychological boxing match. The contrast between the effect of impressions on the weak character and on the strong is drawn exactly as in the later account by Epictetus: the weak person yields to the impression and experiences the relevant emotion; the strong person rejects it through reason and is merely "bowed down" for a moment.

From here Philo proceeds to draw a moral for the progressor. "When something happens against one's will," he says (i.e., when the involuntary impression occurs), one should neither be immobile, "fixed in prayer," nor "entirely rapt and moved and drawn toward this," but should "somewhat gradually go toward it, and retire before the end is reached." As examples of the externals which might move an agent he gives "the possessions of others" and "the divisions of women"—that is, women's genitals. These suggest, respectively, the sins of theft and adultery. To prevent oneself from committing these, men should "think it sufficient to have been struck by these impulses, and . . . move away and take their stand upon the immovable and firm mind." Thus he presents desire as analogous to grief and enjoins the progressor to eliminate that emotion and not merely to moderate or limit it. He does not expect even advanced progressors to be completely unresponsive to stimuli, but he does ask them to withdraw *before* the response develops into desire.

The 'being struck' which Philo allows to Abraham would in the usage of Origen and later writers be called a *propatheia* or 'pre-emotion,' and indeed the later digest-commentaries of Procopius of Gaza and the *catena* tradition refer to Abraham's 'coming to mourn' as "a pre-emotion, not an emotion."[27] Whether Philo himself used that term for an involuntary feeling which precedes emotion is not known, since the Greek text of the *Questions on Genesis and Exodus* survives only in a handful of quoted fragments. However, we do have one such fragment in which he is reported to have used that term for a feeling which precedes one of the *eupatheiai*—for Philo, following the Stoics, posits a class of normative affects which are fully compatible with wisdom and virtue. The fragment comments on Genesis 18:11–12, in which Abraham's wife Sarah laughs at the·promise of a child in her ninetieth year. According to Philo Sarah's laughter indicates hope, which he says is "a *propatheia* of joy," commenting that "before joy there is an anticipation of good."[28] Her reaction cannot be an emotion, for Scripture says that "there ceased to be with Sarah the ways of women," and Philo takes "the ways of women" to mean the ordinary emotions of fear, sorrow, pleasure, and desire.[29] But neither is it joy itself, for joy, which is the chief among the *eupatheiai*, is restricted to God and to the virtuous in contemplation of God, while Sarah, who has not yet attained a state of knowledge, "does not yet know laughter."[30] In contrast to Abraham, whose laughter Philo is willing to call "divine laughter," Sarah is still uncertain; she has "begun to rejoice" but is not actually rejoicing.

Philo is also familiar with the Stoic usage which offers 'biting' as a nonculpable analogue to grief. Commenting on Genesis 9:3, in which God instructs Noah to accept "every reptile that lives" as food to be eaten, he recognizes a difficulty: how can God advocate the consumption of reptiles, given that reptiles function in Philo's interpretive scheme as symbols of the 'poisonous passions' desire, fear, grief, and pleasure?[31] The solution is that the reptiles spoken of here must be a different, 'clean' sort of reptile, representing nonculpable forms of affective response. Each of the four genera of unclean passion-reptiles has a clean genus ranged alongside it: alongside pleasure is 'joy,' alongside desire 'reflection,' alongside fear 'caution,' and alongside grief 'biting and contraction.'[32] The first three of these clean genera are familiar to us as the canonical genus-*eupatheiai* of Stoic theory, for 'reflection' is a reasonable rendering for *boulēsis* (wish). As the paired terms 'biting and contraction' correspond to the passion of grief, they must refer to an affective response that is comparable to grief in the same way as joy is comparable to pleasure or caution to fear. In that this response is 'clean' and can arise in one not susceptible to ordinary emotions, Philo's scheme treats 'biting and contraction' very much as the same terms are treated in Cicero. Philo differs from Cicero, however, in that he gives 'biting and contraction' the status of a fourth *eupatheia*. Evidently he has combined two elements of older Stoic theory, the *eupatheia* doctrine and another which mentioned the terms *dēxis* and *sustolē* in connection with a response which has some features of grief but is exempt from culpability.

Origen knew the works of Philo and undoubtedly drew from them many exegetical principles. But he had no need to draw on Philo for Stoic material, for he had himself read extensively in Stoic works, of logic and physics as well as ethics. His account of what he calls the 'pre-emotion' is expressed with some terminological precision. Anger itself, he says, is 'up to us' and comes about when there is assent (*sunkatathesis*) which accepts that it is appropriate (*kathēkein*) to take revenge on the supposed offender. But the word 'anger' might also refer to a pre-emotion, which is involuntary and takes place, he says, "even in the perfect" in circumstances like those that evoke anger.[33] "The Word knows that there is an anger which is not a sin, one which does not come from what is up to us, is not emotional and does not perform any bad deed."

Thus in interpreting Psalm 4:5, which reads in the Septuagint translation "Be angry (*orgizesthe*), and do not sin," Origen insists that the 'anger' that is meant is only the *propatheia*. Noting that the Greek verb could be either imperative ('be angry!') or indicative ('you are angry'), he argues that it must be the indicative that is intended, since it would make no sense to order someone to do something that is involuntary. He draws further confirmation from Akylas's rendering of the Hebrew word as 'tremble': to command people to tremble, he says, would be absurd. The verse as a whole, then, teaches that when one experiences trembling or the pre-emotion of anger, one should not allow any blameworthy act to follow.[34]

Like Philo, Origen assumes that ordinary human emotions, grief and fear as well as anger, always imply some moral error, so that no emotion can be attributed to the deity or to any virtuous human. For this reason he devotes special attention to New Testament passages which seem to attribute emotions to the incarnate Christ. A key passage is Matthew 26:38–39, which tells how Jesus in the garden of Gethsemane "began to be grieved and agitated . . . and said, 'I am deeply grieved, even to death.'" Origen is concerned that some who read this verse may seize upon Jesus' example as a way of defending ordinary human emotions. Also, he is concerned that Jesus' apparent distress may lead some readers to believe that Jesus was not truly divine but merely human, the error, he says, of "certain heretical sects." In his own comment on the passage, he therefore emphasizes the word 'began.' There is a big difference, he says, between beginning to grieve and actually grieving. Jesus did experience the beginning of grief and fear, but he did not grieve "with the grief of emotion itself."[35] This is exactly the interpretive strategy that enabled Philo to maintain that Abraham did not mourn for Sarah. But there is a polemical edge to the interpretation that we did not find in Philo. Origen is writing for the catechumens of his own school, but as always he is also writing in the midst of controversy. Here, of course, he has in mind Arian Christologies that deny the full divinity of Christ.

At the same time, his treatment of the passage contains the germ of an argument against the opposite error, that of supposing that Jesus is not human at all but a completely divine nature in the shape of a human. Citing Hebrews 4:15, "he was tempted in everything as we are, except that he did not sin," he remarks that Jesus' incipient emotions are an indication of his human nature. Having assumed the weakness of the human body, he "was able to suffer with us in our weakness," and an important part of human weakness is the susceptibility of human nature to emotion. Hence while it is important to recognize that Jesus does not actually grieve or fear, it is equally important to recognize that he does at least experience the beginnings of those emotions. These beginnings teach humility to the disciples, by giving them a concrete illustration of the words he is about to say to them: "the spirit is willing, but the flesh is weak." And they also demonstrate that during his lifetime he does indeed have the sort of mind which is capable of emotions, even if the capacity is never exercised. He is "not altogether without taste of grief." But this is only, in his own words, "even to death." After his death, he will no longer experience even the beginnings of grief.

This second line of argument proved especially useful to those of Origen's successors who were concerned to refute the views of Apollinaris of Laodicea (c. 310–c. 390). Apollinaris had taught many to believe that Jesus did not have the same sort of mind as other humans have, his reasoning processes being entirely divine. The 'rational soul' (*psuchē logikē*) which enables ordinary humans to think and make decisions was in him replaced by the divine Logos, which in the Incarnation took on only as much of human soul as was necessary to endow his flesh with its basic life functions. To combat this view, Apollinaris's orthodox contemporaries lay some emphasis on Jesus' experience of pre-emotions. The argument is best followed in the scriptural commentaries of Didymus Caecus, Origen's successor in the teaching headship at Alexandria.[36] Didymus argues repeatedly that the pre-emotions Jesus experienced at Gethsemane are sufficient proof that he possessed a rational human nature. To have a pre-emotion is to receive the same kind of impression as ordinarily produces fear, anger, desire, or grief, and only a rational being is receptive to this sort of impression. If Jesus had had in his human nature only the sort of soul that an animal has, being otherwise entirely divine, he would not have been able even to begin to grieve. So while it is a fact that Jesus did not actually experience any emotion, that fact is not to be attributed to some superhuman changelessness; it is rather the glorious achievement of an essentially human will.[37]

Didymus is well aware that having a pre-emotion means having a false thought, one which, if it were definitively accepted, would be a moral error. Demons sometimes suggest pre-emotions to us, although this is not the only way they arise.[38] They are, in fact, a kind of impurity, even though no blame attaches to them. In explanation of this he offers an analogy to the faint marks that handling leaves on a shirt: on a shirt stained with use, these go unnoticed, but if it were a shirt fresh from the tailor, they would show.[39] Just as it is possible to imagine a shirt that is never handled, so it is possible to wish for a mind cleansed even of pre-emotions. That this is the wish of Jesus himself can be seen in certain of the Psalms, as when the psalmist says, "I have sinned greatly" or "cleanse me from my secret faults"—for it is to be understood that many passages in the Psalms are spoken "in the person of the Savior." But the implication of Didymus's larger view is that one cannot really expect to avoid some temptation, some handling, as it were, as long as one is in this life. Impressions of the emotive type are integral to what it is to be human; that is, to be a rational creature. What is really required is not that we should cease to have them but that we should withhold assent from them.

A Stoic essential

In the role of unassented feelings in scriptural exegesis we have seen creative adaptation and some themes that are entirely new. The essential features of the concept have, however, remained remarkably consistent. The pre-emotion as we find it in these Alexandrian authors occurs involuntarily and without blame when one has a rational impression of the emotive type. It thus begins the sequence that may generate an emotion. It is phenomenologically similar to a genuine emotion but differs from it in fact, because no assent is given and no action takes place. It may occur in a person of perfect virtue, and that it does so serves to establish that the moral ideal does not exceed the potentialities of human nature as we know it. All these are points made also by Seneca, as we have seen. By inference, they are likely to have been emphasized by Chrysippus as well.

The existence of the pre-emotion concept helps us to understand how Stoic views on emotion can have seemed compelling to so many intelligent persons in antiquity. As long as one uses a single term, 'emotion,' for every sort of feeling there is, it is quite easy to assume that what is true of some of our feelings—that they are involuntary and have no particular influence on our actions—is true of them all. The Stoics draw their distinction in such a way that having an emotion is necessarily more than this. For them, one has not had an emotion until one accepts that the way the emotion presents its object is really true; that is, that that object really is charged with value or disvalue and really does merit a vigorous response. Such acceptance is hardly distinguishable from action and from the excesses to which emotional actions are sometimes carried. By working out a position on feelings without assent, Stoics were able to insist upon the ethical seriousness of this fact.

5

Brutishness and Insanity

The principle that moral accountability is linked to rational assent has an immediate and, for most Stoics, unproblematic application in the way we regard animals. Animals share with humans the capacity for impressions, and they have their own impulses or action tendencies; they are capable, too, of surprisingly complex behaviors—witness the spider building its web—and of certain kinds of inference: the horse trembles at the sight of the whip.[1] One might want to say, then, that inasmuch as animals do have ways of processing and using information, they must have some form of assent. Yet it would be implausible to assert that animals assent in quite the same way as humans do. We may ascribe to them some way of ratifying propositions, but this ascribed assent or 'yielding' is only loosely analogous to the information processing that is evidenced in humans by our use of complex languages. The difference is sometimes explained by saying that nonspeaking animals lack the concept of 'following'; that is, the capacity to recognize and evaluate inferences as such.[2] The horse that is alarmed by the mere sight of the whip does not know it is performing an inference: it can associate one thing with another, but nothing will ever enable it to recognize the associative thought process itself. Hence while many animals can be trained by the use of rewards and punishments, none can recognize that its own choices were amiss or decide for itself to amend its own behavior. This fact will surely make a difference in the sort of agency it can be said to have. Animal behavior is just behavior; it is not volitional action, and the animal is not subject to praise or blame for it in the way that humans are. For the same reason, no response of a nonhuman animal is considered by Stoics to be an emotion.[3] An animal might behave in ways that resemble emotional behavior in humans, but its responses cannot simply be classed with human affective responses as if the differences were unimportant.

A comparison can be drawn between the behavioral capacities of animals and those of some human beings. Not everyone, it can be argued, is capable of volitional action; by the same token, if emotion implies volition, then not everyone is capable of emotion. I am not speaking now of children, though it is true that children were not considered by Stoics to be responsible for their actions. Children are on the path to becoming rational agents and need to be considered in the context of that developmental story. There are some adults, though, whose behavior does not lend itself to analysis by the kinds of models that are applied to human action in general. Alternative models have to be created.

Aristotle reserved a category in his ethics for persons whom he called 'beastlike' or 'brutish' (*thēriodeis*). His examples include horrifying instances of cannibalism such as the slave who consumed another's liver and the woman who had a taste for aborted fetuses.[4] Such behavior, he says, is "outside the bounds of vice": one cannot place it within the regular conceptual framework of his ethics, though one can give some thought to the causes of such conditions. It seems, then, that he exempts these agents from blame on grounds of (as we would say it) mental illness; in fact, the terms 'insane' and 'diseased' both figure prominently in his discussion. And even long before Aristotle, Greek intellectual traditions recognized certain kinds of behavioral dispositions as outside the realm of voluntary action. Already in the earliest Hippocratic texts, various forms of deviant behavior were treated as symptoms of some nonculpable medical condition, attributable usually to humoral imbalance and responsive to changes in diet or to drugs such as white hellebore. Prominent among the causes alleged is the mysterious dark humor called 'black bile' (*melas cholos*), and it is *melancholia*, 'melancholy' or 'atrabiliousness,' that takes hold in the popular imagination. To mention bile on the comic stage, for instance, is to say that someone is out of his wits.[5] Hallucinations, also, are a recurring theme, especially in tragedy: Pentheus sees a doubled sun; Orestes is pursued by Furies whom no one else sees; Ajax slaughters a flock of sheep in the belief that they are Greek warriors.

There is a sharp contrast between these earlier Greek notions of insanity and what we encounter in the often-repeated Stoic teaching that "all fools are mad." That flamboyant claim makes virtually everyone who has ever lived insane—for in Stoic usage the 'foolish' are just those who are not wise, and wisdom is a theoretical ideal that hardly anyone has attained in fact. One point to be established in this chapter is that the general-insanity claim has particular reference to the ordinary person's susceptibility to emotion. To be insane in this paradoxical sense is just to lack knowledge of what is really important. It is when one lacks such knowledge that one assents, all too easily, to the notion that external objects merit emotional response.

The nonwise condition is called 'insanity' by an extension of the Stoic position on loss of control in emotion. As we have seen, Stoic authors beginning with Zeno and Chrysippus found no difficulty in asserting that although emotional impulses are rational in that they are dependent on our capacity for judgment, they can also be called 'irrational' in that they tend to overrule other, better-grounded judgments we make at around the same time. Metaphors drawn from the discourse on insanity can be used to emphasize this point, without conceding any diminution of responsibility for what we do in times of emotion. When Seneca begins his treatise on anger by calling that emotion a *brevis insania* or 'temporary insanity,' he does not mean the angry agent is exempt from blame. On the contrary, he means to stress that the dangers to which the ordinary rational condition is prone are very real dangers and to urge readers therefore to correct their dispositions while it is still possible. Nominally addressed to his brother Novatus, the admonition is meant for every person who retains any tendency to irascibility.

It would be incorrect, even absurd, to suppose that Stoic philosophers ever charged human beings in general with being insane in the sense that Aristotle's beastlike agents are insane, or the unbalanced and sometimes hallucinatory characters of Greek tragedy. At the same time, Chrysippan Stoicism does recognize that some varieties of human behavior are not well described by the usual theory of action, but are better classed and evaluated separately, as manifestations of some exceptional mental condition. Identified usually by mention of *melancholia,* this category of agency includes the deranged condition of Orestes and others who suffer some disruption in their capacity for impressions. For these, the usual understanding of moral responsibility has to be set aside; they are to be tended, not blamed. In such cases the mental operations involved fail to satisfy even the minimal conditions for rational behavior. Unreasonable as ordinary humans can sometimes be, we are still reasoning beings; these persons, though, are something less.

Stoic thought thus provides for two different ways of being insane, one deranged or hallucinatory, and the other relatively ordinary, though not without significance. A distinction of this kind does not appear to be made elsewhere in Greek thought. The Hippocratic texts sometimes contrast insanity (*mania*) with *melancholia,* but they do so in such a way as to make *mania,* too, a specific medical diagnosis; for instance, some physicians have it that *mania* is caused by yellow bile rather than black, or that it is accompanied by fever while *melancholia* is not. In the popular literature, *all* the various terms for insanity are used interchangeably to describe conduct which the speaker regards as lacking in good sense.[6] In Stoic texts, by contrast, we find two conceptions of madness which are not only quite different but actually different kinds of conception. On the one hand, we find a moral and epistemological conception which merely redescribes in a particular way the practically universal human condition of flawed rationality; on the other, a medicalized notion applicable to only a small number of persons. This latter, as the conception directly opposed to ordinary rationality, sets the bearer beyond the scope of responsible action; in effect, it makes one morally subhuman.

The two conceptions thus exclude one another: the ordinary 'insane' person cannot at the same time be melancholically insane, and the melancholically insane cannot be 'insane' in the paradoxical sense.[7] But this is not to say that they are unrelated. There is a conceptual connection derived from the ordinary person's loss of control in emotional impulses. It is this connection that gives plausibility and point to the madness paradox. Further, there is some evidence to suggest a causal link. While the etiology of deranged or hallucinatory insanity could be assigned to black bile or other medical causes, it may also have been a Stoic view that repeated episodes of strong emotion can cause a person to become mentally ill. The resulting condition is called by Seneca 'brutishness,' an echo (though not, I think, a direct imitation) of the term used by Aristotle. This is a frightening possibility for rational creatures, for while it is compared to animal behavior ('brute' in the sense of 'wild beast'), the state of the brutish person is more erratic and wild than that of the most dangerous predator.

Orestes and the *Phantastikon*

Brief discussions of melancholic insanity are provided in a pair of sources on Stoic epistemology. In both of these, mental derangement is treated as a disruption of the capacity to form mental impressions. The report of Aetius attributes to Chrysippus a neat distinction among four related Greek words. In addition to impression (*phantasia*) and the object of impression (the *phantaston*), there is also another mental experience called *phantastikon;* its object is a *phantasma* or phantasm. The *phantastikon* must be what we call a hallucination. Like an impression, it is a kind of seeming, in which something appears present or appears to be the case; this, however, is an 'empty' seeming, with nothing underlying it. Chrysippus explains as follows:

> The *phantastikon* is an empty attraction, a mental experience which comes about without there being anything to produce the impression, as in the case of one who fights with shadows and punches at emptiness. For a *phantasia* has something underlying it, but the *phantastikon* has nothing. The *phantasma* is that to which we are attracted in the empty attraction which is the *phantastikon*. This happens in the case of those who are melancholic and insane. At least, when Orestes in the tragedy says,
>
> > Mother, I beg you, do not set upon me
> > those maidens bloody-faced and snakelike,
> > for they—they are leaping nearer to me!
>
> he speaks as one who is mad and sees nothing but only thinks he sees. Hence Electra tells him,
>
> > Stay calmly in your bed, poor thing;
> > you are not seeing any of those things that seem so clear to you.
>
> So also with Theoklymenos in Homer.[8]

Orestes is 'attracted' to his Furies, not of course in the sense of wanting to pursue them, but in that the nature of his mental experience entices him to believe that they are really there and to pursue a course of action in relation to them. This cannot be a regular instance of impression, for an impression 'reveals both itself and what made it,' but no Fury is present on stage. Theoklymenos in book 20 of the *Odyssey* is similarly given to hallucination. He is the seer who is mocked by Penelope's suitors for his prophetic vision of blood speckling the banquet hall and ghosts thronging the courtyard. Although the poet-narrator represents the vision as veridical, it is clear that other characters in the scene see nothing of the kind; for them, his visions are evidence of an altered mental state.

Orestes serves as an example of madness also in a discussion of Stoic epistemology by Sextus Empiricus, where the center of interest is again a disruption in the capacity for impression. This time Orestes is said to be the recipient of an impression, but one which is "both true and false." Just as when one sees in dreams a person who is alive but far away, the supposed impression is only an empty attraction:

For in that it was as from a real thing, it was true, since Electra was real, but in that it was as from a Fury, it was false, for she was not a Fury.[9]

Later in the same paragraph Sextus indicates that the impressions of the insane may be true and yet not 'graspable' (*katalēptikai*), a Stoic term of art for impressions whose truth is self-evident. Persons who have phrenitis and *melancholia,* he says, may have true impressions "by chance" and not assent to them, even though they are of a sort that most people would accept without question. The details of this account are not quite congruent with what we have from Aetius. Sextus does not use the word *phantastikon,* and while he does include the phrase 'empty attraction,' he treats the hallucination as a skewed impression arising from something which does, in fact, exist.[10] The essentials, though, are secure enough. Both sources clearly have in mind a disruption of impressions which is severely debilitating when it occurs, but which does not occur very often. Orestes is joined by Theoklymenos and, in related sources, by Ajax, Heracles, Alcmaeon, and possibly Pentheus, but there seems no possibility of his being joined by some large majority of humankind.[11] For that would invalidate the point about how impressions normally work.

Repeatedly in these texts we find insanity spoken of in conjunction with *melancholia* or black-bile disease. Phrenitis, literally an inflammation of the *phrēn* or diaphragm, is also mentioned. Both terms suggest an explanation of mental processes in terms of physical interactions. Such an explanation is always at least a theoretical possibility in Stoicism, for while the principal philosophical role of impressions is as content bearers, an impression is also that physical event in which the mind material takes on a certain configuration. Thus Stoics retain the option of dropping down to that material level to explain aspects of function or malfunction which cannot be explained at the intentional level. It should be noted in this context that impressions are classed by Posidonius as "corporeal events in association with the mind," falling into the same category as 'melancholies,' 'lethargies,' and pre-emotional 'bitings.'[12] The causation of insanity may then be comparable to that of dreams, which come about nonmysteriously, through the relaxing of pneumatic tension in sleep.[13] One might also compare it to the effects of alcohol on perception, thought, and speech. Indeed, one brief fragment actually calls drunkenness a 'little insanity,' a short-lived version as it were.[14]

Melancholic loss of virtue

The special status of the insane is confirmed by another Stoic discussion in which *melancholia* plays a significant role. In the encyclopedia of Diogenes Laertius we read as follows:

> Chrysippus says that virtue can be lost; Cleanthes that it cannot. The one says that it can be lost through drunkenness and *melancholia*, the other that it cannot be lost because of secure grasps.[15]

Two other ancient sources seem also to have been familiar with this position of Chrysippus; their reports give some additional detail. In one, it is said to be the Stoic view that "it is possible for the virtuous person to become lethargic or melancholic or darkened or out of his wits, in which states he cannot act in accordance with virtue."[16] The other supplies an explanation:

> Even the Stoics admit that in *melancholiai* and drowsiness and lethargies and in taking medications there is loss of the entire rational condition and along with it virtue itself. [In this case, they say,] vice does not come in to replace it, but the security is relaxed and lapses into what the ancients call the 'middle condition.'[17]

According to this the loss of virtue is not a matter of yielding to temptation or the like: one does not return to being an ordinary, morally flawed agent. The virtuous condition disappears only when the entire rational condition is destroyed by melancholy or equivalent conditions, the latter including drowsiness, lethargies, and the taking of certain drugs. Any of these, it seems, can 'relax the security' of virtue.

The way Diogenes Laertius frames his report would tend to suggest that there was a clear-cut difference of opinion between Chrysippus and his predecessor Cleanthes. The substance of Chrysippus's position, though, sounds less like a departure from his school's usual position than like a relatively minor modification of it in response to pressure from the skeptical Academy. In asserting that virtue cannot be lost, Cleanthes merely has stated a consequence of the Stoics' basic epistemology. Knowledge, for Stoics, has inherent stability: since assent is dependent on the system of beliefs one already holds, possession of a fully coherent system of properly justified beliefs ('secure grasps') should mean that one is no longer inclined to accept any false impression, either practical or theoretical.

There is, then, no basis for error, and the virtuous person (who is also the knowledgeable person) cannot lapse into vice. Chrysippus can, however, concede that virtue would be lost if the wise person were to leave off being a rational creature: animals cannot be virtuous, and people who have degenerated from the usual intellectual capacities of human beings cannot be virtuous either. It does not seem likely that the wise person would ever think it justifiable to allow her own rationality to be impaired. The wise "take wine, but do not get drunk." But the condition might come on without one's consent, due to illness or the forcible administration of drugs or alcohol, or simply because one is half asleep. In such states, even the wise may be "subject to peculiar impressions because of *melancholia* or delirium, not through their own reasoning as to what is choiceworthy, but contrary to [their] nature."[18]

For the purposes of this argument there is no need for Chrysippus to pursue the physiological explanations in any detail. Given Stoic notions of the relation between systematicity of judgment and an optimal level of tension in the mind's material substrate, it would be natural enough for him to describe all the specified conditions as various ways in which pneumatic tension might be relaxed to the point of impairment. But that kind of account is not his present concern. His reference to *melancholia* is no more than a casual appeal to generally accepted medical notions. Had he been writing in our own day, he might have spoken instead of clinical depression or Alzheimer's disease, without any major alteration in his philosophical view. More important for him is that the condition to which one can be reduced by *melancholia* and similar causes is not a condition of vice. One is not acting sensibly, but neither is one behaving badly: if rationality itself is gone, one cannot be a flawed rational agent either. Some kind of custodial care is needed: being 'darkened,' according to one source, means that one "needs to be tied up and to have the assistance of friends."[19] This is quite different from having a moral failing, although, as Aristotle says of brutishness, it is also more to be feared in oneself.

Fluttery ignorance

Nonetheless, there is also a sense in which anyone who has a moral failing can be called insane. For there is a familiar Stoic saying, mentioned in many texts, that "all fools are mad" or that the nonwise condition is itself a sort of insanity. It is this way of talking that gives rise to the complaint of one Diogenianus, an Epicurean of perhaps the second century C.E.:

How is this? You say that except for the wise person, there is no human being who is not equally as insane as Orestes and Alcmaeon. And that there
have only been one or two wise persons—and all the rest are by reason of
their imprudence just as insane as those named![20]

Diogenianus is being uncharitable, or perhaps he is misled by his sources.
Stoic moralists are not in fact open to this particular criticism, the implications of which would be as unacceptable to them as to him. No bona fide
Stoic text ever asserts that the mental state of every human is just the same
as that of an Orestes or Alcmaeon, and none ever refers to *melancholia* or
any other medicalized notion of insanity when speaking of the madness
of humans in general.[21] The generalized *mania* is apparently of a different
order.

"All fools are mad" is a paradox, one of the counterintuitive teachings
for which the school was renowned. Like others of its kind—"only the
wise person is rich," "all fools are slaves"—it runs contrary to popular
opinion (*para doxan*) but becomes plausible when restated in other terms.[22]
It is a conversation opener, a deliberately provocative formulation meant
to arouse the curiosity of the audience, later to be cashed out in a way that
renders it acceptable. We can glean a fair idea of the kind of exposition
Stoic teachers would have supplied from the brief explanation in Diogenes
Laertius:

> All the senseless are mad, for they do not have sense but do everything in
> accordance with madness, madness being equivalent to senselessness.[23]

'Sense' is *phronēsis,* the conventional opposite to *mania* for Greek speakers.
This way of putting it gives the statement a reasonable sound: anyone
who lacks sense would naturally be called senseless or witless. In a Stoic
context, however, the word *phronēsis* cannot be used in any other way than
for the cardinal virtue of good sense; that is, the disposition to act properly
in any and all circumstances.[24] Since practical wisdom, like every virtue,
consists essentially in knowledge, it is to be found in actuality only among
those exceedingly rare persons who instantiate the epistemic ideal. The
extent of non-*phronēsis* is correspondingly broad.

But in order for the teaching to continue in a productive direction, the
Stoic speaker would need also to supply some additional explanation, going beyond the bald equivalence claim to explain what it is that an ordinary lack of wisdom has in common with insanity in the more familiar

use of the word. Without this, hearers would be justified in objecting that while Stoics might not be guilty of reducing humans in general to the level of Orestes and Alcmaeon, they are still guilty of frivolous use of language, having renamed the ordinary condition merely for effect. To make their paradox worthwhile, then, the Stoics needed to identify some defining characteristic or sphere of reference within which it is appropriate to describe the condition of fault as being one of insanity rather than, say, cowardice or injustice. For just as the principal virtues, though coextensive, have each a particular area of applicability, so also with the principal faults, among which madness as 'lack of sense' must be counted.[25] Such an area of applicability is, in fact, specified within the Stobaean account.

> They say that every inferior person is insane, since such people are ignorant of themselves and of what accords with themselves, and that is just what madness is. Ignorance is the fault opposite to self-control, and when in a certain relational state, when rendering the impulses unsettled and fluttery, this is madness. For this reason they also define madness like this: fluttery ignorance.[26]

Again, madness is said to be the same thing as ignorance or senselessness, but now it is ignorance "in a certain relational state"; that is, within a particular frame of reference. Ignorance is madness specifically when it renders the impulses "unsettled and fluttery."

A *ptoia* or 'flutter,' we know from later in the Stobaean summary, is another word for that especially vehement sort of impulse that is an emotion.[27] The word suggests lightness, as of something easily moved, and that is also how 'fluttering' is explained: it is the "ease with which the capacity for emotion is activated" or the way that one is moved 'by chance,' meaning by trivial causes.[28] The nonwise are, in general, 'precipitate' in assent, but our susceptibility to emotion is even more easily triggered: we can be blown about like feathers in a windstorm. And a tendency to succumb to emotions is also a tendency toward irrational behavior, for as we have seen, an emotion, with its absolute notion of value, is just the kind of vigorous impulse which will frequently override one's other judgments about what it is best for oneself to do. Chrysippus makes the comparison explicit when he speaks of the experience of being carried away by anger, love, or even delight as one of being 'beside oneself' or 'in an altered state' or 'not oneself.' When people are stirred by emotion, he says, we treat them as if they were out of their minds, making allowances for them and not trying to reason with them until they are calmer.

> This is also why when people are in love or have some other strong desire, or are angry, one can hear people say things like "they want to indulge their feelings" and "let them be, whether it is better or not" and "say nothing to them" and "they have to do it, no matter what, even if it is a mistake and not to their advantage." . . . They reject the [therapeutic] speech as one whose chastisement is ill-timed and who is no arbiter of the affairs of love, as a human who sees fit to give ill-timed advice at a time when even the gods see fit to let them swear false oaths. "Let us follow our desire," they say, "and do whatever occurs to us."[29]

People who want to do "whatever occurs to them" and want to do it "no matter what," even if it is not to their advantage, are not behaving rationally even by the most basic standards of what it is to act upon reasons or to be responsive to reasoned considerations. Such a person is more like an animal which yields without thinking to its impulsory impressions and which needs to be managed rather than convinced. During moments of strong feeling, or, as Chrysippus sometimes puts it, during the 'inflammation' of the emotional condition, a person might really be like this.[30] But the lover or angry person is nonetheless a rational being, for it was through the normal mechanism of practical reasoning that the emotion occurred.

In using the word 'insane,' then, the Stoics mean to say that the common intellectual and moral condition of humans is disposed toward episodes of irrational behavior, even though ordinary people are at other times fully capable of reflective reasoning and at all times accountable for their activities. Cicero catches the thought exactly when, speaking of the effect of anger in social situations, he remarks:

> It is cases like this, surely, that the Stoics are referring to in their claim that all fools are insane. Set aside the emotions, especially anger, and their position will become ridiculous. But they explain that when they say "all fools are insane," it is like "all bogs stink." Not always! But disturb the bog, and you will smell it. Even so the irascible person is not always angry—strike him, though, and you will see him go mad.[31]

Ultimately the Stoic teacher would want to insist that the conception of insanity being invoked is not, after all, particularly alien to ordinary ways of speaking. Chrysippus is said to have observed in the introduction to one of his treatises that common usage allows Greek speakers to call the ambitious person 'mad about fame' (*doxomanēs*) and the lecherous person 'mad about women' (*gunaikomanēs*).[32] There was even a Greek word that meant 'mad about birds': partridges and cockerels were favored by Athenians as pets, and no doubt some were just as devoted to them as many people now are to their dogs or cats. Emotive dispositions in relation to such specific object-types are called by Stoics *arrōstēmata* or 'infirmities'; technically, they belong to the theory of personality, where they figure among the traits of character. In this particular passage, however, Chrysippus's point is a less technical one, such as would serve to introduce a basic treatise on ethics. Having mentioned the madness paradox as a convenient way of highlighting certain common mistakes in evaluation, he cites these instances of ordinary usage to show that the doctrine does have a certain linguistic plausibility. Everyone who has some commitment to the genuine value of externals is insane in that we are liable to experience the wrong sorts of affect. We may tease those whose ridiculously high estimation of some one object type ties their emotional lives to a partridge or cockerel. But these persons are not more insane than the rest of us, only insane in a more specific way.

Emotions as causes

A number of the themes we have seen so far may also be found early in Cicero's third Tusculan Disputation. Like Chrysippus in the fragment mentioned above, Cicero uses the madness paradox as an opening gambit: a susceptibility to grief and other emotions, he says, is "hardly different from insanity," for the Latin word *in-sania* or 'non-health' is an appropriate term for any mental condition which falls short of the ideal. This notion of insanity is broadly applicable, since it concerns all who are not wise; there is, however, another form of mental aberration which brings about "a complete darkening of the mind" and so renders a person incapable of managing his life in the usual way. This latter he calls in Latin *furor* or 'frenzy,' remarking that while frenzy "would seem to be worse than *insania*," nonetheless the complete darkening of mind "is the sort of thing that can come upon a wise person, while *insania* cannot."[33] The Latin usage, he says, is superior to the Greek, for where Latin says *insania*, Greek has to use the less apt word *mania*, and where Latin says *furor*, Greek is left to speak of *melancholia* or black-bile disease. This is of course the same linguistic habit as we have noticed in our own Greek sources: *mania* in the madness paradox, *melancholia* (or both terms together) for that sort of insanity which requires custodial care.

Such an explicit admission of the difference between one and the other form of insanity is not to be found in other extant sources for Stoic thought. Still, we need not doubt that Cicero is working closely with Stoic material, for while he certainly expresses a preference for his own language and culture, even appealing to the Twelve Tables, Rome's oldest law code, for examples of usage, both his larger argument and the specific terms of his discussion correspond to points made in undisputed Stoic contexts. On one point he is indeed very close to the summary in Diogenes Laertius, where it is said that the wise "are not insane" even though they are at times subject to strange impressions due to melancholy or delirium.[34] It is of interest, then, to see that Cicero in the course of reporting on Greek usage also drops a remark about the causation of melancholic frenzy. So-called *melancholia*, he says, is not caused only by black bile but may also be caused by episodes of strong emotion:

> The Greeks mean the same thing we do, but they do not have a good word for it. What we call 'frenzy,' they call *melancholia*, 'biliousness,' as if the mind were stirred up only by black bile and not by some more serious form of anger, fear, or grief, as happened with the frenzy (as we say it) of Athamas, Alcmaeon, Ajax, and Orestes.[35]

The belief that an episode of some powerful emotion can cause a person to become insane seems to have been widespread in Greco-Roman antiquity; it can be found, for instance, in a fragment of Epicurus and in numerous places in Roman poetry.[36] It is also implied, as Cicero notes, in the mythological histories mentioned, notably in that of Ajax, who is supposed to have been driven mad by his anger over the arms of Achilles. But it would be a different matter if the claim were actually put forward by a Stoic philosopher such as Chrysippus, who has definite commitments on the nature of psychic events and causes. We should therefore take a moment to consider whether it is compatible with Stoic psychology to assume a strictly emotional causation for some cases of hallucinatory derangement.

I argued in chapter 1 that an emotion in Stoicism is not only a judgment but also, simultaneously, an alteration in the *pneuma* of which the mind is composed. Under the latter, psychophysical description, the mental event or 'movement' which is an emotion actually alters the size or shape of the mind material, 'contracting' it in the case of grief, 'uplifting' it in the case of delight, 'stretching it out' in the case of desire, and pulling it back in the case of fear. It is these psychic changes that account for the sensations we identify as mental pain, yearning, upset, and the like. With these in mind, it is easy enough to suppose that an especially powerful, protracted, or much repeated emotion might have some lasting effect on the mind material which would alter its tensional level and hence its rational nature. This would be an effect comparable to those of drugs or alcohol, although produced in a different way.

Obviously, emotional causes cannot be alleged for the onset of melancholic insanity in the wise. In that emotions are dependent on improper assent, they are inherently foolish, rather like getting drunk of one's own volition. If the discussion concerns only the nonwise, however, there is no obstacle. Indeed, it might sometimes be advantageous for a philosopher to point out that strong emotions are dangerous not only in themselves but because of their long-term effects on the psyche.

Brutishness

Such is the intent of a particularly horrifying paragraph in Seneca's treatise on anger. The disposition involved is called by Seneca *feritas*, 'brutishness,' making an implicit comparison to the condition of a carnivorous animal. Seneca writes,

> And now we must ask also concerning those people who rage about at random and delight in human blood, whether they are angry when they kill people from whom they have not received any injury and do not believe that they have—people like Apollodorus or Phalaris. This is not anger but brutishness. For it does not do harm because it has received an injury; rather, it is willing even to receive an injury so long as it may do harm. It goes after whippings and lacerations not for punishment but for pleasure. What then? The origin of this evil is from anger, which, once it has been exercised and satiated so often that it has forgotten about clemency and has cast out every human contract from the mind, passes in the end into cruelty.[37]

The examples of behavior are unusually violent even for this violence-filled treatise. Apollodorus and Phalaris were tyrants who became proverbial for sadistic forms of torture and execution. Hannibal and Volesus, mentioned further on in the paragraph, were generals who found satisfaction in the grisly sights of war. Hannibal sees a trench filled with blood and exclaims, "O beauteous sight!"; Volesus, who has ordered three hundred executions in a single day, views the scene and cries, "O kingly deed!"

These alarming examples are meant to warn the reader away from anger, for while such behavior has lost the distinguishing marks of anger, it also has its origin in anger. Brutishness is caused by anger in the same way Cicero says insanity might be, a way parallel to the effects of black bile or, in other passages, of alcohol or drugs. Repeated episodes of strong emotion have caused one to pass into a different state. Anger itself is temporary insanity; the acts of a Phalaris or an Apollodorus, though, can no longer be considered instances of imperfectly rational minds getting carried away in the heat of a moment. They manifest an entirely new behavioral disposition. Failing to curtail their anger in the short term, these men have managed to obliterate what is most human in themselves. In them clemency is forgotten, and the 'human contract,' the natural sense of fairness which all human beings share, has been thrown away.

The difference between angry behavior and brutish behavior is not merely a matter of degree. Anger is more than aggressive violence: it is by definition a response motivated by the supposition that some sort of retributive action is justified by injuries received. One who lacks this characteristic motivation is not angry, any more than a predatory animal is angry when it leaps upon its prey.[38] Angry persons desire to harm those who have offended them; brutish agents desire just the harm itself, in which they find a perverse kind of pleasure. Neither do they have the facial expressions typical of anger. "They laugh, then, and rejoice, and experience great pleasure. Their expressions are very different from those of angry persons, for they are savage for fun."[39]

Though called beastlike, this is not the mental state of the nonhuman animal. Animals may not reason in a conscious way, but their actions do exhibit a certain rudimentary logic: they act in accordance with their own natural interests. The feral human is more dangerous in that he rages about indiscriminately, 'at random.' Rather than harming because he has been harmed, he is willing even to receive an injury in order that he may hurt another. The ordinary kinds of connections between behavior and self-interest have broken down; rational agency is compromised. Even the manner of conceptualizing visual inputs is bizarre. What Hannibal and Volesus think they see is drastically different from what they are really seeing. Their case is not altogether different from that of Orestes when he looks at his gentle sister and sees an avenging Fury. They can speak, as could Orestes; what they say, though, is nonsensical when compared with their situation.

The cruelty exhibited by these killers is distinguishable from the vice all too common in ancient rulers; that is, the tendency to go overboard in one's punishments. The latter sort of cruelty is commonly and rightly associated with anger.[40] The difference is explained in Seneca's work *On Clemency*, composed not long after *On Anger*. Seeking to define clemency, Seneca inquires into its opposite. That opposite is not severity, he says, for severity is also a virtue; instead, it is the vice of cruelty, defined as 'harshness of mind in exacting penalties.' The interlocutor objects: what about people who are not exacting penalties and yet are cruel, people like the tyrant Busiris, or Procrustes (he of the uncomfortable bed), or the notorious Mediterranean pirates, who torture their captives for no reason at all? That too is *crudelitas*, says Seneca, but not the kind of *crudelitas* picked out by the definition. If needed for the sake of clarity, one could give it a different name.

> This is indeed cruelty, but it falls outside the bounds of our definition, since it neither follows vengeance (for it has not been harmed) nor is angry at any wrongdoing (for no crime has preceded). The definition included psychic intemperance in exacting penalties. We can say that this is not cruelty but brutishness, which finds savagery pleasurable. We can call it insanity, for insanity is of different kinds, and none more certain than the one which goes so far as to kill and mutilate human beings.[41]

This insane form of *crudelitas* is perhaps not well described by our word "cruelty," for cruelty in English usage is compatible with great intelligence. A better rendering might be 'bloodlust.' The account here reminds us that *crudelitas* in its etymological sense is a primitive state, the state of those who eat their meat raw: it is the nominal form of *crudus*, meaning 'raw' or 'uncouth,' and is related also to *cruor* meaning 'blood.' It is a word that can be used of a savage dog or a Cyclops.[42] In Moral Epistle 83, the bloodthirsty Mark Antony, who required the severed heads of princes to be exhibited to him at feasts, exemplifies the *crudelitas* of the far-gone alcoholic.[43]

We might compare this behavioral disposition with the condition now usually called psychopathy or antisocial personality disorder.[44] Persons with this disorder regularly violate social norms, often torturing animals in youth and in adulthood gleefully preying on other people in a variety of ways, some of them violent. They are often glib talkers and do not immediately appear insane, but their grandiose ideas, lack of interest in moral notions, and complete lack of sympathy for their victims lead those who have had longer acquaintance to describe them as scarcely human. They can be said to lack empathy even with their own past or future selves, a crucial factor in developing behavioral inhibitions. Hence they are, as

Patricia Greenspan puts it, "prone to self-sabotage": they are so far unde-
terred by any memory or expectation of punishment as to bypass even
obvious considerations of self-interest.[45] Persons with these characteristics
were undoubtedly to be found in ancient societies as well. In Seneca's 'insane' form of cruelty, we find the same lack of empathy, the same grandiose ideas, and the same indifference to prudential considerations as have
been described in modern case studies.

Both in the ancient and in the modern context there is some question
whether persons who exhibit this unsophisticated kind of cruelty should
be considered vicious or merely debilitated. At least some contemporary
philosophers have argued that psychopaths who are impaired in their ability to recognize and allow for inhibitory moral reasons cannot be held
responsible even for heinous acts of violence.[46] For the Stoics, similarly,
the notion of vice or suboptimal rationality requires the imputation of
volitional competence. If the brutish agent lacks even the ordinary human
capabilities for practical reasoning, then he or she may actually be free of
vice—not in any enviable way, of course, but in the way that the melancholically insane person (who may recently have been the virtuous person) is free of vice. Aristotle places brutish insanity "outside the bounds of
vice," and Seneca could consistently hold the same view. But he does not
bring out the implication, and given the extent of bloodshed in his description, it is understandable that he would be reluctant to do so. His purpose,
after all, is not to excuse the psychopath or even to explicate his thinking
but to expose the risks of indulging one's own tendencies to anger.

At the end of the passage he notes that while the new condition is not
anger, it is "a greater evil, and an incurable one." This is like what Cicero says of melancholic *furor,* that it is worse than the paradoxical sort of
insania; that is, worse than the ordinary flawed condition. It is not technically blameworthy, since it can come upon the wise through no fault of
their own; for those who enter that condition, though, it is a very great
misfortune. Because rationality is the best and most characteristic human
capacity, the loss of rationality affects us more deeply than any other loss.

Seneca's three movements

The observations just made concerning brutish insanity have a bearing
also on the interpretation of an important but disputed paragraph in the
same part of *On Anger.* This is the passage that makes the transition from
the preliminaries to emotion studied in chapter 4 to the brutishness discussion just quoted. Although it comprises only one short paragraph, it

will be worth our while to study this passage with care, for an incautious reading of it has too often suggested interpretations which are contrary to Seneca's real purposes and misleading for Stoic psychology as a whole.

The paragraph, numbered 2.4, comes immediately after the passage quoted on page 97 of chapter 4, and is immediately followed by the alarming paragraph 2.5, on brutishness. I now present both paragraphs together.

> Let me tell you how the emotions begin, or grow, or get carried away. The first movement is nonvolitional, a kind of preparation for emotion, a warning, as it were. The second is volitional but not contumacious, like this, "It is appropriate for me to take revenge, since I have been injured," or "It is appropriate for this person to be punished, since he has committed a crime." The third movement is already beyond control. It wants to take revenge not if it is appropriate, but no matter what; it has overthrown reason. That first impact on the mind is one we cannot escape by reason, just as we cannot escape those things which I said happen to the body, such as being stimulated by another person's yawn, or blinking when fingers are thrust suddenly toward one's eyes. That second movement, the one that comes about through judgment, is also eliminated by judgment.
>
> And we must still inquire concerning those people who rage about at random and delight in human blood, whether they are angry when they kill people from whom they have not received any injury and do not believe that they have—people like Apollodorus or Phalaris. This is not anger but brutishness. For it does not do harm because it has received an injury; rather, it is willing even to receive an injury so long as it may do harm. It goes after whippings and lacerations not for punishment but for pleasure. What then? The origin of this evil is from anger, which, once it has been exercised and satiated so often that it has forgotten about clemency and has cast out every human contract from the mind, passes in the end into cruelty.

By reading continuously from 2.4 to 2.5, we allow for the possibility that the two paragraphs are closely connected in sense. The structure of the passage in fact suggests that there is such a connection. Having devoted the preceding two pages to the explication of just two mental events, namely, anger (or any genuine emotion) and the preliminary feeling or pre-emotion, Seneca here announces, quite unexpectedly, that there are not two but three events to be considered. He then supplies a brief explanation for the first event, then the second, then the third; then, again for the first, then for the second, and the paragraph ends. It seems reasonable to expect that the paragraph following will continue the flow of thought by again describing the third movement. And if the third movement is the one which has not yet received any detailed explication, then one would expect that following paragraph to explain at some length what that further event is and how it differs from genuine anger. This, I mean to argue, is exactly what happens. The first and second movements are the two which have already been treated; that is, the preliminary feeling and the genuine emotion of anger, respectively. The third movement, which is now introduced for the first time, is brutishness, i.e., the acts of the brutish condition, as described in paragraph 2.5.

But the scholarly tradition on this passage has not in general taken this approach but has instead assumed a sharp break of sense at the end of 2.4, looking only within the confines of that paragraph for explication of what the three movements are. Within these constraints it is inevitable that one will take the third movement, which is clearly the worst of the three, to be anger itself. One is therefore forced to conclude that Seneca here introduces a new, intermediate mental event between the preliminary movement and the emotion of anger. Interpretations vary as to what exactly that second event is supposed to be. There seems to be general agreement, though, that it must be some response less damaging than anger, with anger in the full sense of the word occurring only in the third movement.

An important point in support of this anger-third approach to the passage is that when Seneca introduces the three movements he speaks of "how the emotions begin, or grow, or get carried away" (*quemadmodum incipiant adfectus aut crescant aut efferantur*). Since the first movement is clearly described as a beginning, it is hardly to be doubted that "grow" and "get carried away" are to be associated with the second and third movements respectively. But the expression "get carried away" is one that is especially appropriate to anger because of the tendency of that and every emotion to override one's calmer judgments. Seneca has just explained this point in paragraph 2.3, where he says that anger is "that movement which overleaps reason and drags reason along with it."[47] The verb *efferantur* is even cognate with the Greek verb *ekpheresthai*, which Chrysippus uses more than once in his treatment of emotional recalcitrance.[48]

The reminder that anger is liable to get carried away is both frequent and important in *On Anger* and should not by any means be overlooked here. Other elements of the anger-third reading are more problematic, however. The biggest stumbling block is in the treatment of this passage by Richard Sorabji. Sorabji understands Seneca to have said that there is a point in the sequence of events leading up to anger at which one endorses the full cognitive content of anger but is not yet disobedient to reason. One is angry and yet not carried away by anger. Sorabji realizes that there is nothing like this in any surviving fragment of Chrysippus. But he suggests, as have some scholars before him, that Seneca may have modified the Chrysippan view or perhaps taken over a modification by some intervening author.[49]

The problem with this interpretation is that it finds Seneca to be committed to a notion which his treatise is otherwise very eager to combat. Repeatedly in *On Anger* he strives to show that once people get angry at all, there is no turning back. In both book 1 and book 2 he argues at length against the (loosely) Aristotelian view upheld by some Hellenistic thinkers, that anger can be moderated and made useful.[50] Anger, he says, is like falling off a cliff (1.7), like letting a besieging army through a city gate (1.8), like a sword that sticks in the enemy's wound and cannot be pulled back (2.35). This is a standard Stoic position, as we have seen, but it is also Seneca's position. For him as for Chrysippus, there is no such thing as a way of responding in an angry mode without getting carried away. That would be equivalent to a kind of running that does not involve momentum.

It would be strange, then, if Seneca were to create (or uphold) a modification of Stoic psychology in which a person can go only partway to anger, having some substantive reaction and yet stopping short of the full anger response. It would be stranger still if he should introduce such an idea without making any effort to develop it or explain its moral implications. Yet no trace of the supposed intermediate response is to be found even later in this same book of *On Anger* (though it would certainly have application there), and neither is anything made of it in his later works. Seneca comes out a whimsical philosopher indeed, who revises an explanation which is centrally important to his own larger concerns and then proceeds as if the original explanation were still in force.

One could try to maintain the identification of the third movement with anger by interpreting the second movement in a different way which would be more consistent with Seneca's thought overall. Stoicism allows for actions based on nonaffective considerations, when one determines that something is appropriate to do without also regarding the relevant object as unconditionally good or evil. Seneca is familiar with this class of impulses, and he does hold that they may be a valid alternative to anger. 'Selection' is the correct term for the impulses of the virtuous person who leaps forward to defend a parent from an assailant but does so without anger.[51] But the second movement cannot be merely nonaffective action, for such action is not part of a sequence leading to anger; rather it is what one does when one is *not* reacting emotionally.

Alternatively, one might seek to identify the second movement with the assent of anger as distinct from the impulse of anger.[52] Seneca is clearly interested in the propositional content of anger, and it is conceivable that he might wish to distinguish that intentional aspect of the emotion from its practical aspect, in which judgment is manifested as observable behavior. The difficulty with finding that distinction here is that it cannot be made to accord with the way Seneca has introduced the paragraph, as identifying three countably distinct events. Assent to an impulsory impression is not an event which occurs prior to impulse; it is just the impulse itself, analyzed at the intentional level. It will not do for Seneca to promise three events and then deliver one event (impression) plus one event under two different descriptions (assent / impulse). Of course Seneca might be confused or careless about the implications of the statements he is making. But we should not charge him with that philosophical lapse if an alternative explanation is available.

What I want to suggest is that when Seneca speaks of three movements he has in mind already the terrible consequences of indulging one's anger which will be described in the paragraph on brutishness. He therefore presents anger as the *second* event in a temporal sequence which culminates in the behaviors of people like Phalaris and Volesus. Having already distinguished anger as a true emotion from the preliminary feelings accompanying impressions, he will now go on to distinguish it from the actions of the psychopath. Anger is thus flanked by two things which are not anger. Neither the first nor the third movement is a rational phenomenon, though for different reasons: in the one case, the feeling is not rational because it occurs without assent; in the other, it is not rational because it occurs in one who is no longer a competent rational agent.

Because anger has now to be distinguished from forms of aggression which are actually insane, there is need to describe it in a way which emphasizes its dependence on the ordinary reasoning abilities of human beings. The second movement meets all the conditions for anger as described in the preceding section, but it is not yet beyond remediation in the way that psychopathic behavior is beyond remediation. In the second movement, the mind says to itself, "It is appropriate for me to take revenge, since I have been injured," or "It is appropriate for this person to be punished, since he has committed a crime." This is exactly what anger says earlier in book 2: to be angry is "to take in an impression of injury received, and conceive a desire for revenge, and to link together the two ideas, that one ought not to have been wronged and that one ought to take revenge."[53] The second movement is volitional and comes about through judgment, just as we have been told repeatedly about anger in the preceding paragraphs.[54] The second movement can also be eliminated through judgment, just as anger "will succumb to reason" (i.e., to argument, 2.2.1) and "is put to flight by precepts" (2.2.2).

To say these things about anger is to emphasize that anger is a function of the rational (though not *optimally* rational) mind. Hence the second movement, in that it is contrasted with the third, is also "not contumacious" and wants revenge just when it thinks revenge is appropriate, not indiscriminately. *Contumax,* meaning contumacious or obstinate, is applicable in Latin usage to anything which moves forcibly and unthinkingly against the restrictions imposed by reason. A horse or mule is *contumax* when it throws its rider; a flood is *contumax* when it bursts a dam; hunger is *contumax* in that one cannot reason oneself out of it.[55] In the present passage, where anger is contrasted with an impulse which is "beyond control" and "wants to take revenge not if it is appropriate, but no matter what," the claim that anger is 'not contumacious' reminds us that anger itself is a decision by the reasoning mind, however refractory it might be in relation to a normatively rational judgment.

Nothing which has been said brings about any change in the point made earlier, that anger is itself a wild thing with its own inherent tendency to override one's better judgment. Anger may be noncontumacious in comparison with insane or psychopathic aggression and still contumacious in itself. Indeed contumacy is one of its distinguishing features.[56] From a broad perspective, the second and third movements have a great deal in common. There is a resemblance between them, as well as a causal relation, and that resemblance is indeed Seneca's main point. At least some of the confusion which has been created by the 'three movements' paragraph results from its author's efforts to bring out this resemblance even as he establishes the distinction. Thus his account of the third movement as one which "has overthrown reason" recalls what was said about anger in 2.3.5, that it "overleaps reason." *Evincere,* 'to overthrow,' is a stronger word than *transsilire,* 'to overleap': a literal translation would be 'to conquer utterly,' whereas 'overleap' suggests rather a temporary besting of reason as if in some athletic competition. But the resemblance between the two is undeniable.

A similar point can be made about the connection noted earlier between being 'carried away' in the third movement and being 'carried away' in Stoic accounts of emotional recalcitrance. Appearing just as the new idea is introduced, the term is at first ambiguous; after all, we have just been told that anger itself "drags reason along with it." It quickly becomes clear, though, that the notion of being carried away is now being taken to a new level. The resemblance of Seneca's chosen word *efferantur* to Chrysippus's verb *ekpheresthai* may be a deliberate echo, for Seneca retains many Greek expressions in mind and may expect some readers to remember them also. But there is another and more ominous verbal game going on entirely in Latin. *Efferantur*, from *efferre*, 'to carry away,' differs by only one letter from the corresponding form of another Latin verb, *efferari*, which means 'to become brutish'; the latter is the verb-equivalent to *feritas* in the paragraph following. Although *efferari* is less common than *efferre*, it is by no means rare; indeed, it is something of a favorite of Seneca's both in the prose works and in the tragedies.[57] For one who is familiar with both words, the resonance between them produces a peculiarly chilling effect, like watching one thing turn into another before one's very eyes. The recalcitrance of the ordinary emotion is seen to anticipate something even more dangerous and far less human.[58]

Seneca is not, then, proposing any modification in the Stoic theory of action. That his views are in accordance with those of Zeno and Chrysippus is not something it would have been safe to assume as a premise, for although his intention to remain within school tradition is generally clear enough, he also makes some claim to intellectual independence. In this instance, however, he remains within the ambitus of early Stoic thought. His account gives us, in a typical case of angry behavior, just two mental events, impression and assent; the third event (when things go so far) comes on some subsequent occasion. His point about emotional overriding is the same point as was made by Chrysippus. It is true that Seneca's further point concerning the actual loss of rationality in extreme cases is one not attested for Chrysippus in this form. It has elements in common with the treatment of bestial states in Aristotle and other Greek philosophers. Probably we should assume that some general account of brutishness was a rhetorical commonplace of Hellenistic Athens.[59] As such, it may have been adapted to suit Stoic purposes already in some treatise lost to us, or Seneca may have made the adaptation himself. For there is nothing in it which presents any necessary contradiction with Stoic thought.

What is important, though, is that on this reading Seneca's thought is coherent, his points adequately developed, and his rhetoric strong. He wants to insist on the rational nature of the anger response; at the same time, he wants to show where anger is headed. As the preceding paragraphs illustrated various possibilities for mental events which stop short of the conditions for rational behavior, so these indicate what lies on the other side, where rationality is no longer. The scope of admonition lies between the two. The person who assents to the impressions typical of anger is behaving as a rational creature, exercising mental capacities characteristic of humans. But that seemingly tame impulse is also a dangerous impulse, and not only for the reason explained earlier, that anger overleaps reason and cannot be checked by it. It is dangerous also because if such impulses occur frequently they may be destructive to one's rational nature, eventually rendering one incapable of anger or any other human feeling. One thus has a powerful motive to learn ways of eliminating or at least decreasing the frequency of anger by the methods Seneca goes on to suggest, like examining one's conscience, correcting one's values, asking friends for help. For these are the means of preserving one's humanity.

6

Traits of Character

Let us now consider a more nuanced emotion narrative, one which compares two different flawed agents—for although these agents are goddesses, they are behaving at the moment very like human beings. The story is from book 4 of the *Iliad*. The gods are sitting in council; Hebe pours the wine, and all gaze down at the beleaguered city of Troy. Zeus, on a whim, begins to needle Hera. "Here are you and Athena," he says, "the supporters of Menelaus, sitting at your ease, while Aphrodite busies herself protecting Paris. Perhaps it's time to give up: make peace for real, and let Troy stand." Both Hera and Athena are angered at this, for both have labored for many years to bring about the destruction of Troy. But Athena does nothing but murmur and glare at her father; it is only Hera who bursts into a torrent of angry words. Moreover, Hera's subsequent tirade against her husband is of a pattern with her violent anger, well beyond provocation, toward Priam and the people of Troy. She would eat them alive, if she could, and so the city must be sacked after all.[1]

How is one to explain the difference between Hera's response and that of Athena, who has received equal provocation? In both ancient and modern analyses the usual appeal is to differences of character.[2] Rather than speaking only of emotions or other mental events as they occur in any given moment, one refers to patterns of behavior over time and to lasting traits of character that are manifested in those patterns. It is not just that Hera becomes angry on many occasions but that she is *irascible:* she is disposed toward angry responses by some feature of her mental constitution which another person might not possess, or might possess only in lesser degree. In recognizing this, we feel that we have come to understand something about Hera as an individual. Given sufficient means of observation, we could perhaps produce a list of all the traits she exhibits to any appreciable degree. We would then have given a comprehensive account of her character or personality.

Character in this sense bears the entire weight of moral responsibility in the Stoic system. The principal reason a cylinder rolls when pushed is that the cylinder is round, and the principal reason for my tendency to moral error is something about me, my moral character. But Stoics are not usually given credit for any very subtle account of how character can vary from one individual to the next. Always primary in this ethics is the distinction between virtuous and nonvirtuous characters, and this distinction is expressed in absolutes. Anyone who is virtuous exhibits all the virtues together, and not in greater or lesser degree, but each of them entirely. Similarly with vice: it is all or nothing. As long as Achilles is not the Stoic sage, he is, technically, a coward; Aristides "the Just" is technically unjust.[3] If one considers only these primary ethical divisions, the view seems to be that the world is populated by only two sorts of people, with one sort being extremely scarce and the rest of us all sharing the same depressing list of faults. In these terms there is little to be gained by apportioning responsibility on the basis of character: each of us behaves, contingent upon opportunity, in ways that manifest a single very general personality type, the flawed or 'vicious' personality of the nonwise.

It is of interest, then, to find that Stoic theory also had other ways to speak about character which suggest an interest in the attributes of individuals as such. Such an interest is expressed not only in the diffuse and rhetorical Stoicism of Panaetius but also, and more to the point, in detailed technical accounts which show a concern with the underlying psychology.[4] These indicate, as we shall see, that there are traits of character which differ from the virtues in that they do not interentail and can vary in degree. It thus becomes possible to describe a person's character in ways specific to the individual. Just as one may observe variations in the sea floor without disregarding the fact that all of it is equally underwater, so it is possible in this system to differentiate one personality from another even where all concerned have the same overall moral standing.

These differentiable or, as I shall term them, 'scalar' traits may be entirely benign. They are exhibited even by the wise, in what are called the *epitēdeumata,* the 'habitudes' or specialties of the normative human being.

These reassure us that the acquisition of wisdom does not result in loss of individuality. Perhaps, too, they indicate that variance in traits, abilities, and habits is not in itself unnatural or problematic even among the non-wise. In theory a person should be able to devote time and energy to some specific interest on the basis of true beliefs, acting as do the wise while still on the way toward wisdom.

What the Stoic discussions emphasize, though, is that among the non-wise the scalar traits of character are generally *not* benign. Described by such terms as 'sicknesses,' 'infirmities,' and 'proclivities,' they are, above all, conditions disposing us to experience specific kinds of emotion, or emotions in response to specific kinds of stimuli. As we will see, they consist in pernicious forms of false belief which relate directly to our practical experience, controlling our reactions in many of the situations of everyday life. Left unchecked, they can become powerful emotion generators that ruin our chances for happiness.

Eventually it will be necessary to add a developmental story, showing how these dangerous traits are acquired and how they intensify over time. However, this question, and the difficulties it creates for Stoic providentialism, need not concern us just yet. For the moment our concern is to see how character traits are described in Stoic psychology and how they work to determine our reactions.

Scalar conditions of mind

The importance in Stoic moral psychology of notions of epistemic coherence can hardly be overstated. Consistency in belief is an essential requirement for knowledge and is what guarantees the infallibility and impassivity of the wise.[5] If asked to state in just a few words the difference between the ordinary person and the person of perfect understanding, the answer one should give is that the person of perfect understanding has established relations of logical harmony among all his or her judgments and beliefs, while the ordinary person has not. If what one wants, however, is to give some account of possible variations within one or the other of these conditions, then coherence is not a standard one can usefully apply. For coherence is, like pregnancy, not a matter of degree: one is either in that state or not; there are no intermediate possibilities. It is, then, a 'non-scalar' condition. Our sources like to remark at this point that every bent stick, no matter how it is bent, is equally not straight—and, likewise, that everyone who is anywhere below the surface of the sea is equally without air; or that a puppy is just as blind the day before it opens its eyes as it was at birth.⁶ This is just to say that there are some conditions that cannot be approximated: to fall short of virtue at all is to fall altogether short of it.

But to recognize what is absolute and invariable about straightness is not to say that all straight sticks are identical. The same stick that either does or does not exhibit the invariable property of straightness may also exhibit varying degrees of some other property such as length or hardness: it may have scalar properties in addition to the one nonscalar property. A helpful passage in one of the Aristotle commentators gives the Stoic terminology for distinguishing these two kinds of attributes:

> They [the Stoics] say that *hexeis* can be heightened and reduced, but *diatheseis* cannot. This is why the straightness of the stick also is called by them a *diathesis*, even though it can easily be changed, since the stick can be bent. For the straightness cannot be reduced or heightened, nor can there be more or less of it, and that is exactly why it is a *diathesis*. It is in this way that the virtues are *diatheseis*, not because of their stability but because they cannot be heightened and do not admit of increase. But the skills (*technai*) are not *diatheseis*, even though they are not easily altered.⁷

Like Aristotle, the Stoics use the words *hexis* and *diathesis* for two different kinds of condition. In Aristotle, though, the distinguishing factor is stability, with the *hexis* being the stable type. In Stoic usage, by contrast, the distinguishing factor is whether the condition is scalar or nonscalar. It is true that the virtues—which are the most familiar examples of *diatheseis*—are stable conditions: as it happens, the virtues once acquired can never be lost except with the loss of rationality itself. But stability is not what makes a condition a *diathesis*, for there are also some stable conditions that are not called *diatheseis*, and some *diatheseis* that are not stable. Instead, a *diathesis* is a nonscalar condition, a condition which does not admit of increase or decrease, and a *hexis* is a scalar condition.

To avoid confusion in dealing with some passages, it is helpful to realize that the word *hexis*, for which I use the translation 'condition,' has both a broad and a narrow signification. In some passages, it serves as a general-purpose term for conditions of any sort; it refers, that is, to a lasting state as opposed to an event. The class of 'conditions' in this broad sense can be subdivided into one subclass called *diatheseis* and another called simply 'conditions.' (There are a number of Stoic terms that work this way: a genus is subdivided into two species, one of which has a distinguishing mark and gets a special name, while the other keeps the same name as the genus.)⁸ So a *hexis* may be either a condition as opposed to an activity, or a scalar condition as opposed to a nonscalar condition—a 'mere condition,' as it were.

The report in Stobaeus explains in more detail how the distinction between scalar and nonscalar conditions is applied in ethics. In the schematic manner typical of this text, the Stoic author treats first goods, then evils, dividing each of these broad categories into three subcategories: first the two sorts of conditions, then activities.

> Some of the goods having to do with the mind are *diatheseis*, some are *hexeis*, and some are neither. All the virtues are *diatheseis*, but the habitudes (*epitēdeumata*). like prophecy and so forth, are *hexeis*, while activities in accordance with virtue, like a prudent action, an exercise of self-control, and so on, are neither.
>
> Likewise, some of the bad things having to do with the mind are *diatheseis*, some are *hexeis*, and some are neither. All the vices are *diatheseis*, but proclivities, like enviousness, tendency to grief, and so on, are *hexeis*, as also are the sicknesses and infirmities. Activities in accordance with fault, like an imprudent action, an unjust action, and so on, are neither.[9]

The most basic distinction here is the one between mental conditions generally, all of which are long-term properties or states, and mental events, which Stoics call either activities or 'movements' (*kinēseis*). The activity is that event which actualizes some capacity, the thing one is disposed to do or undergo, as riding a horse actualizes the skill of horsemanship. What actualizes a good or bad condition is itself good or bad accordingly. But there is also room for a further distinction among the conditions, between the nonscalar *diatheseis* and other conditions which are called simply *hexeis*. By exclusion, the latter must be scalar conditions.

The passage lists a number of examples of scalar conditions: on the good side 'habitudes' (*epitēdeumata*). and on the bad side 'proclivities,' 'sicknesses,' and 'infirmities.' The items on this list, I contend, are our best candidates in Stoicism for bona fide traits of character. They are lasting attributes of persons that help to explain feelings and behavior, and they are also variable from one individual to the next: they can be present in one person and not present, or only very little present, in another.[10] Let us therefore examine some further evidence about what these traits consist in and how they determine our behavior.

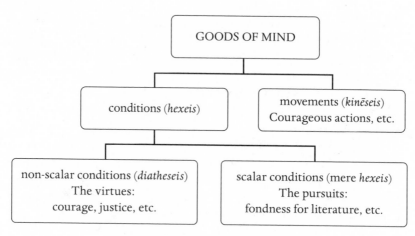

Figure 6. Classification of psychic goods.

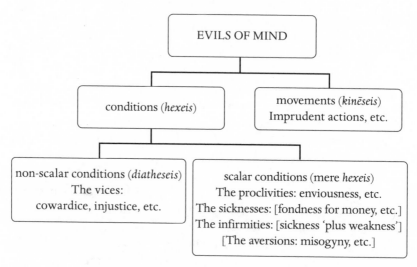

Figure 7. Classification of psychic evils.

Fondnesses and Aversions

The Stobaean text lists three classes of scalar conditions in ordinary persons: 'proclivities,' 'sicknesses,' and 'infirmities.' Among these, the condition about which we have the fullest information is the one called a 'sickness' of mind, a *nosos* or *nosēma* (plural *nosēmata*). Here the explanation given by Stobaeus is confirmed by technical material in Cicero's fourth Tusculan Disputation, which names Chrysippus as the source.[11] The *nosēma* is defined as a single belief of a particular kind, an opinion that some object is very much worth pursuing when in fact it is not. Likewise the inverse condition, called a *proskopē*, is an opinion that something is very much worth avoiding. In other words, it is what we call in English an aversion.

> A 'sickness,' they say, is a desirous opinion which has hardened into a condition and become entrenched, according to which people suppose that things which are not choiceworthy are extremely choiceworthy; for instance, fondness for women, fondness for wine, fondness for money. And there are conditions opposite to these which come about through aversion; for instance, hatred of women, hatred of wine, hatred of humanity.[12]

The restrictive clause "which are not choiceworthy" indicates that the objects in question are externals, and the examples offered bear this out: one is fond of such externals as money, reputation, food, wine, or the opposite sex; averse to guests or to people generally, or again to the opposite sex.[13] So these are traits which orient a person's behavior in relation to various types of external objects, or as the Stoics say, 'indifferents.'

To say the indifferents are 'not choiceworthy' does not mean we should cease to pursue them, or rather to pursue some and avoid others. Even the wise prefer some external objects to others and act on those preferences in what are called 'selections' and 'disselections.'[14] But the beliefs called *nosēmata* and *proskopai* regard their objects in a way the person of perfect understanding would not. They evaluate them unconditionally, as goods inherently worth pursuing or as evils inherently worth avoiding. Furthermore, these are mistaken evaluations which have "hardened into a condition and become entrenched." "Hardened into a condition" indicates that the sickness is a persistent state rather than a single event; "entrenched" suggests, further, that the erroneous belief is unusually difficult to eliminate, one which cannot be corrected without some wrenching readjustment of the personality.

Closely related to the 'sicknesses' is another type of condition called 'infirmities' (*arrōstēmata*). Stobaeus indicates that the infirmities are a subclass within the sicknesses: they are "sicknesses that occur together with weakness."[15] This definition, which also appears in Cicero and in Diogenes Laertius, matches well with the attested term: *rhōmē* or 'strength' is sometimes mentioned as a quality of mind, and *arrōstēma* adds a privative prefix to this; hence an infirmity is literally a 'lack of strength.'[16] It is not clear, though, how the mention of 'weakness' does anything to modify the definition of sickness already given. 'Weakness' is mentioned often enough in Stoic texts, usually as a characteristic of assent in the nonwise: to assent 'weakly' or 'out of weakness' is to endorse a proposition that a person with a 'strong' or fully coherent belief set would not endorse.[17] It follows, for Stoics, that *all* the mistaken views we hold are held 'weakly'—and thus that the sicknesses already satisfy the definition for infirmities. At most, the difference between them will be a matter of emphasis, as that an infirmity is a sickness in someone who is somehow especially tolerant of self-contradiction.

It is easy to see how the sicknesses and aversions, and similarly the infirmities, are related to the causal history of emotions laid out in chapter 2. I argued there that a dispositional belief about the value of indifferents is a necessary though not sufficient condition for affective response to the object type evaluated. Each of these three scalar conditions is just such an evaluative belief and will certainly dispose its owner to emotions concerned with its object. This is exactly what we should expect from an account of character by philosophers who give an intellectualist account of action. Since traits are dispositions toward various kinds of feelings and behavior, we should expect them to consist in beliefs of the sort that regularly enter into practical reasoning. The trait exerts influence through the agent's implicit recognition of logical relations between his or her long-term beliefs and new impressions that arise.

But it does not follow that everyone who ever has an emotion in connection with a certain object type must also have the trait of character associated with that object type. The causal account does require that before a person experiences any emotion in relation to (for instance) money, he or she must have formed a belief to the effect that "It is a good thing for me to acquire money." Most of us probably do believe something like this, at least sometimes and to some extent. But the person with the *nosēma* of money-fondness holds a stronger version of the belief and gives it greater importance in practical reasoning. He may have unusually strong feelings where money is concerned or become emotional about unusually small sums. No doubt he will also give such priority to the possession of money that his emotions about that object will take precedence over other emotions he might have had: he will be much more upset about his veterinarian's bill than he is about his dog. Other people may be baffled by his reactions, even though they themselves are capable of similar responses on a smaller scale.

Thus the 'sicknesses' and related conditions are emotional dispositions whose potency varies in accordance with their perceived saliency in practical reasoning. They are not required for emotional response, but for many individuals they establish a pronounced pattern of unjustified reactions to events. Of course, the person who exhibits one of these traits may not analyze the matter as we have done. He or she may well experience the emotions as involuntary forces arising from some mysterious region of the self. But a reflective observer will still say with confidence that it is the especially strong evaluative belief that is at fault.

As the *nosēma* in these cases is by far the most significant causal factor in emotion, there is some justification for the punning or 'catachrestic' usage by which Chrysippus conflates these powerful dispositional beliefs with the occurrent acts of judgment which are the emotions themselves. One example of this Chrysippan usage has already been mentioned. In the summary by Diogenes Laertius, Chrysippus is reported to have said that the *pathē* are simply ascriptions of value, examples being "fondness for money, . . . drunkenness, stubbornness, and so forth."[18] Another clear example occurs in book 4 of Chrysippus's treatise *On Emotions,* as quoted by Galen. In that passage he is comparing the practice of philosophy to that of medicine: just as the doctor must have intimate knowledge of the illnesses (*pathē*) of the body, so also the 'doctor of the mind' must have intimate knowledge of a variety of conditions of the mind.

> For we do also say in reference to the mind that some people are strong or weak or have good tension or lack tension, and also that they are sick or healthy, and it is also in the same way that we speak of illness (*pathos*) and infirmity and things like that in the mind.[19]

There is some wordplay: the usual sense of *pathos,* which predominates in other fragments of this work, can hardly have been forgotten. Chrysippus perhaps feels that an overlap between *pathos* in the sense of 'emotion' and *pathos* in the sense of 'medical symptom' gives more point to his metaphor of philosophy as a healing art for the mind. In this somewhat rhetorical passage, he is not concerned about maintaining the distinction between condition and movements.

Echoes of Chrysippus's pun—or perhaps his equivocation—can sometimes be heard in later authors. Cicero has been criticized for insisting, in his account of the Stoic theory, that *morbus,* 'disease,' is the appropriate Latin translation for what Stoics mean by *pathos.*[20] The Latin *morbus* is an obvious equivalent for *nosēma* and is Cicero's preferred translation for that word in explaining the Stoic theory of emotional personalities. But it is not otherwise used to refer to episodes of anger, fear, desire, and so on, as *pathos* is in Greek. Cicero may have been misled by Chrysippus's play on words, or he may have been trying rather clumsily to reproduce it. Errors along the same line can be traced also in some of the later Greek handbooks. Thus Stobaeus lists *philēdonia*, *philoploutia*, and *philodoxia* as examples of desire; and pseudo-Andronicus names as emotions no fewer than eight items which seem really to be *nosēmata*.[21]

Proclivities

The Chrysippan material on scalar conditions also includes as evils of mind a group of conditions called *euemptōsiai* or 'proclivities.' Examples in the passage cited above include 'enviousness' (*phthoneria*) and 'tendency toward grief' (*epilupia*). Another portion of Stobaeus explains that a proclivity is a tendency toward some specific emotion; alternatively, it is a tendency toward some action contrary to nature.

> A proclivity is a proneness to emotion, as to one of the actions contrary to nature. Examples include a tendency to grief, irascibility, enviousness, a tendency to wrath, and things like that. There are also proclivities toward other actions contrary to nature, such as toward theft and adultery and violence, in accordance with which persons are called thieves, adulterers, or violent characters.[22]

Irascibility, for instance, is the condition of those who are easily angered: they are not angry all the time, but they become angry more often than other people. Similarly, a person might be timid, that is, have a proclivity to fear, even when he is not actually afraid, and so on with grief, anxiety, envy, and other similar dispositions.[23]

The proclivities bear an obvious resemblance to the sicknesses, since both types of condition predispose an individual to experience some emotions rather than others. However, the pattern of predisposition is different for the proclivities. A person with a 'sickness' is especially concerned about some one object type and experiences a range of emotions concerned with that object. Someone with a proclivity, by contrast, experiences one emotion more than all others and must therefore experience it in connection with a wide range of objects. The one cares deeply about, say, birds and may become mad or sad or glad about them; the other has no special concern with birds, money, men, or anything else but just gets mad, mad, mad about them all. Hence while the names of specific sicknesses are usually derived from those objects—*philodoxia* from *doxa* or

SICKNESSES / INFIRMITIES	AVERSIONS	PROCLIVITIES
fondness / craziness for fame (*philodoxia, doxomania*)	hatred of women (*misogunia*)	enviousness (*phthoneria*) irascibility (*orgilotês*)
fondness for money (*philarguria*)	hatred of humanity (*misanthrōpia*)	timorousness (*deilia*) tendency to pity (*eleēmosunē*)
fondness / craziness for women (*philogunia, gunaikomania*)	hatred of wine (*misoinia*)	tendency to grief (*epilupia*) tendency to wrath
craziness for food (*opsomania*)	aversions to guests (L. *inhospitalitas*)	(*akrocholia*)
fondness for wine (*philoinia*)		anxiety (L. *anxietas*)
fondness for pleasure (*philēdonia*)		desirousness (L. *libidinosum esse*)
craziness for birds (*ornithomania, ortugomania*)		

Figure 8. Scalar conditions in the nonwise.

reputation, *gunaikomania* from *gunaikes* (women), and so on—the names of the proclivities indicate only the nature of the response: *epilupia* is a proneness to *lupē* (grief), *orgilotēs* a proneness to *orgē* (anger). Further examples are given in figure 8.[24]

A comparison can be drawn between the person with some proclivity and the one who has trouble with sinus infections or intestinal cramping. These are chronic conditions, such that we say the condition exists even between bouts of nasal congestion or abdominal pain. Moreover, not everyone who ever gets a stuffy nose is said to have chronic sinusitis: one can suffer from something like that now and then without being especially prone to that ailment more than any other. In the same way, one can experience anger now and then without having the proclivity called irascibility, or fear now and then without being considered timorous. This last point, I take it, is the one made by Chrysippus in this connection. We know that he made the disease comparison, because Cicero spells it out in the technical passage already mentioned, and also because Galen criticizes him for it.[25] Further, the treatise *On Emotions* by Posidonius, on which Galen reports in detail, included an elaborate critique of Chrysippus's statements on proclivities.[26]

If we assume that Chrysippus's position was as I have just described it, then it is possible to understand and resolve Posidonius's objection. Posidonius complains that on Chrysippus's analogy, a body which lacks any tendency to one form of illness more than others must be like the mind which is not susceptible to emotion at all—that is, the mind of the

sage. This, he says, is not an accurate comparison, since the minds of
sages are actually proof against emotion, while every body, even a healthy
one, retains some susceptibility to disease. Thus in his view it would have
been better to compare the mind's 'ill health' to the body's *health*. "For
bodily illness is a condition already diseased, but the sickness Chrysippus
is talking about is more like a proclivity to fevers."[27] As I understand him,
though, Chrysippus did not intend to contrast ordinary susceptibility with
the stable affective health of the wise, but to explain that some of the nonwise are more inclined than others to experience certain emotions upon
small provocation. In that case, the minds which are analogous to healthy
bodies are those of ordinary people who, as Posidonius says, remain susceptible to emotions generally but who are not especially prone to any
one emotion. Posidonius fails to understand this, and so his objection is
not well taken. But Chrysippus should have made his point explicit, rather
than leaving the analogy to do the work.

In what exactly do the proclivities consist? Like every attribute of mind,
they must have some material substrate, say in one's body type or mix of
constitutive humors. But there ought to be an intentional-level account
as well, as there is for the sicknesses, infirmities, and aversions. Let me
therefore venture a suggestion. We have seen that the *nosēmata* are cognitive conditions consisting entirely in a particular sort of belief. They are
in fact deeply ingrained and reinforced versions of the first premise in the
pathetic syllogism, which in its most general form runs like this:

1. Objects of type T are either goods or evils.
2. If either a good or an evil is either present or in prospect, it is appropriate
   for me to undergo some sensed psychophysical movement.
3. Object O, being of type T, is now present.

It is now appropriate for me to undergo some sensed psychophysical
movement.

Now, it could be that the proclivities, too, consist in belief. Specifically, a
proclivity might consist in a strong commitment to some version of premise 2 above. For instance, a person with the proclivity called 'timorousness'
might have an especially well-developed belief that fear, or withdrawing
of the spirit, is the appropriate response to prospective evils. A person with
this commitment would not be very concerned about any one object type;
rather, his belief would be that his favored response, the fear response,
is appropriate in an unusually wide range of situation types. While any
nonwise person might think fear is an appropriate response some of the

time, this person thinks it is the right reaction to the rumble of a subway train or the growl of a Pekinese. As a result, he will indeed be afraid of all of those things, whenever the relevant circumstances arise, whether or not he himself recognizes that his cognitive makeup is such as we have described. And this is just what it is to be timid.

This is an attractively neat account of the proclivities. It gives the Stoics a strongly cognitivist understanding of all three of the nonwise conditions attested as differentiable. Our evidence is thin: no proper definition for the proclivities is extant, and so the interpretation given here cannot be regarded as secure; still, in the absence of clear evidence to the contrary, it is the style of explanation we should prefer. And the interpretation in terms of appropriateness beliefs has a further advantage in that it can be extended to cover tendencies toward other sorts of actions contrary to nature, as also mentioned in the Stobaean account. A proclivity to adultery, for instance, can be explained by the operation in one's everyday practical reasoning of a premise that "sleeping with other people's spouses is an especially appropriate thing for me to do," and so also with tendencies toward other action types such as theft or violence.

Habitudes of the wise

Finally we return to the attributes belonging to the normative human life and to the group of conditions called *epitēdeumata,* that is, 'habitudes' or 'pursuits.' Examples of these appear in another portion of the Stobaean account:

> Fondness for music (*philomousia*), fondness for literature (*philogrammatia*), fondness for horses (*philippia*), fondness for hunting with dogs (*philokunēgia*), and, in general, the things that are said to be encyclical skills are called by Stoics 'habitudes' but are not said to be forms of knowledge; rather, they are classed among the worthwhile conditions. Accordingly, they say that only the wise person is fond of music and fond of literature, and analogously with the others. And they give an outline account of the 'habitude' as follows: 'a road that leads toward what is in accordance with virtue through a skill or through part of a skill.'[28]

What strikes the eye immediately is the similarity of nomenclature between the examples of 'habitudes'—*philomousia, philogrammatia, philippia, philokunēgia*—and the 'sicknesses' considered earlier: *philarguria, philogunia,* and so on. Why should 'fondness for horses' have a different moral standing from 'fondness for birds'? There would be no reason at all, if it were not that the habitudes are defined quite differently from the sicknesses. Sicknesses and infirmities have as part of their definition a mistake about the value of externals: they take some object to be choiceworthy that is in fact not choiceworthy. A habitude does not involve any such mistake; nor could it, since habitudes belong to the inerrant wise. Thus while a nonwise person might well be fond of dogs or literature in an ordinary way, thinking of a day of hunting, or of reading Euripides, as a genuine good, that would not be the sort of fondness that counts as a habitude.[29] To be a habitude, one's engagement with the preferred object must be 'a road that leads toward what is in accordance with virtue through a skill or through part of a skill.'

To understand this definition, it is helpful to know that the word *hodos*, 'road,' also means 'method': a sensible means of achieving some end. Also, we have a definition of 'skill' as 'a system of accurate cognitions trained together toward some good end.'[30] Accurate cognitions, also called *katalēpseis* or 'grasps,' are instances of reliable judgment. Thus we are again dealing with the area of belief, though these beliefs are not the precipitate and unstable opinions (*doxai*) of the nonwise but the wise person's fully justified beliefs, also describable as items of knowledge. A habitude should therefore be the kind of item that can work together with a set of interrelated beliefs to guide one's actions in one direction rather than another. I suggest, then, that a habitude must itself take the form of a belief (in this case a reliable 'grasp') with specific content. Logically it should be related in content to the *katalēpseis* comprised by the skill, without being one of them. That is, it should not just register some reliable bit of information concerning, for instance, horses but should direct a person's actions in that direction. This would be the case if the content grasped included something about the appropriateness in one's own case of preferring activities related to horses where circumstances permit and where no other more pressing obligation stands in the way.

Thus a habitude is indeed a road or method, in that it guides a person toward actions in accordance with virtue. It should be remembered, though, that in the Stoic system *all* the actions of a wise agent are necessarily in accordance with virtue. We cannot think, then, that the habitude leads toward what is in accordance with virtue by directing one away from what is in accordance with vice: the wise person would not need such direction. Rather a habitude must offer a principle of selection among a number of possibilities for virtuous action. It must give the justification for devoting one's time to literature rather than public service, or sports rather than music.

We are told that a habitude is not a form of knowledge but rather a 'worthwhile condition.' The significance of this assertion is that as worthwhile conditions, the habitudes do not have to characterize all wise persons equally. Knowledge in Stoicism is a property of a person's overall epistemic makeup, and it is a *diathesis*: it is present whenever someone holds all beliefs in a fully systematic way, as all the wise do. The virtues are forms of knowledge, and as such they interentail, so that every wise person possesses all the same virtues.[31] However, the Stoics did not assert that every wise person has the same experience or knows exactly the same things.[32] There is room for individuality in the account of skills, for while the virtues (in the sense that applies here) are also skills, not every skill is also a virtue. Skills are concerned with particular areas of experience: they are defined by specific good aims rather than by more general epistemic characteristics such as internal consistency or stability. It is quite possible, then, that each wise person may differ from all others in the specific skills that he or she possesses. Likewise, each may have his or her own habitudes.

The habitude, then, is a characteristic of the wise person as an individual different from others who are also wise. Related in content to her individual skills, it gives her activities a specific focus which is no more virtuous than many alternative possibilities, but which is nonetheless legitimately favored by her. For instance, being 'fond of music' would mean that she believes—with full justification—that it is appropriate for her to spend many hours a day practicing, studying, or listening to music. Such an appreciation is not in itself a virtue, and it is not by any means necessary for virtue that a person have either that appreciation or any specific appreciation at all.[33] One wise person may be fond of music but not of dogs, while another, equally wise, devotes herself to horses, or to a variety of pursuits. Such preferences are not what it is to be wise; rather, they are personality traits of the wise, products of their varied experience.

※

The personal characteristics of the wise thus present an instructive contrast to those of ordinary flawed human beings. They are traits we might like to have, and if our lives were perfected we would have them—for by including this class of traits in the account, the Stoics indicate that it is natural and good for people to have *some* individual characteristics. But this is not the sort of trait that figures prominently in the Stoic account of our nonwise personalities. For us, the traits of character that matter are the ones that shape our emotional lives: the *nosēmata, arrōstēmata,* and *proskopai* disposing us to respond emotionally to various object types, and the proclivities disposing us to various emotion types. The wise have personalities: they have their varieties of experience, their areas of expertise, their favorite pursuits. But these personalities are not structured around the affective experience of the wise in the way that nonwise personalities are structured around emotion. Those who are wise invariably recognize that the objects of their favored activities are inconsequential to happiness, and do not waste their eupathic responses on them. They can be fond of music and still understand that playing music is not in itself a good thing, and that being thwarted in a wish to practice is not an evil.

Why is it, then, that the rest of us so consistently fail to get this right? The reasons are to be sought in the developmental account of character, in the many-layered process of maturation and perversion that produces an ordinary human being. We now turn to consider that developmental account.

7

The Development of Character

The history of an emotive personality is approached quite differently from that of a single episode of emotion. In tracing the causes of occurrent emotions, the Stoic founders sought to defend their understanding of the functional unity of the human person, and along the way to eliminate the bad-faith excuse that behavior can be caused by forces beyond one's control. For these purposes it was most important to explain our feelings and their behavioral expression as having been caused by elements of our own character, beliefs that we hold and habits of mind we have formed. Returning to an earlier analogy, one might say that the causal history supplied for emotional responses addresses the question "Why does the cylinder roll?" and answers it, in brief, by pointing out that the cylinder is round. By contrast, the causal history of character addresses the question "Why is the cylinder round?" That is, it seeks to explain the origin of those characteristics which dispose us to react emotionally when the relevant circumstances arise. And because for Stoics the principal determinants of emotion consist in certain kinds of belief, this portion of the inquiry must ask, in particular, about the origin of those powerful and deeply held beliefs.

In keeping with the interests of our sources, I pursue the inquiry at two successive points. First to be considered is a question concerning the sources of moral error as a widespread phenomenon in human intellectual development. Stoic providentialism asserts that the mind is geared toward the acquisition of correct knowledge throughout one's life. Although we are not born with knowledge or even the rudiments of knowledge, we do have innate tendencies which give some guidance to our intellectual development, and these necessarily point us in the direction of wisdom rather than of error. Despite nature's beneficent plan, however, we acquire many erroneous beliefs along the way. Moreover, we exhibit marked tendencies toward certain errors of evaluation rather than others. As the hymn of Cleanthes makes plain, human "witlessness" in the face of Zeus's beneficent regime regularly takes the form of excessive concern for either reputation, money, or pleasure. It is not that we are inherently wicked: at some level people do consistently long for the good; that is, for real goods as Stoics understand them. But they are deluded, over and over, by these same few objects:

> Wretched creatures! Though ever longing to possess good things,
> they do not see, nor do they hear, god's universal law . . .
> but witless, they act for various bad ends,
> some in contentious zeal for glory,
> others disorderly, bent upon gain,
> others for ease and bodily pleasures.[1]

If Stoic philosophers are to defend their view of nature's intentions for our species, they must offer some explanation why these particular errors occur with such frequency among us.

The obvious strategy would be to point out how many false messages are conveyed to children in the course of their education, and to adults from the mistaken assumptions of their culture. Plato offers an answer of this kind in the *Republic,* blaming especially the direct teaching of those whom he calls 'sophists' and referring also to the praise or blame of popular assemblies.[2] Epicurus makes a similar claim when he cautions his followers to "shun *paideia*"; that is, to keep clear of insidious cultural influences and especially of the usual instruction in poetry and drama.[3] But the Stoics realized that this sort of answer is not adequate to the question. Transmission from one person to another may be the easiest way that erroneous values are contracted, but it can hardly be the only way. Before there can be transmission, there must be something to transmit. Stoics from at least the time of Chrysippus therefore sought to explain the most prevalent forms of human error both by transmission and independently of transmission, through what they called 'the persuasiveness of impressions.' It will be my task in the first part of this chapter to piece together the account of that transmission-independent cause and with it the full

Stoic explanation for moral error as a general phenomenon of human life.

The second part of the chapter considers the process by which the mis-evaluation of one or another object type becomes entrenched or 'deep-rooted' in the emotive personality of the individual, resulting in the *nosē-mata* and other faults treated in chapter 6. Here the emotions themselves play a central role in the explanation, for the Stoic claim is that emotions are habit-forming: repeated episodes of desire give rise to greed, and re-peated episodes of fear give rise to timorousness. I suggest here that such repeated episodes exercise their influence specifically in their character as judgments, by altering our long-term views about matters of value and importance. In this way they lead us gradually to a point where even the most trivial provocation seems inevitably to produce a powerful emotional response. However, it is also possible to reverse the process of entrench-ment through the exercise of reason, by means of self-coaching and vari-ous techniques of cognitive therapy.

It is at this point that the Stoic developmental account becomes most closely entwined with issues of long-term responsibility for one's own character and actions. The initial constitution of one's character is hardly one's own doing; genetic predisposition, upbringing and education, and sheer opportunity all have a role to play. Yet the intellectual resources pro-vided by nature give us opportunity to shape our own emotional person-alities. One does not have to retain characteristics which turn out to be maladaptive: one can rid oneself of them by the exercise of the reasoning faculty. Thus Chrysippus does not hesitate to say that some negative traits such as irascibility may be inborn in a person.[4] Framed in accordance with the Stoics' carefully layered analysis of causation, his claim acknowledges the role of genetic and environmental factors without abandoning his po-sition on moral responsibility.

Empiricism and corruption

I begin with the native endowment of human beings as explained by Ci-cero's Stoic spokesman 'Cato' in book 3 of *On Ends*. This is a central wit-ness for Stoic thought on intellectual maturation and is usually treated as authoritative, for Cicero makes explicit mention of "Zeno and the Stoics," and the substance of his account is corroborated from other sources at many points.[5] Cato begins with the mental characteristics of infants and very young children. He denies that infants have any natural commitment to pleasure for its own sake; instead, what one has from birth is only an orientation to one's own constitution; that is, a sense of attachment to one's natural way of functioning, both physically and psychologically, and a preference for the kinds of objects that tend to preserve it. At the most basic level these objects must be the minimal necessities for health and safety, things like appropriate nourishment and secure places to rest.[6] But the wish to understand and make connections is also part of our native endowment. Even young children are pleased when they figure something out, says Cato, regardless of whether they derive any material advantage from it. Similarly we dislike being deceived and are unwilling to accept what is false or incongruous.

This is not very much—far less, for instance, than the innate knowledge posited by Socrates in Plato's *Meno*—and yet it suffices for a course of development which has its culmination in the full flowering of virtuous knowledge. Cato explains in some detail how the mind progresses. At first one seeks merely to preserve oneself; then, to select things that accord with one's nature; then, recognizing a pattern in one's own preferences, one begins to try to preserve and perfect that pattern for its own sake, bringing it into harmony with the natural order of which one is a part. Natural preferences for self-preservation, for understanding, and for order and control thus work together to establish in one's life the stable and coherent systems of belief and action which constitute the human good. Coming to understand the good and coming to instantiate the good thus happen at the same time, as one transfers one's allegiance from external goods to those objects which are integral to one's rational nature.[7]

It should be emphasized that while this account of intellectual maturation employs a broadly empiricist model of knowledge acquisition, it also makes use of innatist elements, preferences and tendencies which are simply part of human nature. The philosophical significance of this fact is demonstrated by Dominic Scott in *Recollection and Experience*.[8] Reports of Stoic epistemology speak of the mind at birth as being like a blank sheet of paper which has yet to form even those rudimentary concepts by which we make sense of perceptual inputs.[9] Learning takes place entirely through experience of one's environment and without mysterious inputs. But the empiricist commitment is consistent with the mind's having been constructed in such a way as to favor some decisions over others. There can be a bias in favor of a choice that will, in the long run, promote a development toward knowledge and virtue. Scott compares this innate bias to genetic factors favoring such illnesses as asthma or breast cancer, conditions one does not have at birth but may be primed to develop in the usual course of events.[10] There is some irony in this, for in Stoicism the condition one is primed to develop is not an illness but mature psychic health, and the genetic factor is shared by all rational creatures. The important point, though, is that an empiricist system can find a naturalistic basis for minds' developing in one direction rather than another.

Thus the native tendencies described by Cicero's Cato must be very closely allied with the 'starting points toward virtue' (*aphormai pros aretēn*) spoken of by Cleanthes.[11] In the Stobaean summary we are told that "one has from nature starting points toward discerning what is appropriate, toward stabilizing the impulses, toward enduring, and toward fair distributing"; in other words, toward the cardinal virtues of prudence, temperance, courage, and justice.[12] Another work of Cicero, the treatise *On Duties* (better called *On Appropriate Actions*), makes the connection even more plain: prudence develops out of an innate preference for understanding, justice from an innate tendency toward sociability, and courage and temperance from similar propensities for mastery and for order.[13] Thus while the *aphormai* are not in themselves positive epistemic attainments, they do point us in the right direction, toward objects that tend to promote our healthy functioning and accurate understanding, and away from their opposites. Given an unimpeded course of development, it seems that every human being should in time attain to wisdom and virtue.

This is encouraging at the level of theory: at least there is nothing posited of human nature which must necessarily incline us toward vice. But it has to be acknowledged that what we actually encounter, both in ourselves and in those around us, does not accord very well with the orderly progression Cato describes. If virtuous wisdom is where we are headed, then the vast majority of us seem to be taking a long detour along the way. This is not to say merely that the immature mind makes some mistakes. That in itself might not require much explanation: learning from experience is inherently a matter of trial and error. One might make many mistakes in dealing with the complexities of lived experience and still end up in time with a reliable set of concepts.[14] The problem is rather with the regular occurrence of certain specific kinds of error, namely, strong or uncompromising evaluations of such external objects as money, pleasure, fame, and their opposites. When overwhelming numbers of people make the same kinds of error repeatedly in the course of their development, one does need to offer some explanation for the source of those errors. Otherwise, pointed questions may be asked about the real nature of our innate endowment.[15]

The twofold cause

The summary by Diogenes Laertius gives evidence of an attempt to provide such an explanation:

> The rational animal is corrupted sometimes by the persuasiveness of things from without, sometimes through the teaching (*katēchēsis*) of our associates. For the starting points which nature provides are uncorrupted.[16]

Two causes are named for our perversion: first the persuasiveness of "things from without" (whatever those might be) and second the teaching of one's associates. The second of these must be the important one in real cases, for children absorb most of their values from adults: once the mistaken beliefs are established, there are a hundred ways they may be passed on to the next generation. (*Katēchēsis,* the word that later became 'catechesis' as in religious instruction, is literally a dinning of something into one's ears.) But of course there must be some more fundamental cause. Our associates can transmit to us only what has already been transmitted to them. It must be to prevent the obvious regress objection that the Stoic thinker here represented has included also an appeal to "the persuasiveness of things from without." Nothing has yet been said, however, about what that ultimate cause is supposed to involve.

A clear attribution for this Stoic doctrine is given by another familiar source, Galen's *On the Precepts of Hippocrates and Plato.* Galen is again criticizing certain positions taken by Chrysippus in his treatise *On Emotions,* which he has read together with another work on the same subject by Posidonius; in the latter, if we can believe Galen's account of it, Posidonius too expressed sharp criticism.[17] Galen is here stating his own position on the natural inclinations of children, in opposition to the Stoic view as he understands it. How can it be, says Galen, that children have a natural orientation toward moral excellence? For if they did, then faults could not arise in them from within, but only from without, whereas what we actually observe is that even if children are reared in good habits and properly educated, never seeing or hearing any example of fault, they still go wrong sooner or later. Chrysippus himself admits this, says Galen, for "he did not dare to falsify the phenomena." And he also offers an explanation for it: he says (and here Galen seems to be quoting his exact words) that "the cause of perversion is twofold: one comes about through transmission from many people, the other through the very nature of things."[18] The phrase "through the very nature of things" is hopelessly vague; it is shortly to be restated, however, as "the persuasiveness of impressions," the same cause as is named in Diogenes Laertius. The terms 'perversion' and 'transmission' also match exactly with our other source. We therefore have confirmation not only that Chrysippus treated the perversion issue but also, given the context, that he regarded it as highly relevant to the study of emotion.

Galen also provides some hints as to how Chrysippus developed his points. Continuing his attack, he writes,

> But I am puzzled about both of these. First, about the one arising from persons near at hand: when they see and hear some example of fault, why do they not hate and avoid it, given that they have no orientation to it? This strikes me as baffling. And it is even more baffling when they are deceived without having seen or heard any example of fault, through the very nature of things. . . . When he says that perversions concerning goods and evils come about in ordinary persons both through the persuasiveness of impressions and through transmission, we must ask him, "What is the reason why pleasure gives us the persuasive impression that it is a good, and pain the persuasive impression that it is an evil? And likewise, why is it that we are readily persuaded when we hear the many praise and congratulate people for having statues put up of them, as if that were a good thing, and speak of defeat and dishonor as if they were bad?"[19]

Exactly how an impression can be persuasive is not explained; indeed, Galen would like his readers to believe that no explanation is possible. We do, however, gain some examples of the kinds of objects that are supposed to produce these mischievous impressions: they include pleasure, pain, praise (as expressed in the putting up of statues), defeat, and dishonor. All these are points which Galen means to challenge and which he claims Posidonius challenged before him. They must therefore be elements already included in the Chrysippan account.

A more coherent statement of the Stoic position can be found in a late source, a Latin commentary on Plato's *Timaeus* by a scholar named Calcidius, writing somewhere around 400 C.E. Calcidius's knowledge of the topic is impressive: he supplies clear Latin equivalents for the terms 'corruption,' 'transmission,' 'the twofold cause,' and 'the circumstances themselves,' and his account is also close to Galen's in its emphasis on pleasure and pain and on the praise of the many.[20] This suggests that he has access to material derived from the same Chrysippan treatise as used by Galen. Calcidius may not have consulted that work himself; it is likely, though, that he worked closely with earlier *Timaeus* commentaries which supplied him with good information.[21]

Calcidius states clearly that what Stoics call 'the twofold cause' is meant to explain how false values become established among people whose nature is to pursue the good. He describes this twofold cause as follows:

> This arises both from things themselves and from the transmission of ru-
> mor. For the very experience of being born involves some pain, because
> one is moving from a warm and moist place into the chill and dryness of
> the surrounding air, and as a remedy for this the midwife provides a warm
> bath and swaddling to recall the womb, to ease the young body with pleas-
> ant sensation and quiet it. Thus . . . there arises a kind of natural belief that
> everything sweet and pleasurable is good, and that what brings pain is bad
> and to be avoided. Older children learn the same thing from the experience
> of hunger and satiety, and from caresses and punishments.
>
> As they mature, they retain this belief that everything nice is good,
> even if not useful, and that everything troublesome, even if it brings some
> advantage, is bad. Consequently they love riches, which are the foremost
> means of obtaining pleasure, and they embrace glory rather than honor.
> For humans are by nature inclined to pursue praise and honor, since honor
> is the testimony to virtue. But those who are wise and engaged in the study
> of wisdom know what sort of virtue they ought to cultivate, while people
> do not know about things and so cultivate glory, that is, popular esteem,
> in place of honor. And in place of virtue they pursue a life steeped in plea-
> sures, believing that the power to do what one wants is the superiority of
> a king. For humans are by nature kingly, and since power always accompa-
> nies kingship, they suppose that kingship likewise accompanies power. . . .
> Similarly, since the happy person necessarily enjoys life, they think that
> those who live pleasurably will be happy. Such, I think, is the error which
> arises 'from things' to possess the human mind.
>
> But the one which arises 'from transmission' is a whispering added to
> the aforementioned error through the prayers of our mothers and nurses
> for wealth and glory and other things falsely supposed to be good, and a
> disturbance from the bogeys which frighten young people very much, and
> from comfortings and everything like that. Yes, and think of poetry, which
> shapes the minds of older children, and of the impressive productions of
> other authors! How great an influence concerning pleasure and suffering
> do they exert on the novice mind! What about painters and sculptors? Do
> they not deliberately lead the mind toward sweetness?[22]

Unlike Galen, Calcidius admits that the Stoics have provided an explanation for what it is that makes pleasure, riches, and the like so appealing to people, without their being good in fact and independently of transmission from the previous errors of others. All these objects have a tendency to co-occur with objects that one is indeed inclined by nature to pursue. The warm bath and swaddling clothes provided by the midwife "as a remedy" are things which ease and quiet the newborn body; they would count, then, as restorative of the natural constitution and so worth pursuing. But most (though not all) restorative experiences are also pleasurable, and it is hardly surprising if the infant fails to realize that drinking milk or taking a bath is to be pursued qua healthful rather than qua pleasurable. The same can be said of an older child's experience of nourishment or of a parent's embrace. Because these things both promote our temporal well-being and provide pleasure, it is easy for a mind which has not yet formed the requisite concepts to assume that it is the pleasure involved, rather than the benefit to the natural functioning of our bodies and family units, that is of value. Some epistemic confusion is practically inevitable; it is "a kind of natural belief" and yet not a true belief. And one's early experience of pain has the opposite effect.

It is no surprise that a Stoic author should take this stand in regard to pleasure. It is a view attested for Chrysippus that pleasure is a concomitant or by-product (*epigennēma*) of activities that restore one's natural constitution; that is, that it supervenes on them.[23] Less familiar is the apparent implication that other objects mistakenly valued similarly supervene on one's natural goals. This is most clearly stated in the sentences on power and what Calcidius calls 'kingship.' Part of our native endowment is a predilection for mastery, which motivates us to assume control over our surroundings. But not every exercise of power is a manifestation of the human being's proper controlling role; rather, power supervenes on that role just as pleasure supervenes on the flourishing condition.

Where honor and glory are concerned there is an additional level of confusion to be sorted out. Humans are by nature inclined to pursue praise and honor, for honor, says Calcidius, is "the testimony to virtue": it has a reliable connection to virtuous action and for that reason constitutes a legitimate object of choice. But humans frequently make the mistake of cultivating another form of praise which is here called "glory" or "popular esteem," deceived apparently by the resemblance between justified and unjustified praise. Thus popular esteem stands at two removes from the real source of value: honor is derived from virtue, and popular esteem is then confused with honor.

The extra attention devoted to the topic of reputation is in keeping with the interests of Stoics in the early period. Separate definitions were given for honor (*timē*) and for repute (*doxa*): honor, we learn from the Stobaean summary, is a genuine good restricted to the virtuous, while repute is merely a preferred indifferent.[24] Cleanthes is said to have composed a short treatise on each.[25] Calcidius's report helps to bring out the significance of the distinction within the developmental story. As the young person matures, he or she is expected to begin to value praiseworthy behavior for its own sake, no longer being deeply concerned for reputation, though still perhaps pursuing it as a preferred indifferent. But that new understanding of what behavior is praiseworthy has been derived largely from observations of what behavior tends to be praised in fact. During the period when one's own concepts of justice and integrity are still in the process of formation, there is no way to correct mistakes in this area. It is an inherently risky procedure.

Once the spontaneous or point-of-origin cause of error is in place, the transmission from person to person happens quite easily. There was in the earlier paragraph no implication that the midwife acts improperly in bathing and swaddling the baby. Error in that case arises spontaneously, from babies' misinterpreting what happens to them. Here, by contrast, the caregiver is already in error, and the child has only to absorb and remember her values. Most false beliefs are transmitted verbally, from the "whispering" of those who pray in the child's hearing for the supposed blessings of wealth and reputation, or from tales of bogeymen intended to frighten the child into good behavior. Poetry and drama, mainstays of education in antiquity, are deeply implicated. So also are the visual arts, though these must convey their messages through symbolism or other nonlinguistic means of representation.

Cicero's hall of mirrors

Yet another version of the twofold origin of error can be traced out in the writings of Cicero, in a segment of his work *On Laws* and again in the preface to Tusculan Disputation 3. Here we must proceed with caution, for in neither context does Cicero attribute his argument clearly to the Stoics, and we know that he was open to other intellectual influences, especially Platonic influence. Yet because of close similarities to accounts we have already seen, I believe that a large share of his thinking does derive from some early Stoic treatise. The likeliest sources are Chrysippus's treatises

On Laws and *On Emotions,* which are known to have supplied arguments for other portions of these two Ciceronian works.[26]

The point at issue in book 1 of *On Laws* is whether humans possess a universal sense of justice.[27] Cicero argues the affirmative, but he does not mean to say that all people actually behave justly or even know what justice is. The claim about human nature is in fact quite minimal: it is only that humans possess, even without teaching, a kind of 'initial and inchoate intelligence' which favors the development of justice in each person. This *prima et inchoata intelligentia,* also referred to in the plural (*intellegentiae*), is not "intelligence" in our sense of the word, and it is not what Cicero calls *intelligentia* in *On Ends* 3.21, that is, a full-scale concept. Rather it is a natural endowment which equips us in some way to form the concepts out of which justice is built.[28] The process by which one comes to understand justice is therefore self-starting, but its success is not guaranteed, for humans in general are also subject to perversion (*depravatio*) through "customs and [false] opinions."[29] This corrupting influence is so great that it extinguishes the 'sparks' given to us by nature and allows faults to become established.[30] The result is that people resemble one another not only in what they get right but also in their perversions of the right (*pravitates*).

The cause of these perversions appears at first to consist simply in the influence of other people, their various ill-founded views and pernicious cultural practices. A reprise of the perversion theme at 1.47 mentions "the parent, the wet nurse, the teacher, the poet, the stage," and, in general "the views of the many." These "take us when we are young and inexperienced and give us whatever shape and color they wish." But Cicero appears more interested in another means of perversion, one that comes about not through cultural transmission but through one's own impressions of certain object types.

> For all people are also attracted to pleasure, which has something in it similar to what is good by nature even when it is an inducement to shameful conduct. For it so delights us by its smoothness and sweetness that it is construed as something healthful, through an error of the mind. It is by a similar misunderstanding that people flee death as being a dissolution of nature and pursue life as preserving us in the state in which we are born. Pain is considered to be one of the worst evils both because of its sharpness and because it is seen to accompany destructions of our nature. And there is a resemblance between moral excellence and glory, which is the reason

why those held in honor are regarded as fortunate and those in disgrace as unfortunate.[31]

Cicero names six objects which people mistakenly regard as goods and evils: pleasure and pain, death and life, honor and disrepute. Each of these is closely associated with an object for which we have some natural affinity or disaffinity: on the positive side health, the preservation of one's natural state, and moral excellence; on the negative side bodily harm, the dissolution of one's nature, and (by implication) moral turpitude. Our errors arise from our tendency to confuse objects in the first group with the corresponding objects in the second group. We fail to make distinctions between things that are in fact distinct.

But why should we make such mistakes? Cicero twice speaks of the confusion in terms of a resemblance between one thing and another. Pleasure, he says, "has something similar" to what is good by nature and so is "an imitator of the good."[32] Glory, also, is said to resemble moral excellence (*honestas*). However, the language of resemblance is not entirely transparent. Ordinarily we think of resemblance as a sharing of properties: to perceive a resemblance is to observe the same properties in two distinct objects, each of which is already fully conceptualized. That is not quite what is happening in this case, where the relevant concepts are still in the process of formation. Here as in Calcidius, the salient epistemic challenge must be that of sorting out experiences which regularly occur together. The difficulty that confronts the developing mind is that of recognizing that the objects in question are in fact different, making distinctions it has not previously made, so as to form the boundaries of its concepts correctly.

This alternative (and philosophically preferable) explanation is expressed in the passage just quoted, in connection with the confusion between pain and the destruction of our nature. Pain, says Cicero, is thought to be an evil both because of its sharpness and because it is seen to accompany (*videtur sequi*) destructions of our nature; i.e., instances of harm to our natural constitution.[33] Being injured is not at all the same thing as being in pain, yet because pain does regularly accompany injury, it is easy for the undeveloped mind to assume that it is the pain itself that is to be avoided. Hence the difficulty of persuading a child to accept some necessary but painful medical treatment. With greater experience of the world, the child may come to realize that there are two object types to be kept straight, those which cause pain and those which harm the body, and to regard these things in different ways. Until then, the frequency with which these co-occur will be misleading. Likewise pleasure comes to be understood as a distinct object type from that which promotes health, and good or bad reputation as distinct from reputable or disreputable conduct. Even life itself—that is, the mere continuance of one's existence as an animate organism—is to be distinguished from a proper object, the preservation of one's natural state or (as we might say it) of one's wholeness as a person. A mature person does not necessarily believe that death is to be avoided at all costs.

%

Cicero's last and most elaborate treatment of the perversion theme appears in the preface to the third book of the *Tusculan Disputations*. There, again, he is seeking to maintain the beneficence of our native endowment in the face of what might seem like overwhelming evidence to the contrary. The skewing of our values was never a foregone conclusion: although we were endowed at birth with only the smallest beginnings of mental capacity, "the tiniest sparks of understanding," these if not perverted would be sufficient to enable us to grow into beings both virtuous and wise. "Seeds of the virtues," he says, "are inborn in our characters, and if they were allowed to mature, nature itself would lead us to perfect happiness."[34] It therefore becomes necessary to explain how it is that those sparks are extinguished, overwhelmed by our 'wrongful habits and beliefs.' This occurs in the first place through the influence of associates, the list of whom is identical to that given in *On Laws* 1.47: the wet nurse, the parent, the teacher, the poet, the public. Each of these is described, with emphasis given especially to the last. It is when we meet with society at large, says Cicero, that we "become thoroughly infected with corrupt beliefs and secede from nature absolutely."

But the explanation is not yet finished, for the ultimate origin of perversion has not been identified. Cicero therefore proceeds to a second mode of explanation, although he makes no effort to mark it as such. He observes that while developing humans are mainly influenced by the opinions of others, there are also certain people who have made up their minds for themselves what is to be valued. These people are intellectual leaders, though misguided ones; the rest of us merely acquiesce in their judgment. It seems also that they are political leaders, men perhaps like Cicero himself, for their interest is specifically in civic and military honors:

> As a result, we think the meaning of nature best understood by those who
> have made up their minds that public office, military commands, and the

glory of popularity are the best and most honorable goals a person can have.[35]

And it is mistakes concerning honor and glory which will be the principal target of the explanation. Desires for money and pleasure will be mentioned at the end of the passage, but only summarily: if the erroneous pursuit of glory can be explained, these will follow in its train.

Always important for Cicero, the glory theme here has a distinct (though unacknowledged) Stoic coloring.[36] Those whom he calls "the noblest among us" have come to an erroneous conclusion about glory through failure to sort through a double set of distinctions. These are just the same distinctions as reported by Calcidius. A false glory, also called 'popular acclaim,' is to be distinguished from true glory, and the latter must still be kept distinct from moral excellence and the right actions in which it is displayed.

> These things attract the noblest among us, so that even as they pursue that genuine distinction which is the one chief aim of their nature, they spend their lives in great emptiness, chasing not a solid figure of virtue but only a shadow-shape of glory. For real glory is a solid thing, clearly modeled and not shadowy at all: it is the unanimous praise of good persons, approval sounded without bias by those who know how to judge excellence of character. It is, as it were, the reflection or echo of such excellence, and there is no need for good men to disown it, since it is the regular accompaniment to right actions. But there is another sort of glory, which pretends to imitate the first, and which is rash and ill-considered, frequently praising misdeeds and faults. This is popular acclaim, which offers a perverted caricature of the beauty that belongs to true distinction, and people are blinded by it, so that they do not know where to find or how to recognize the fine things they desire.[37]

The relation between true glory and excellence of character is somewhat like the relation we observed in Calcidius between pleasure and health and between power and kingship, and in *On Laws* between pain and bodily harm: the one regularly accompanies the other. With this pair, though, the connection is especially reliable, for true glory is praise spoken by the wise, knowledgeable observers who can be counted upon to dispense approval on exactly the right occasions and in exactly the right degree. Thus true glory is a concomitant or 'regular accompaniment' (*comes*) to appropriate actions.[38] This implies that justified praise never merits avoidance, as Cicero also says: any state of affairs in which such praise is heard is also an object worthy of pursuit. The difficulty, it seems, is that the undeveloped mind identifies the wrong feature of appropriate acts as making them worthy of choice. Rather than valuing those acts as being in accordance with nature, it values them as being praiseworthy; in effect, it values the praise itself. This opens the door to further error. For praise coming from ordinary observers might be virtually indistinguishable from the praise that would be spoken by a person of perfect understanding, if one happened to be present. The words spoken might be the same, and they might be spoken with the same inflection and ring of sincerity. Only one who had the wise person's own sensitivity to the epistemic state of others would be in a position to assess the mind of the speaker and determine whether he spoke from knowledge. Putting it in real terms (since actual wise persons are rarely to be encountered), we might say that even where the praise a young person receives is justifiable, one whose concept of the good is not yet fully formed will have no reliable way to distinguish such praise from that which is accorded to misdeeds and faults. It is therefore very unsafe to draw any inference from the praise of the fallible multitude to one's real merits. But this is a risk the young progressor will invariably have to take.

The imagery is worth dwelling on. Real glory is "a solid thing, clearly modeled"—we are meant to think of statues in bronze or terracotta—but solid as it is, real glory is itself only a "reflection or echo" of something yet more substantial.[39] Popular acclaim, in turn, is a shadow cast by true glory—a shadow of a reflection, as it were. Those misled by it find themselves pursuing only shadows, and distorted shadows at that, "perverted caricatures" that trick our vision and leave us blundering around in the dark of our own blindness. The multiple image-original relations recall Plato's cave analogy in book 7 of the *Republic,* where ordinary people compete for honors while striving to identify regularities in the progression of shadows cast by statuelike images of people and animals. The point of the allusion (which is perhaps Cicero's own embellishment of the theme) is that the Stoic account of epistemic corruption is more than a little reminiscent of Plato's stated concern with "our nature in its education and lack of education."[40] Like Plato, the Stoics regard moral error as a result of confusion and lack of guidance, rather than of any evil inherent in our nature.

The establishment of traits

We now have in place the essential groundwork for the Stoics' developmental account of character—the account which is supposed to explain why certain kinds of external objects so often produce wrongly emotional responses in the nonwise. The Chrysippan 'twofold cause' yields a comprehensive account of human development in that it gives thought to every stage in a person's intellectual growth, from babyhood to the early stages of a working life, and to every person that is likely to have an influence, from the humblest of working women to the most prestigious representatives of high culture. At the same time, it is intended to be a very general account which will explain the presence of erroneous evaluative beliefs across the broad spectrum of humankind. It is based in natural propensities which all people share, and the specific views it explains are ones that need explaining precisely because they are widely held.

Something more is needed, then, if the Stoics are to provide a causal history for individual traits of character such as we encountered in chapter 6. That money is a good is something very many people believe; the greedy individual, though, believes this in a special way which is manifested in a pronounced pattern of behavior. To supply an explanation for the presence of such individual traits or, collectively, profiles of traits, it is not sufficient to appeal to the processes of misperception and transmission described above. There must be some further process at work by which the sorts of errors that play some role in the thinking of every ordinary person become, in some individuals, the very armature around which their behavior is structured. That process, whatever it is, will be invested with great significance in ethics. For it is individual patterns of response which give meaning to the notion of agent responsibility.

In what way, then, do the individual traits of character differ from the erroneous evaluations shared by humans generally? The definitions studied in the preceding chapter suggest, for at least the most important types of trait, that the difference is in the extent to which the former are ingrained or 'entrenched' beliefs. The 'sicknesses,' 'infirmities,' and 'aversions' are not just any mistaken evaluations; each is an opinion "which has hardened into a condition and become entrenched."[41] I want therefore to call attention to the mechanism by which those beliefs become ingrained. Cicero in his treatment of traits of character in Tusculan Disputation 4 provides the following brief etiology:

They [the fondnesses and proclivities] arise from desire and from gladness. When a person has conceived a desire for money, and when there has been no immediate application of reason—the Socratic medicine, as it were, which might have cured that desire—then the evil works its way into the veins, and settles in the vital organs, and comes to be a sickness and an infirmity. Once it has become habitual, the sickness cannot be removed, and its name is 'greed.' It is the same with the other sicknesses, such as desire for glory or liking for women. The contraries of these are thought to arise out of fear. Examples include hatred of women and hatred of the whole human race, such as we have heard of in the case of Timon, who is called 'the Misanthrope'; also hostility to guests. All these infirmities of mind arise from some kind of fear of those objects which the persons in question dislike and avoid.[42]

Since this account is presented by Cicero as a summary of a longer treatment by Chrysippus, it is a fair guess that a similar but somewhat more precise account by Epictetus also derives from that source, although it is attributed by him only to 'the philosophers.'

When once you have desired money, if there is an application of reason, which will lead you to recognize the evil, the desire stops and our directive faculty (hēgemonikon) governs as at the start, but if you do not apply anything in the way of therapy, it no longer returns to the same [condition], but when it is again stimulated by the corresponding impression it is kindled into desire more quickly than before. And if this keeps happening, it thereafter becomes callused, and the infirmity gives stability to greed.[43]

The two versions agree in that they attribute the ingraining of such beliefs to repeated episodes of strong emotion. So, for instance, a person who accepts provisionally that money is a good may find that belief powerfully reinforced after having felt strong desires for money a number of times, and one who has been frightened by women over and over may develop an aversion to all women. Both authors also argue that a trait can be prevented from forming by a quasi-medical 'application of reason,' but that the opportunity will narrow and eventually close altogether as the trait becomes fully formed. Epictetus is somewhat clearer than Cicero about the effects of repetition: it is when the desire episodes keep happening that one comes to develop the arrōstēma of greed. But the same thought may lie behind Cicero's remark about the sickness's becoming 'habitual' (inveterata).

The two texts together give evidence of a Stoic account in which occurrent emotions are counted as causes of the related long-term dispositions. If reason does not intervene, desire itself brings about an alteration
in the mind's condition such that subsequent episodes of desire are more
frequent. To be sure, one would not have experienced any emotion in the
first place if mistaken evaluations of external objects did not already have
some place in one's thinking. To that extent, the misevaluation is causally
prior. But the repeated experience of emotions may also have an effect on
the evaluative belief, causing it to become hardened into a trait of character.

The causal claim may at first appear vacuous. If a trait of character
were nothing more than a pattern of behavior—a certain prevalence of
anger responses, for instance—the Stoics would have said nothing more
than that a frequent reaction is made frequent by one's having it especially
often. But a trait is more than this. Epictetus's comparison to a callus helps
to bring this out. Calluses are produced by repeated contact, but having
a callus is more than having had repeated contact with something: once
formed, it alters one's sensitivity to subsequent contacts, and it is also mea-
surable by other means. A trait of character, likewise, is not just a string
of similar responses but an increased receptivity to the potential triggers
for responses of that kind. Desire will be felt at the first hint of a possible
profit; waves of hostility at the mere suggestion of company for tea. Further, the analogy may imply that the trait is detectable by means other
than merely counting the frequency of certain responses. Even in periods
of calm the greedy person or the misogynist should reveal himself by his
conversation or choice of pastimes. The claim must be, then, that occurrent emotions of a certain type bring about some definite change in the
mind, either by adding new beliefs or by changing the manner of one's
believing.

The metaphors of 'callusing' and 'settling into the vital organs' do not
give us any very clear idea of what it means for a belief to become entrenched. We can see, though, that the process is one that can be coun-
teracted by reason. Presumably, then, we should be thinking of a process
which can be described in intentional terms (though it might bear a material description as well). One could, for instance, describe it as a change in
the structure of the belief-set which ensures that that belief is consulted
especially often in one's practical reasoning. An ingrained belief about the
value of money would then be one whose network of associative links
to other beliefs is unusually extensive. Each time one completes the kind
of practical syllogism that is implied in the desire impulse, one becomes

aware of additional links between the value of money and other presumed facts about the world, so that in time the misevaluation comes to be a point of reference for a great many of one's judgments.

Alternatively, one might speak of an additional second-order belief about the significance of the evaluation. The second-order or salience belief would refer to one's memory of strong feelings in connection with the relevant object type. Timon, the misanthrope, remembers having had many unpleasant feelings toward other people. Whatever his original reason for having these emotions, he has since come to believe that *being around people is bad for me* is the one value out of all the values he holds that should most often determine his actions. Competing considerations, thoughts which might dispose him to respond to new situations in ways other than by shunning human contact, seem to him unimportant in comparison with these thoughts whose importance has been reinforced by strong feeling. Revision of the view becomes increasingly difficult.

We should observe, further, that both in Cicero's and in Epictetus's version the Stoic account lays great emphasis on the capacity of rational agents to reverse their emotional commitments and prevent vicious dispositions from forming in themselves. For Timon and others like him whose mistaken views have already become deeply entrenched, there may be no hope: in them the trait has taken on stability and can no longer be removed.[44] But the usual situation is less extreme. The process of trait formation is not so rapid as to leave no opportunity for reflective self-examination to intervene. It takes many repetitions of the occurrent emotion to establish a stable characteristic, and each of those repetitions depends upon beliefs a thoughtful agent can learn to recognize as false. Even if one has erred in the past, then, one can still counteract the cognitive aftereffects of those errors by an early exercise of the rational capacities one has as an adult human. In this way each of us can take charge of the formation of a healthful character for ourselves. Conversely, if we fail to take charge in this way, we contribute by omission to the vice-ridden character we end up with. For however it was that we first fell into error, it is only through subsequent laxity that the error becomes entrenched.

Autonomy and luck

The formation of traits of character thus depends on two quite different kinds of causes. Traits are formed by the repeated occurrence of the relevant emotions, but because the activity of reason can also prevent them from being formed, it seems that the imperfectly rational nature of the mind being formed is also causally implicated. Suppose Crassus is greedy. One cause of his greed is that he has desired money frequently in the past: his desires have altered the subsequent character of his mind. Also very important, though, is that during the period in which the trait became ingrained, Crassus was a rational creature, fully capable of self-examination and amendment of view. The trait that formed in him would have gone out of existence if at any point he had engaged in those characteristically rational activities. So the fact that he has persisted in doing otherwise counts as a cause of its continuance.

This account of trait formation is consistent with what we otherwise know about Stoic thought on the causation of qualitative states. The relevant doctrine is lucidly explained by Susanne Bobzien in connection with a basic distinction between change and the maintenance of a change. Whenever an object exhibits some qualitative state, there are two quite different questions to be asked about the causation of that state. One might ask why the object changed in the way that it did when it first acquired that characteristic, or one might ask why it continues to exhibit that characteristic over time. Causal questions of the second kind are answered in accordance with the postulates of Stoic physics, by appeal to the 'active principle' or 'designing fire' which works continuously upon all things in the universe. As a rule, the states of objects manifest the activity of the designing fire in each, operating through the *pneuma* inherent in that object. Insofar as the *pneuma* is responsible for the object's continuing to exhibit some state, it is called the 'sustaining cause' of that state. This is a cause that operates simultaneously with the effect it produces. By contrast, the cause of the object's coming to be in that state must precede, at least in part, the time during which the effect obtains. It is therefore called an 'antecedent' cause.[45]

The two kinds of causes are different both in the effect they produce and in the time at which they operate. Bobzien writes,

> States can be said to have antecedent causes only in the indirect sense that they have been *brought about* by antecedent causes, i.e. that the states are the result of a change caused or part-caused by those antecedent causes. It is important not to confound the direct causes of states, which sustain the states, and the indirectly responsible causal factors that bring the states about. For without the internal sustaining causes, whatever qualitative state has been brought about by antecedent causes would immediately deteriorate.[46]

Thus while every state must necessarily have been brought about by one or more antecedent causes, the operation of the sustaining cause is far more important. This cause, also called the 'complete' cause, is specified a priori and always in the same way. For every state or characteristic of an object, the sustaining cause is just the portion of *pneuma* that is present in that object.

Since causes in Stoicism are always bodies, it is helpful to remember that the human psyche is also a certain amount of *pneuma* and that mental events, including emotions, are also describable as bodies, that is, as the *psuchē* in the moment of undergoing certain alterations.[47] A Stoic can therefore say both that a string of occurrent emotions causes a trait to form and that the mind itself causes the trait by maintaining it. One and the same discrete quantity of *pneuma* is involved, but in different roles and at different points in time. Thus Crassus's experience of desire is a body—it is the *pneuma* in Crassus undergoing a certain alteration—and that body, considered for its contribution to Crassus's becoming greedy, is also an antecedent cause of his greed, though not by any means the only such cause. Further, Crassus's psyche during the time he exhibits the trait of greed is, again, a body, and that body, considered for its contribution to the maintenance of his greed over time, is also the sustaining cause of that trait. Finally, Crassus's psyche, considered for its role in taking on the characteristic of greed, is also the body to which the effect is caused.[48]

It is the psyche's role as sustaining cause of its own traits that is most important for questions of individual autonomy. As we have seen, Chrysippus's position on autonomy in a determinist system is that we are responsible for our actions and emotions just because impulse implies assent, and assent is determined by one's own moral character. To this it is easy to respond that if that is all that can be said, then the notion of autonomy thus established is exceedingly thin. Unless it is also shown that one is responsible in some meaningful way for the character that one has, the problem has only been shifted back a step.[49] Plutarch is especially indignant about this. On the Stoic system, he says, it is unfair that anyone should be chastised for vice, for by Chrysippus's own assertion all the states (*scheseis*) of every part of the universe come about in accordance with Zeus's providence. Thus Zeus himself is responsible for the faults that cause us to behave badly, including the *nosēmata* of *philarguria*, *philēdonia*, *philodoxia*, and cowardice.[50]

The Stoics' distinction between antecedent and sustaining causes gives them a way to respond to these concerns. They can allow that a person's character is the product of a variety of formative influences; indeed as determinists they should insist on this.[51] Such influences always have to be taken into account, for some of them begin to work upon us even during childhood, well before we become rational beings capable of assent. Each of us is shaped at least in part by genetic factors, as well as by the physical environment, by the way we are treated within the family, and by our education, role models, and so forth. Rarely do we have any control over these matters which, collectively, supply the makings of our adult selves. One could consider them a form of luck. On the Stoic scheme, however, all these influences which are outside our control come under the category of antecedent causes, not sustaining causes. As such they are not the direct causes of those ongoing states of mind we call character traits, even if they initially caused those states to form. The direct cause is always the sustaining cause, which maintains the state over time, and that cause consists in one's own psyche.

In fact the Stoic founders themselves drew attention to the fact that there are antecedent causes for a person's character. Cleanthes drew a useful argumentative premise from the fact that children resemble their parents not only in body type but also in "emotions, characters, and dispositions," and Chrysippus is known to have followed him on this point.[52] Such resemblances were explained by saying that the ratio of psychic components in the offspring is determined by the qualities of the 'seed,' i.e., the genetic material, coming from the parents.[53] Among environmental influences, Chrysippus mentioned the atmospheric conditions at one's place of birth. The point is reported to us as part of a discussion concerning the Stoic doctrine of *sumpatheia,* the complex interconnectedness of causes which ties the lives of individual humans to things and events in the larger world order. Chrysippus holds that the characteristics of places have an influence on the inhabitants: Athenians are smart because of their rarified air, Thebans fat and healthy because their air is dense, and so on. Just as some people delight in sweets, while others prefer slightly bitter tastes, so some people are "lustful, irascible, cruel, or haughty" because of various kinds of causes; that is, various kinds of *antecedent* causes.[54]

On Chrysippus's way of thinking the inclusion of this sort of cause in the account of character does nothing at all to reduce the autonomy that we have as agents. Because it is the indwelling *pneuma* that sustains a trait of character once formed, it is that same bit of *pneuma* that is responsible for the trait. This is not a trivial answer. Of course it is true also of a cockroach, or even a rock, that the *pneuma* inherent in it is responsible for the traits it exhibits. But the good and bad traits of a human being are traits that belong to rational creatures as such. To say that we are rational creatures is to say that we are *capable* of reviewing and correcting our own beliefs, whether or not we do so in fact.[55] In other words, autonomy and responsibility are inherent in the very notion of rationality.

The point is neatly expressed in narrative form in a curious anecdote about Socrates, which although it did not originate with the Stoic school is cited by Cicero in connection with their views. Socrates is confronted in the midst of a group of students by a certain Zopyrus, who announces from his knowledge of physiognomics a list of Socrates' personal faults. These he claims to have deduced from "certain hollows around the collarbone"; they include that he is thick-witted and overfond of women. The company is amused, not having seen any evidence of these faults; Alcibiades even bursts into a loud guffaw. Socrates himself, however, supports Zopyrus, saying that the faults "were indeed inborn in him, but that he had cast them out by reason."[56] For Stoics who told this story the point must have been that Socrates, who is as much the moral exemplar as anyone who ever lived, was produced by the same sorts of antecedent causes as produce every flawed human being. Just as the shape of Socrates' collarbone was determined by genetic or environmental factors, so also may his mental capacities and inclinations have been shaped by antecedent causes. But the morally significant traits differ from the collarbone in that they can also be reshaped by reason.

This still leaves a role for luck in moral development, since Socrates' readiness to amend his faults through philosophical reflection must itself be the product of antecedent causes. Perhaps that readiness was also written in his physiognomy and Zopyrus, if he were an infallible observer, would have seen it there, just as Zeno was said to have discerned a man's sexual preference from hearing him sneeze.[57] For Stoics the merits or demerits of the individual belong just as much to Zeus's design for the cosmos as they do to ourselves. But the hard work that produces a Socrates is still his own, caused in a principal sense by his own agency.

8

City of Friends and Lovers

> Some things are transformed by growth. After many additions which merely increase them in size, the final addition works at last a change: it imparts to them a new state of being, different from before. It is a single stone that makes an arch—the keystone, which is slotted in between the sloping sides and by its coming binds them together. Why does the final addition accomplish so much, though small in itself? Because it is not only an addition but a completion.[1]

Seneca's analogy has an important point to make about what it might be to perfect the human mind. Consider the final stage in the construction of an arch. The finished arch is quite different from an unfinished arch, even one only a day or an hour from completion. The moment the keystone is set in place, there is a tremendous accession of strength and stability, new properties that emerge with the fulfillment of the design. In just the same way, human maturation is not merely an improvement on our present condition—that is, not merely an increase in desirable qualities we now have. Rather, it is the realization of structural possibilities which as yet are only latent in us. The myriad of opinions that direct our lives are then brought into harmony: at last, each makes sense in light of all the others. No longer is there any inclination to give assent to what is false, no longer any reason to do what is wrong. New properties emerge, properties like stability of impulse and inner beauty.

Understanding what this condition is like requires some exercise of the philosophical imagination. Wisdom is not something any of us is likely to have experienced, either in ourselves or in others. Chrysippus himself did not claim to be wise, nor to have found wisdom in his Stoic predecessors; historically speaking, the wise person was said to be as rare as the phoenix of Ethiopia.[2] It is not from observation that Stoics derive their conception of what wisdom is and why it is valuable, but from careful reflection on the nature of intellectual and moral excellence. To see what the wise person would do or feel, we have to work out by reason what it would mean to be completely free of intellectual and moral error. It is a kind of thought experiment.

It is important to realize, though, that the Stoic investigation concerning the wise person is also meant to be an investigation into the nature of ordinary human beings. Again, the arch analogy is helpful. The unfinished arch is made of the same materials as the finished one and has the same design and purpose. But one cannot comprehend this fact unless one has in mind what is not yet in existence, the way those materials and that arrangement are to function in the completed structure. Until then, the unbalanced stack of stones appears useless, even dangerous. In the same way, there may be features of our present experience which take on an entirely new significance when considered as imperfect versions of experiences posited for the wise.

Such is the case with an important group of emotions which may be loosely grouped as social or relational responses: tender concern for family members, appreciation and regard for friends, and romantic love toward a partner or spouse. All these are in some sense natural to us, in that they are grounded in an innate behavioral orientation of the human animal which leads us to seek association with others of our own kind. But the love and friendship of the wise are qualitatively different from similarly named forms of affect in ordinary persons. Like other varieties of eupathic response, they come about in accordance with the remarkable epistemic capabilities of the perfected agent and express the thoughts and values that belong to the normative condition.

This means, for the Stoics, that while philosophical reflection on bonds of intimacy and affection may well begin from observations of actually occurring behavior, it cannot end there. One needs also to reflect on the kinds of friendly or loving relations that might exist among persons of thoroughly good character—what those people would find to value in connections with others of equal attainments, and what feelings and behavior would ensue. These are theorized relations, for given the scarcity of even individual wise persons it seems unlikely that two or more of them could ever come to know one another in fact. But if we can work out what those theorized relations would be like, we will gain in understanding of ordinary social relations as well. As in Aristotle,[3] but in a more utopian vein, the meaning of friendship as a whole is derived from the friendships of the good.

Concern for others

Once again the best point of entry is suggested by Stoic claims about the innate psychological endowments of human beings. It was noted in chapter 7 that while knowledge and belief are acquired empirically, ethical and intellectual development is also guided by certain innate preferences or tendencies, called the starting points (*aphormai*) of virtue. Among these is an innate orientation (*oikeiōsis*) toward the interests of others. This, also called a starting point "toward fair distributing," is the seed from which the virtue of justice may in time develop.[4]

Thus Chrysippus asserted in more than one of his works that just as we have from the outset a natural orientation to our own bodies, so also we have a natural orientation to other human beings.[5] This latter orientation manifests itself especially in the devotion of parents to their children but extends also to other people generally. The speech of Cato in the third book of Cicero's *On Ends* expresses the point in very much the Chrysippan manner:

> It cannot be consistent that nature should intend us to have offspring and not be concerned that those offspring should be tended. The intent of nature can be clearly seen even in animals. When we see how they labor to produce and rear their young, we seem to hear the very voice of nature. Therefore, just as it is clear that we have a natural aversion to pain, so also is it obvious that nature itself induces us to love those we have engendered. From this it is concluded that humans have in common a natural orientation toward one another.[6]

The fragmentary treatise of Hierocles even suggests a terminology: one's orientation to self is 'well-intentioned orientation,' to possessions 'acquisitive orientation,' and to kindred 'devoted orientation.'[7] These orientations might be initially nothing more than a verifiable tendency to behave in one way rather than another, as when infants smile more often at their parents than at strangers. In time, though, as one begins to perceive the regularities in one's own conduct, one begins to acquire a sense of fitness or appropriateness in one's dealings with others. Thus other-regarding behavior has a basis in our innate endowment just as self-preservation does.

The tendencies observed in infants and their parents manifest themselves also in the formation of cities and assemblies. The fact that nearly all humans live together in organized groups is not just a result of our contingent need for mutual assistance. It is also an expression of a deep-seated preference which is characteristic of our species. The Stobaean source indicates that marriage and political action are in accordance with the nature of humans as creatures who are not only rational but also communal (*koinōnikos*) and gregarious (*philallēlos*).[8] The treatise of Hierocles supports a similar assertion from the ease with which social ties are formed.

> But we are the kind of animal that has a herd instinct and a need for one another. This is why we live in cities. For every person without exception is part of some polis. In addition, we form friendships easily. For by sharing a meal or sitting together in the theater . . .[9]

Unfortunately the papyrus tails off in mid-sentence, but it is clear enough what the argument must have been: if we can feel connected to another person from so slight an acquaintance as sitting next to one another at a performance, we must indeed be companionable beings. Taking a different tack, Cicero's Stoic spokesman in the third book of *On Ends* offers examples of social behavior among animals, including the symbiotic relationship of the pea crab and the oyster and the more complex hierarchies of ants, bees, and storks. Just as it is in the nature of these social animals for each to behave in ways that promote the interests of the group, so it is natural for humans to act sometimes on behalf of others.[10]

From this it is inferred that every person has an obligation to consider the interests of others in determining how to act. In theory, that obligation should extend not only to others in existing social systems (the polis within which one is born) but also to every human being, since all rational beings are in fact united in a single cosmic community under the rule of Zeus.[11] Progress in ethical understanding is in large part a matter of increasing one's awareness of the extent of this obligation. "Every human being should regard every other as akin *just because* they are human," writes Cicero.[12] Another fragment by Hierocles speaks of a sense of kinship (again, *oikeiōsis*) as something that can be intensified by conscious effort. Hierocles thinks of the individual as surrounded by concentric circles representing successively the self, the nuclear family, the extended family, the neighborhood, city, country, and finally the whole human race. It is a mark of character, he says, "to somehow pull the circles toward the center in one's proper treatment of each person, deliberately transferring those in the outer circles to the inner ones." As one comes to think of the persons in the wider circle as truly belonging to oneself, one will be increasingly motivated to behave toward them in the way the wise person would do.[13]

Until wisdom is actually attained, however, the usual epistemic limitations remain in force. The natural sense of attachment is subject to perversion, as are all the starting points, and for this reason the imperfect person's sense of what is appropriate in dealing with others is quite unreliable. Thus Zeno states rather curtly that only the wise exhibit proper familial affection and that the nonwise are enemies to one another, even parents to their children.[14] These harsh observations make it clear that instances of ordinary emotion toward friends or family members are still being counted as moral errors. Being anxious for family members' welfare, longing for their company, and grieving when they die are all wrong actions insofar as they are causally dependent on the belief that objects outside one's own sphere of agency can be unconditionally good or bad for oneself. Nothing in the theory of natural orientation justifies that belief. The Stoic position remains that the only objects that are invariably beneficial or harmful to a person past the period of childhood are objects integral to that person's own character or behavior. So we cannot read Chrysippus's statements on concern for others as encouraging us to be emotionally involved with them in the usual way.

Nor do we have to have such involvement in order to behave appropriately toward those around us. Health care professionals regularly do their utmost to assist persons toward whom they feel no personal affection. Parents, too, continue to feed and care for their children at times when their emotions are otherwise engaged. Indeed for many responsibilities the more dispassionate performance is the more effectual. This is obvious enough in a surgeon or police officer; less obvious, perhaps, in a parent. But a parent may be called upon to remain at the bedside of an afflicted child, offering calm assistance or encouragement at a time when a full emotional response would mean becoming dysfunctional.[15] This, from a Stoic perspective, is not only the more sensible course of action but also a truer expression of concern for the child's welfare.

It is with this point in mind that we should read Epictetus's advice to love other people in full awareness of their mortality. Just as one can be fond of a vase or goblet and yet not be devastated if such a fragile thing should happen to break, so, says Epictetus, one should train oneself to love a child, a sibling, or a friend without unrealistic expectations, remembering that death is a regular fact of human life.[16] In so doing one is not being callous or selfish. Considered in their original context (as found in the *Discourses*, not the elliptical *Handbook*), Epictetus's words assert that only by taking this calmly rational view can we properly fulfill our responsibilities as citizens and friends—responsibilities we have 'to everyone' but also, of course, to the family members themselves. It is no service to them if in our emotional engagement we are "laid low, or shattered, or dependent on the other, or reproachful toward god or humankind." A certain affective detachment will enable us to care for them more effectively.

Proper friendship and the wise community

Nonetheless detachment is not the attitude Zeno and other Stoics elevate to an ethical ideal. Their person of perfect understanding is not limited to discharging obligations in a dispassionate way. Under certain circumstances, he or she may become affectively involved with others, either with others who are also wise or with those who are not wise but show promise of attaining wisdom. But let us first consider relationships between those who are of equal stature in virtue and wisdom. For there is evidence to suggest that between themselves the wise form strong friendships, friendships rich in feeling, and that they themselves regard those friendships as unqualifiedly good.

Surviving texts repeatedly tell us that genuine friendship, the sort worthy of the name, is found among the wise and nowhere else.

> They [the Stoics] also say that friendship is only among the righteous, because of the likeness among them. They say that it is a sharing in the things of life, when we treat our friends as we do ourselves. And they claim that the friend is choiceworthy for his own sake and that having many friends is a good.[17]

> They [the Stoics] allow friendship to remain only among the wise, since it is only among them that concord arises concerning the things of life. Concord is knowledge of common goods. For friendship which is genuine (and not falsely so called) cannot exist apart from loyalty and stability.[18]

In approaching these texts, one should keep in mind that this friendship claim, like all Stoic claims about the righteous or wise person, is made at a normative and theoretical level; it is not a description of historically instantiated relationships. If even the individual wise person is as rare as the phoenix, it is hardly to be expected that two such people would ever exist at the same moment in history. But the claim made here does not concern what has happened or might happen but only what ought to happen. Relationship entails plurality; in order to treat the idealized form of human relationship, Stoics must take plurality as a given and proceed from there.

What, then, would relationships among the wise be like if they were to come together, as in theory they might? The above passages sound several important themes: that there is a likeness or similarity among all wise persons; that wise friendship is in essence a 'sharing' or commonality (*koinōnia*) which involves treating the other as oneself; and that there is concord (*homonoia*), defined as a recognition that goods are held in common. To these points may be added further statements made in the same context by the Stobaean witness. These indicate that wise friendship includes a level of affective engagement.

> The righteous person is companionable, tactful, encouraging, and in companionship is liable to seek after good intent and friendship. . . . And they also say that cherishing, welcoming, and being friends belong only to the righteous.[19]

Of significance here are the terms 'good intent' (*eunoein*), 'cherishing' (*agapān*), and 'welcoming' (*aspazesthai*). For *eunoia*, *agapēsis*, and *aspasmos* are all terms known to us in the context of Stoic affective theory, where they are named as species of eupathic response, the type of affective response found in the wise; specifically, they are all species of the eupathic genus *boulēsis* or 'wish.'[20] Their occurrence here suggests that the ideal form of human relationship is conceived not only as a mutual disposition to act in one another's best interests but also as a disposition to respond affectively to one another. We are to imagine the wise interacting with one another in daily life and, in the context of those interactions, experiencing feelings of warmth and affection.

A very early Stoic claim was that all the wise are automatically friends to one another, even sight unseen.[21] In the Stobaean account, however, that view is replaced by one which allows friendship to be more clearly a personal relationship. Proper civic relations between people who are not personally acquainted do not have to be considered friendships, although it is still true that all wise persons, wherever they happen to live, regard one another as fellow citizens and regulate their actions accordingly. Friendships arise when people who are wise also come into contact with one another and acquire knowledge of each other's character as individuals.

> All the righteous benefit one another, although they are not in every case friends of one another, nor well-intentioned, approving, or accepting of one another, since they neither know one another nor dwell in the same place. Still, they are of a disposition to experience good intent, friendship, approval, and acceptance for one another.[22]

Again these friendships are characterized by occurrent affective responses on various particular occasions in their shared experience. Among the responses listed in the last sentence, only good intent is otherwise attested as one of the *eupatheiai;* however, approval and acceptance are near synonyms for the attested 'cherishing' and 'welcoming'. Friendship, too—that is, the Greek *philia*—appears here as an affective response, that of liking or warm affection. All the wise are, as it were, *potential* friends to one another; given proximity and mutual knowledge, they become friends in fact, and it is then that they experience the feelings typical of friendship.

If we accept the implication that wise friendship includes some eupathic elements, then we must also ask ourselves about perceived goods within such friendships, how they are related to the wise person's own character and purposes. I argued in chapter 2 that the objects of eupathic response are necessarily objects integral to one's own agency. Only goods or evils which are 'real and the mind's own' are evaluated by the person of perfect understanding in the uncompromising way which engenders responses of the affective type. We should therefore expect on theoretical grounds that every affective response in a wise person would be a response to some feature of his or her own character or conduct: the possession of some good quality, the prospect of performing some good act, or, on the negative side, the possibility—always in fact unfulfilled—that one might do something shameful or wrong. What, then, are the goods the wise person perceives in friendship, and to whom do they belong?

Of course one always has the option of saying on the Stoics' behalf that what makes friendship valuable is just the opportunity to exercise certain companionable virtues such as generosity and kindness. An answer of this kind puts the emphasis on what one brings to the friendship, rather than what one gets out of it. Friendship becomes a matter of being a friend rather than having a friend; its purpose is to exercise the friendliness that is in oneself, "lest so great a virtue lie hidden."[23] This approach is helpful where there is need to distinguish the ideal form of friendship from the friendship based on mutual utility, in which people call themselves friends because they provide each other with financial gain or political favors. As such it figures prominently in Seneca's epistle on friendship, and it may be found also in the Stobaean account, where the goods of the psyche include "the friendship which concerns oneself, in which one is a friend to one's neighbors."[24]

Important as it is, however, the above answer is not the entirety of what Stoics have to say about value within friendship. For if their claim were that the good of friendship consists solely in the chance to derive additional value from one's own good qualities, then the friend herself would have to be classed as a merely instrumental good, something which is valuable only for what else it enables one to do. This is not, I think, what is meant by those texts which classify the friend as a 'productive' good: those are concerned rather to point out that a friend is, like oneself, a whole person and an agent.[25] But even if Stoics do want to say that friends are valuable to one another in an instrumental way, they also hold that a friend is intrinsically valuable, 'choiceworthy for his own sake.'[26] Cicero is familiar with this claim and also with an especially strong position taken by some Stoics, that in wise friendship each person "values his friend's reason equally with his own."[27] Not every Stoic author would go so far; Cicero also knows of some who maintain that one's own reason is always of most value. Clearly, though, there were Stoic philosophers who held that the stronger view can be defended in consistency with the school's general position on moral value.

A way of maintaining that consistency is suggested by a seemingly casual remark recorded for Zeno. When asked, "What is a friend?" Zeno replied simply, "Another I."[28] The phrase sounds proverbial; Aristotle says something very similar.[29] It may be, though, that Zeno intends 'another I' to be taken literally, as a way of saying that true or normative friendship actually expands the sphere of what is integral to oneself to include the qualities and actions of one's friends.[30] A view of this kind is suggested by the strong interest of our sources in notions of commonality (koinōnia) and concord (homonoia). Commonality, which might also be translated 'sharing' or 'community,' is said to mean that the wise have all their goods in common, so that any benefit done to any of them is done to them all.[31] Suppose Dion and Theon are both wise. The goods Dion has are his own good qualities—courage, self-control, and the rest—together with his actions which put those qualities into effect. These goods benefit Dion; they are something in which he can legitimately rejoice. But they also benefit Theon, since they are benefits to a larger community of which he is a part.

For Dion and Theon, in their friendship, form one whole, the Dion-Theon community as it were. Anything which is a good of either of them is also a good of that larger community and belongs to all the members alike. When the eye sees clearly, the hands benefit as well.

Closely related assertions can be made on the basis of concord or *homonoia*, literally 'sameness of intent.'[32] Although it need not be the case that every person of perfect understanding knows exactly the same things as every other, still the judgments of each are necessarily compatible with those of the others. As far as concerns their common life, they will have the same overall aims and purposes in any situation that might arise. Theon will not be displeased with any choice made by Dion: it is something he too would choose, not for himself to do—for his own situation and capabilities may be different—but for Dion. To that extent he thinks of himself as a kind of co-agent with Dion: there is a community of motives as well as a community of interests. He will wish for Dion to exercise the particular virtues that Dion has, and he will wish this in the same wholehearted way that he wishes to exercise his own virtues. A good description of his attitude can be found in the definition of eupathic good intent (*eunoia*) as 'a wish for good things for another for that person's own sake.'[33]

Concord and commonality are well attested as political terms, and it is evident that the sharing of goods and intentions between wise friends replicates a relational pattern which is supposed to obtain among all members of the normative polity. The notion of a community of the wise was important in Stoic political thought at all periods, whether that community was conceived as in Zeno's *Republic,* as an idealized version of existing Greek cities, or in a broader sense as comprising all wise persons wherever they happen to live.[34] Where wise individuals are widely scattered, however, relations of concord and commonality can exist among them only in potentiality. Community is then a matter of being well-disposed toward persons one has not met and is not likely to meet. Concord and commonality find active expression only in cases where multiple wise persons come to know one another and act within the same setting. But when that does happen, as in theory it might, then the bonds among the wise turn out to be affectionate as well as mutually beneficial.

Friendship and self-sufficiency

Perhaps the most radical element in the Stoic theory of friendship is the claim that relations among good people can be warm and genuine without also compromising the self-sufficiency of the individual. An important feature of the normative human in all ancient accounts is that he or she has the resources to live happily in any and all circumstances. Real happiness should be such as cannot be destroyed by any possible kind of loss. It follows that the wise person should be unalarmed by the mortal illness of a friend and should not grieve when friends die. While there might be some tears and a certain amount of pain—for these can come on involuntarily, as a 'biting and small contraction'—there is no possibility that the wise will enter fully into grief.

The claim that friendship is compatible with self-sufficiency could be defended in two ways. One could argue, first, that the ability to rise above the loss of friends comes of the wise person's accurate understanding of what it is for a thing to be good. The value of the commonality between friends is in its harmonious nature, and this is not dependent on numbers or diminished by the removal of one person. Alternatively, one might argue that while the wise value friendship in general, they are unconcerned about the identity of any one particular friend. A wise friend of one who is gone will turn immediately to other friends or potential friends, finding in them the same source of satisfaction as existed before.

Both of these lines of argument can be traced in Seneca's ninth Moral Epistle, the letter on friendship. We find the first in section 4 of that letter. For Seneca as for other Stoics, a natural inclination to form attachments is universal in human nature: when circumstances permit, the self-sufficient wise person will be as eager as anyone else to marry, raise children, and form friendships. What wisdom adds to this is that if circumstances require it, the person of perfect understanding is able to find happiness within, in the company of his own thoughts. It is not that he is always aloof or driven 'within his own skin'; that is not what self-sufficiency means.[35] Rather it is possible to be content after the loss of friends and family in just the same way as it is possible to be a whole person after the loss of a hand or eye.

> Here is what it means to say the wise person is self-contained: there are times when he is content with just part of himself. If infection or battle took off his hand; if an accident cost him an eye, or even both eyes, the remaining parts of himself would be sufficient for him; he would be as happy with his body diminished as he was with it whole. Still, although he does not feel the want of the missing limbs, he would prefer that they not be missing.[36]

The choice of analogy is significant: it illustrates not only the rationale for imperturbability but also the depth of the connection that existed. The relation of the wise person to friends is not a cool or distant relation, as to a piece of baggage that can easily be laid aside; rather, it is as intimate as one's attachment to one's own body. The friend is to the self as part of the same organic whole, which only some violent invasion could break apart. The person of perfect understanding can survive such an invasion without loss of well-being, but only because he or she is able at need to redefine the boundaries of the self to encompass a smaller but still harmoniously integrated whole.

Less satisfactory is Seneca's way of explaining the second argument, that the wise will always be able to make new friends to take the place of those who are lost. His comparison this time is to the sculptor Phidias, creator of the great statue of Zeus at Olympia.

> But in truth he will never be without a friend, for it rests with him how quickly he gets a replacement. Just as Phidias, if he should lose one of his statues, would immediately make another, so this artist at friend making will substitute another in place of the one who is lost.[37]

The Phidias analogy does not preclude recognition that one's friends are individuals, each different from every other. Phidias is able to part with his work because he knows his capacity to sculpt is undiminished, and yet his willingness does not imply that he lacks real interest in his statues or thinks they all look alike. But the comparison is still troubling in that it seems to imply that friends are merely the passive recipients of one's own artistry as friend maker. Asymmetry need not be incompatible with friendship: it can be argued, for instance, that Seneca's endeavor in the *Moral Epistles* as a whole is to engender a notional friendship between himself as author and Lucilius—or any potential reader—as aspirant to wisdom. Outside the literary context, though, one would like to have some assurance that a Stoic wise person also thinks of the friend as an equal whose existence is as important as his own.

Although that line of thought is not to be found in Seneca, it is not by any means absent from the Stoic tradition. It is suggested by the Stoic claim we noted earlier in Cicero, that the wise person "values his friend's reason equally with his own." More dramatically, it is implied by the willingness of the wise person to allow another person to survive in place of himself. This last point is explained by the second-century Stoic Hecato, using the artificial scenario of two people, both wise, stranded by shipwreck on a plank big enough to support only one.[38] In such a case, argues Hecato, the wise person will be quite prepared to let go of the plank and drown, subordinating his own continued action in the world to that of the other, if it should happen that that person's particular skills are likely to be of more use to the state. This is just what we should expect from one who is prone to the friendly *boulēsis* of good intent. His wish is for prospective goods, but since that wish is expressed in self-cancellation, it can only be for goods that will be realized by another.

Optimistic love

Closely related to the position on friendship is the Stoic claim that the person of perfect understanding will also fall in love. Erotic love was an important theme for early Stoic authors. Treatises specifically on erotic love were written by Zeno, Cleanthes, Chrysippus, Persaeus, and Sphaerus, and the topic was addressed in other works as well, notably the *Republic* of Zeno.[39] As we know little about these treatises, we cannot rule out the possibility that some portions of them were negative in tone, expressing objections to various cultural misconceptions about what kinds of behavior are appropriate in intimate relationships. Enough survives, however, to show that the prevailing position on love was strongly positive, so long as that love is of the right sort, experienced without false convictions and expressed without abusiveness or exploitation.

Our secondhand reports indicate that there were in fact two different conceptions of what erotic love is. The clearest statement is the following:

> There are two senses in which one may speak of the 'erotic person'; one in reference to virtue, as one quality of the righteous person, and one in reference to vice, as if blaming someone for love madness.[40]

The *erōs* named "in reference to vice" is that experienced by ordinary persons when they are powerfully and (they would say) uncontrollably drawn to someone. "Like a wind that swoops down on mountain oaks," says a poem of Sappho, "so did love shake my heart."[41] This sort of love is certainly an emotion, a form of desire as its name implies: *erōs* in some Greek authors can refer to a powerful hunger of any sort. But there is also a normative *erōs,* a love that in theory both could and should be experienced by the perfected human being. It is this conception of love that is expressed in the usual Stoic definition (reported verbatim in many sources) which makes it not a form of desire but 'an effort to form a friendship because of an impression of beauty.'[42]

The Stoic definition and associated doxographic material seem designed to preserve a recognizable relation between the philosophical notion of *erōs* and the assumptions which prevailed in the surrounding culture. Literary texts, historical anecdotes, and the visual arts give ample evidence of what those assumptions were.[43] It was, for instance, assumed by many Greeks that the usual object of love is a person who is physically fit, smooth-skinned, and quite a bit younger than oneself. In some circles it seems to be the expected thing for a male adult to be attracted to a teenage boy—one in his time of 'bloom,' when the beard is just beginning to grow—and to court his favor through gifts and conversation. This might be a youth he has met at the gymnasium or, even more likely, at a dinner party, where wine and a festive atmosphere loosen inhibitions. Given this cultural backdrop it is undoubtedly significant that some Stoic definitions specifically state that wise love is directed at young persons who are in their time of bloom. Stoics also preserve the association of erotic love with dinner parties and social drinking. "It is their doctrine," says the Stobaean author, "that the wise person behaves not only in the manner of a thoughtful and philosophical person but also in the manner of a convivial and erotic one." The report goes on to explain that "convivial virtue" means "knowledge regarding what is appropriate at a dinner party, how to conduct the party and how one ought to drink with others," while erotic virtue is "knowledge of the chase after young persons of good nature."[44]

But while wise love is meant to be comparable to a certain culture-specific notion of falling in love, it is also carefully marked out as an experience the Stoic sage need have no reservations about. This is evident in that wise *erōs* is said to be not a form of desire but a different future-directed impulse called an *epibolē*, an effort or resolve.[45] Definitive of this impulse is that its object is not intercourse per se, but friendship. Since only the wise and virtuous are friends, this implies not only that ideal love seeks a relationship of real companionship and mutual respect but also that the younger person is expected to become wise at some point in the future. That expectation is at least a major part of the attraction, for fuller accounts suggest a strong interest in aptitude for virtue:

> The wise person will fall in love with young persons who through their form give an impression of a good natural endowment for virtue. . . . And love is of friendship, and is not to be blamed. For it is the bloom of virtue.[46]

> They say that love is an effort to form a friendship because of an impression of beauty in young persons at their prime. That is why the wise person

is also an erotic person and will fall in love with those worthy of love, ones who are of good breeding and good natural endowment.[47]

> The person worthy of love is the one worthy of righteous love. . . . Erotic virtue is knowledge of the pursuit after young persons of good nature, and is a protreptic toward virtuous matters and, in general, knowledge of how to love honorably. That is why they also say that the person of perfect understanding will fall in love.[48]

Beauty even by conventional standards is not entirely on the outside; it may also take in qualities of bearing and deportment. The person of perfect understanding is expected to be sensitive to these to such an extent as to be able to form an accurate assessment of the beloved's potential to become a mature and reliable friend.

For a Greek speaker this understanding of what it is to perceive beauty in someone would be made easier by the usage of the word *kalos* to mean both 'beautiful' and 'morally excellent.'[49] This does not mean that the two things are the same; one may suspect equivocation. It may be, though, that what is meant by 'beauty' is *strictly* the perceptible manifestation of those qualities which make the young person suitable to acquire virtue. Stoic postulates about the material basis of mental states and processes imply that everything about a person's character should in theory be available to perception. Hence a person's character is said to be "graspable from his form."[50] The visible indications might be very subtle, but the wise person should have the level of insight needed to interpret them. This does not have to be construed as an arcane capability in physiognomics.[51] It may be more in the spirit of the Stoic discussion to say, as we do also, that some people are unusually perceptive in their judgments of character.

One may be inclined to wonder whether love in this revised conception is supposed to be an affective response at all. Given that wise *erōs* is not a form of desire, there is some temptation to try to classify it with action tendencies of the calm 'selective' type and to conclude that the wise person is devoted to erotic activities only as preferred indifferents, in about the same way as he might be devoted to studying literature or hunting with dogs. Against this it should be noted that the object toward which this love is directed—that is, the forming of a friendship—is an object the wise person recognizes as a good, albeit a good which is to be realized at some time in the future. This is the primary mark of a specifically affective response, as opposed to a merely 'selective' impulse, that it depends on an evaluation of the unconditional sort. For this reason alone we should not hesitate to interpret Stoic *erōs* as having a place among the *eupatheiai*. As a future-directed *eupatheia*, it can be classified as a subspecies of wish (*boulēsis*), alongside the friendly responses of good intent, goodwill, welcoming, and cherishing.[52]

If love is indeed eupathic then there is no reason to deny that it, like other eupathic responses, involves feelings similar in kind and intensity to the feelings ordinary people experience in emotion. In general what distinguishes the *eupatheiai* from the *pathē* is not the kind of the psycho-physical change they produce but their correctness as judgments: pleasure is irrational uplift, joy rational uplift. As a judgment, eupathic love is very different from desire, for it is directed at an object that really is a prospective good according to the Stoic theory of value. As a feeling, though, it may be very similar to what ordinary people call love, including feelings of sexual arousal as well as any other sensations lovers feel. Sexual conduct per se is not its object: sex itself is neither good nor bad in the Stoic system, and the wise would know better than to pursue it as one of the things that really matter. But a eupathic eagerness for a deep level of intimacy with the right person could undoubtedly lead to sexual behavior on suitable occasions.[53]

Malcolm Schofield argued in a foundational study that the Stoics, especially Zeno, conceived of eupathic love as having an educational purpose; that is, that the wise lover's wish is not only to form a friendship with a young person seen as potentially wise but also to supply whatever teaching is required to realize that potential. That eupathic love should foster educational endeavor is an attractive hypothesis, especially in view of the age difference between the lover and the beloved.[54] In view of the Platonic parallel—for Diotima in *Symposium* 206c–207a is similarly concerned with intellectual reproduction—we are probably justified in finding this thought in the remark in Stobaeus that *erōs* is "a protreptic toward virtuous matters." If Zeno thought that love relations between the wise and younger persons who are not yet wise would encourage the latter to study moral philosophy, then it is easy to see why he would have held that love "contributes to the security of the polis."[55] The 'security' would then mean sure continuance over time, as each wise person is moved to train one or more younger persons to replace him.

But we should be careful not to conclude that the educative dimension of the love relationship is what justifies wise *erōs* in the eyes of Stoics. *Erōs* does not require justification; it is a good thing in its own right, as are all the *eupatheiai*. The wise fall in love for no other reason than that it is their nature to want to be intimate with those whom they see as beautiful. A wish to impart wisdom might be part of their endeavor; how could they not want the beloved to acquire what they value for themselves? But it is the intimacy itself that is their object.

Ordinary affections

I have argued here that the friendships and love relations which would be found among the wise are not, for Stoics, entirely austere relations but are rich in affect, charged with powerful responses to the goods exhibited by the other or, in the case of the immature beloved, to the nature which is well-suited to develop those goods. If this is correct, then there is an implication to be drawn concerning the affective dimensions of ordinary flawed affections as well. Just as builders look at a diagram to understand the structure they are trying to complete, so, in Stoic ethics, one may look at the experiences that are posited for the normative agent in order to gain a new philosophical understanding of friendship and erotic love as they exist even among nonwise persons.

Of course, the Stoics have sharp questions about all versions of ordinary emotional response, and the responses belonging to bonds of intimacy and affection are not exempt from this. But it is not their view that these affective elements are illegitimate merely because of the kind of response they are. Proper human functioning does not mean that we should promote the interests of others only in a dispassionate way, having no lively concern for any object outside our own skin. What is proper to us is not only other-concern but affectively engaged other-concern. In our present state we cannot reliably identify the objects toward which our affective engagement should be directed, and for this reason we can sometimes do more for others by setting our feelings aside. But the occurrence of strong feelings is not in itself an indication of error.

Further, the principal Stoic claims in this area suggest that certain structural features of our most intimate relationships are accepted by the school as signs of ethical promise rather than of degeneracy. The linking of interests, intents, and indeed of the very sense of selfhood that sometimes occurs among friends or erotic partners is something that occurs also among the wise, when they respond with joy to one another's accomplishments and with eagerness to one another's prospects. It does not have to be assumed that every case of deep engagement with other people's minds and actions is an indication of dependency and weakness. An affectionate disposition may instead be a disposition of strength, the capacity to identify one's own needs and motives with those of a larger social unit when circumstances allow this.

Finally, there is matter for reflection in the kind of objects with which wise friends and lovers are said to be concerned. If the ordinary person's affectionate impulses are in every case instances of moral error, this is primarily because we tend to take a wrong view of the objects toward which our affections are directed. We think most often of the physical nearness of friends, of their temporal well-being, or, in love relationships, of the opportunity to touch and caress them. The wise, in Stoic thought, regard these matters as preferable but inconsequential: for them, the object of concern is rather the qualities and activities of others as agents, and in particular the reasoning powers of those others. This might suggest that in our case also a deep concern for our friends as agents and reasoning beings is warranted, subject to our own epistemological limitations. In lovers, too, a tender interest in the personal and intellectual development of the other is in accordance with the Stoic model, to the extent that we are able to assist in that development. To be sure, the deficiencies in our understanding may prevent us from exercising that concern in any way which is genuinely beneficial by Stoic standards. But we are at least not wrong to care about reason in others for those others' own sake. In this, at least, we fulfill our design as rational and political beings.

The Tears of Alcibiades

There is one more story that needs to be told. It is an anecdote that goes back to Socrates' earliest followers but that was recounted many times thereafter, by a wide variety of philosophers and rhetoricians. It concerns Pericles' ward Alcibiades, at nineteen the handsomest and most ambitious of all Socrates' young associates. Gifted not only in music and athletics, the usual diversions of his class, but also in intellect, he listens thoughtfully to his first extended lesson in ethics. He attends to the reasoning by which Socrates concludes that good looks, wealth, and fashionable accomplishments are of no inherent value and that a false pride in them may prove disastrous for the state. Of course he does not know how well that conclusion describes his own future of self-aggrandizement and eventually treason. Yet at least in this moment he does embrace the standard Socrates has set; he does perceive the grave errors and vices that are within him. The realization is devastating. Unable to look at his teacher, Alcibiades slumps forward and rests his forehead on Socrates' lap. Weeping, he begs for assistance in amending his life.[1]

Reactions of the kind depicted in the anecdote pose a structural problem for the Stoic analysis laid out in this book. As we have seen, the sharp distinction drawn by the founding Stoics Zeno and Chrysippus between the affective responses of ordinary persons and those of the normative person or sage has a great deal to do with a difference of objects. The ordinary emotions are concerned with externals such as wealth or reputation or the health of a family member, while normative or eupathic response is directed at integral objects; that is, at virtue and virtuous activities, vice and the activities of vice. The experience of an Alcibiades resists this classification. His feeling of remorse or compunction would not be the very feeling it is if it were not directed at evils within his own sphere of agency, his deficiencies of character and inappropriate choices. Thus with respect to the status of its object it bears a resemblance to the *eupatheiai*. Yet a response of this kind is emphatically not the response of a wise person, for the recognition of one's own moral inadequacy is essential to it, whereas the Stoic wise person is the very paradigm of moral excellence. There is some question, then, as to how such affective responses should be described and evaluated by a philosopher of Stoic commitments.

The difficulty might be evaded, if one were prepared to claim that the emotions represented in the story are mere fictions—that neither the historical Alcibiades nor anyone else has ever experienced them in fact. The second-century Stoic Posidonius is known to have taken such a position. Posidonius says flatly that while it would indeed be proper for students of ethics to be overcome with fear and immoderate distress because of their faults, in reality we do not ever observe this.[2] The neat correspondence between emotions and external objects is thus maintained, but with loss of verisimilitude, since Posidonius's appeal to the phenomena is easily falsified. And as will be seen here, Posidonius is an isolated instance, for there were important Stoics who did concede the occurrence of responses like those described for Alcibiades. Chrysippus accepts them among the phenomena to be considered by a viable theory of consolation, and Cicero, speaking from his knowledge of Stoic thought, does the same. Seneca, Epictetus, and certain Stoics known to Plutarch go even further: they actually seek to make use of their pupils' remorse and shame as promising developments in a course of ethical therapy. None of these authors is in any doubt that remorse and the related feelings—fear of future errors, desire for ethical improvement—are real psychological events.

It seems the classification must be expanded. It may well be the case that ordinary flawed agents are disposed to respond affectively to external objects and that much of our emotional experience has this basis. Assuming a Stoic system of value, it is also logically necessary that the person of perfect understanding would respond affectively to integral goods and evils and only to those. But ordinary persons, too, are capable of recognizing integral objects as good or bad for themselves. That recognition may be incomplete and unstable, but it can nonetheless be emotionally powerful. Affective responses generated on this basis may include, at least, an 'Alcibiades distress' whose object is a present integral evil, an 'Alcibiades fear' whose object is an integral evil in prospect, and an 'Alcibiades desire' whose object is an integral good in prospect.

The term 'moral emotion' is sometimes used to bring out what is distinctive about this group of feelings.[3] In a Stoic context, however, that term is less useful, since it offers no way to distinguish between the emotions that are in question here and the eupathic responses of the sage. In this chapter, then, I will follow the practice of those Stoic authors who concern themselves with this category of response, and refrain from using any single broad term. Instead I will approach the question through one important emotion that unquestionably belongs to that category. This is the response called by Greek Stoics *metameleia;* a near English equivalent is 'remorse.'[4] We will consider the role, or potential role, of remorse in Stoic philosophy, understanding that emotion as representative of a larger class of emotions which share its structure.

Wisdom and remorse

The summary of Stoic ethics in Stobaeus gives us both a definition of *metameleia* and a brief description of what that emotion is like:

> Remorse is distress over acts performed, that they were done in error by oneself. This is an unhappy emotion and productive of conflict. For the extent to which the remorseful person is concerned about what has happened is also the extent to which he is annoyed at himself for having caused it.[5]

It is significant that remorse is defined here as a form of distress. This tells us that remorse is conceived as an affective response, one which involves a psychophysical 'contraction' of the psyche and which is sensed as 'biting' or mental pain. While remorse is not among the numerous species of distress that are listed in our major sources on the *pathē*, it does resemble other sorts of distress in the kind of sensation it produces. And the Stobaean account indicates also that remorse is not compatible with wisdom: it is 'an unhappy condition' and produces conflict, whereas the wise are happy, free of emotion, and at harmony with themselves and others.

That remorse is excluded from the experience of the wise is indicated also by the observation that the remorseful person is annoyed at himself for having caused the present situation. Annoyance at what one has done implies that one has now revised a previous decision. I feel remorse today if and when I come to believe that the choice I made yesterday was wrong, and not just wrong as a matter of hindsight (i.e., considering what has happened since) but wrong at the time, on the basis of information I had at the time of choosing. The wise have no need to repent of their decisions in this way: by definition, the decision made by the wise person is the correct decision for that situation.

> They hold that the person of perfect understanding does not repent, since repentance is considered to belong to false assent, as if one had misjudged before.[6]

It may be that circumstances have altered since a decision was made, but the person of perfect understanding would not consider a subsequent change of circumstances to render a previous judgment invalid. Besides, he or she would have had in mind all along the possibility that things might go awry, for the clause 'provided there is no impediment' is implied in every one of the wise person's decisions.[7] Repentance (*metanoia*) and remorse (*metameleia*) are thus very closely related. While the Stobaean author does distinguish them, roughly as we might distinguish a change of mind from a change of heart, it is safe to say that for Stoics, the one always implies the other.[8] Where there is no possibility of reversing a previous judgment, there can be no occasion for the pain of remorse.

The structural principle that is at work is the same principle as restricts the affective responses of the wise to three genera rather than four. We noted in chapter 2 that the *eupatheiai,* like the *pathē,* are classified on two parameters: whether they evaluate their objects as goods or evils, and whether they view them as present (i.e., as fulfilled) or as prospective (not yet fulfilled). This analysis gives room for four genera, but the space for present evils is left empty, on grounds that nothing which the person of perfect understanding would recognize as evil—that is, no integral evil—can be fulfilled in one who is in the ideal human condition. The 'missing' genus of response is, as it were, crowded out by joy, for just as no real evil is ever present in the normative condition, so also real goods are continually on hand. In the wise condition there is simply no occasion to lament one's own defects, whereas every moment of the day gives some new reason to rejoice in the exercise of virtuous dispositions.[9]

For similar reasons one would expect that remorse would be a very frequent experience for the nonwise, provided they see their situation with some degree of accuracy. From the standpoint of theory, the ordinary person is always in line for remorse, since everything ordinary people do is an expression of our flawed epistemic state.

But the inferior person, being without experience of the right use of things, does everything badly, acting in accordance with the disposition he has, and is also much disposed to change his mind and on every occasion filled with remorse.[10]

This is the point at which the subjective experience of the ordinary person diverges most sharply from that of the wise. The ordinary person is barred from eupathic joy, for the many varieties of knowledge and of virtuous action are not yet a part of our experience. If one were to construct a genus grid of the ordinary person's affective responses, not toward externals as with the standard *pathē*, but toward integrals as for the *eupatheiai*, there would again be only three genera. This time, though, it is the quadrant of present goods that remains blank. In our case, it is remorse that is the preeminent reactive response toward integral objects.[11]

The question, then, is whether in the ordinary person, assuming all the epistemic limitations ordinary people have, remorse and the related forms of desire and fear may not sometimes be entirely appropriate. Presumably remorse implies the same judgment as is implied in other forms of distress, that 'it is now appropriate for me to experience mental pain.' What position do Stoics take on the truth or falsity of this judgment? For if they hold that it is necessarily false, then they must be finding some flaw in it other than the error of evaluation identified in chapter 2. But if it may sometimes be true—even if asserted not as an item of knowledge but only as true opinion—then Stoic philosophers are not bound to try to eliminate remorse in the way they seek to eliminate other forms of emo-

EUPATHIC GENERA

	present	in prospect
good	JOY	WISH
evil		CAUTION

ANALOGOUS GENERA IN THE NONWISE

	present	in prospect
good		DESIRE for improvement
evil	REMORSE	FEAR of future error

Figure 9. Eupathic genera / analogous genera in the nonwise.

tion. And this would surely affect the way we understand their norm of
apatheia.

Strategies for consolation

As a way to sharpen the focus I want now to consider a suggestion made
by Chrysippus concerning practical strategies for consolation. Philosophical consolation—that is, the discovery of arguments to alleviate
various forms of mental distress—was in antiquity a regular assignment
for ethical advisors of all schools, and one's manner of approaching the
task could be illustrative of underlying assumptions about the validity of
mental pain.[12] According to one report, that of Cicero in *Tusculan Disputations* 3.76, Chrysippus took a position on consolatory method which
at first seems to imply that for him, a distress like Alcibiades' always
depends on at least one false premise. On closer examination, however,
the report turns out to be inconclusive on that point.

The paragraph in question seeks primarily to demonstrate the merits
of a dual-cause analysis of grief. Because grief, like other emotions, is held
by Stoics to be dependent on false ascriptions of value, a Stoic approach
to consolation might proceed by attempting to correct those mistaken
evaluations. This, says Cicero, is the method of Chrysippus's predecessor
Cleanthes, who seeks only "to teach the sufferer that what happened is
not an evil at all." However this method holds only dim prospects of success, for persons in time of bereavement are not likely to listen to anyone
saying that the loss of a family member makes no difference to happiness.
Moreover there is a theoretical difficulty, which Cicero illustrates by retell-
ing the Alcibiades anecdote.

> Besides, it seems to me that Cleanthes does not take sufficiently into ac-
> count the possibility that a person might be distressed over the very thing
> which Cleanthes himself counts as the worst of evils. For we are told that
> Socrates once persuaded Alcibiades he was unworthy to be called human
> and was no better than a manual laborer despite his noble birth. Alcibi-
> ades then became very upset, begging Socrates with tears to take away his
> shameful character and give him a virtuous one. What are we to say about
> this, Cleanthes? Surely you would not claim that the circumstance which
> occasioned Alcibiades' distress was not really a bad thing?[13]

With a grief like that of Alcibiades, the Cleanthean method will not serve,
for no Stoic could argue that the object of this distress is anything but

a genuine evil. However there is an alternative method available. This is the method proposed by Chrysippus: rather than addressing questions of value, one seeks "to get rid of the person's belief that mourning is something he ought to do, something just and appropriate."[14] In other words, one persuades the sufferer that even if his circumstances really are evil, still it is not appropriate for him to cry or to experience distress.

These two Stoic approaches to consolation may be compared with the causal analysis of grief laid out in chapter 2 of this book. That analysis identifies two different necessary conditions for grief; namely, the two belief conditions whose content is specified as premises 1 and 2 of the distress-specific version of the pathetic syllogism.

1. Objects of type T are evils.
2. If an evil is present, it is appropriate for me to contract my psyche.
3. Object O, being of type T, is now present.
It is now appropriate for me to contract my psyche.

Where the Cleanthean method of consolation recommends eliminating distress by undermining the sufferer's commitment to the first premise, the Chrysippan method offers instead to undermine the second, leaving the question of value untouched and arguing, instead, that contraction or mental pain is not an appropriate way to respond to evils. Since both premises are necessary conditions for the response, elimination of either should have the desired effect. Thus the Chrysippan strategy should, in theory, be efficacious both against the usual sort of distress and against the kind experienced by Alcibiades.

Now, although Cicero does not claim to have taken the Alcibiades example directly from Chrysippus, we should allow for the possibility that he did so and that Chrysippus himself envisioned the application of his consolatory method to remorse as well as ordinary grief. One can hardly suppose, though, that Chrysippus was seriously concerned about finding ways to dissuade young reprobates from feeling sorry for their misdeeds. The function of the anecdote for him would be to distinguish clearly between the two belief conditions upon which, according to his analysis, all forms of distress are based. In this way he demonstrates that his assault upon the second of these constitutes a distinctively new method which offers certain theoretical advantages over that of Cleanthes. The capability to deal with remorse and related forms of affect may be one such advantage, but it is not the only one or the most important.

Of greater practical significance is that the Chrysippan method of consolation enables a Stoic philosopher to assist people who are not ready to accept his position on the value of externals. A fragment from the fourth or 'therapeutic' book of Chrysippus's *On Emotions* points out this advantage, with application not only to grief and distress but to emotions of all kinds. For Chrysippus it is the duty of the philosophical therapist to alleviate the emotional ills of all people, including those who adhere to the Peripatetic view that there are three classes of goods (goods of the body and of estate as well as of the soul), or to the Epicurean view that pleasure is the good. But those who are in the grip of strong emotion are likely to resist assaults on their systems of value. It is therefore very helpful, says Chrysippus, if one can proceed in a way that avoids confrontation with their evaluative beliefs.

> For even if it should be that there are three classes of goods, even so one should work to cure the emotions. But during the critical period of the inflammation one should not waste one's efforts over the belief that preoccupies the person stirred by emotion, lest we ruin the cure which is opportune by lingering at the wrong moment over the refutation of the beliefs which preoccupy the mind. And even if pleasure is the good and this is the view of the person who is overcome by the emotion, one should nonetheless assist him and demonstrate that every emotion is inconsistent, even for those who assume that pleasure is the good and is the goal.[15]

Here the belief that 'preoccupies' a person stirred by emotion must be a belief about perceived goods or evils, either a general belief (e.g., "pleasure is the good") or a more particular belief, as that "taking pleasurable revenge on So-and-so would be a good thing right now." While the emotion is going on, says Chrysippus, it is wasted effort to try to address this sort of belief—in our schema, the evaluative premise 1. Instead, one should "demonstrate that every emotion is inconsistent," i.e., that it is inconsistent with the person's own doctrines. This can only mean that the therapist should direct his efforts against the relevant version of our premise 2. Just as in consolations one must 'get rid of the mourner's belief that mourning is something he ought to do,' so also in anger one should remove the belief that seeking revenge is the appropriate response, and so on with other emotions.

The alternative method makes allowance for the phenomenon in which people are 'carried away' or 'overridden' by their emotive judgments. We saw in chapter 3 that among Stoic philosophers Chrysippus was particularly concerned with this phenomenon and developed an explanation for it. The word 'inflammation' (*phlegmonē*) which he uses here is one of the ways he refers to this same phenomenon. Achilles, for instance, goes through a time of inflammation in his grief for Patroclus, during which he weeps and rolls on the ground and his thoughts are concentrated on that loss.[16] In such moments there is very little that philosophical argument can achieve in any case, and nothing at all to be gained by framing the issue as being about the irrelevance of Patroclus to Achilles' true well-being. The sensible philosopher will keep that observation to himself. If there is any success to be had, it will come through the less direct approach.

It was noted above that this fragment of Chrysippus's *On Emotions* recommends using his therapeutic strategy not only for emotions of the distress genus but for all types of emotion. In this, too, he receives a warm endorsement from Cicero. Writing in his own voice about therapies to be used for every kind of emotion, Cicero recapitulates the points made earlier about consolations for distress, again favoring the Chrysippan approach. He then continues,

> To be sure, all emotions of that sort could be washed away by that form of consolation which teaches that the circumstances which give rise to gladness or desire are not goods and those which give rise to fear or distress are not evils. But the specific and more reliable cure is when you teach that the emotions are wrong in and of themselves and have nothing either natural or necessary about them. The other method of address, the one which eliminates the false belief and the distress along with it, is indeed more useful; however, it works only in rare cases and cannot be applied to the uneducated. Besides, there are some forms of distress which cannot be relieved by this medicine at all. Suppose a person is upset about his own lack of virtue—his lack of courage, say, or of responsibility or integrity. The cause of his anxiety is indeed an evil! In that case, some other remedy would have to be applied.
>
> But that remedy could be the same for every school of philosophers, despite their disagreements in other areas. For all of them ought to agree that it is a fault when the mind is moved contrary to right reason. Even if the circumstances which arouse fear or distress really are bad, and those which arouse desire and gladness really are good, still the movement itself is a matter of fault.
>
> . . . So as I said before, there is one method of cure which belongs to all schools of philosophy, namely, to speak solely about the emotion itself, say-

ing nothing at all about the status of the things which arouse emotion. . . . Some say the highest good is moral excellence, some pleasure, some a combination of the two, and some the 'three classes of goods,' yet all should make use of the same discourse to chase away the too-vigorous impulse, even if it is an impulse toward virtue itself.[17]

Cicero's way of describing the recommended approach is less clear than it might be: he speaks vaguely of arguing against 'the emotion itself' or 'the movement itself.' But he has already made an effort to explain the structure of the method in the preceding paragraph, using as an example the person who is distressed about having become poor. In such a case, he says, one might proceed (*a*) by arguing that poverty is not an evil, or (*b*) by arguing that one should never become upset at all. From a practical standpoint, *b* is preferable, since, if an attempt to argue against the evaluative belief should fail, one would have to concede that distress is permissible, and similarly with other types of emotion. His position, then, is that the best form of therapy is the one which works against the emotional person's commitment to premise 2, the belief that some particular psychic movement is appropriate under some circumstances.

Here again Cicero indicates that the Chrysippan method of therapy has utility not only against the usual sort of emotions but also against emotions directed at integral objects. As before, it can be used to relieve the distress of one who is upset about his present moral deficiencies, and now in addition Cicero suggests using it to quench a desire for virtue. This last, surprising suggestion raises what is potentially a serious issue concerning the proposed therapy. To what extent must the philosopher who uses it believe that feelings are wrong and must be eliminated in themselves, regardless of their objects?

Take the case with which we began, the remorse of Alcibiades, and imagine for a moment that a philosopher of Chrysippan commitments is seriously attempting to alleviate this distress. As in the usual sort of consolation, the argument will be directed against premise 2, the belief that mental pain is the appropriate response to a present evil. But although the argumentative strategy is much the same, the motivation of the philosopher in choosing that strategy must now be rather different. In consoling an Achilles, he goes after premise 2 for reasons of tact, to avoid having the door slammed in his face; he is, however, privately convinced that premise 1 is false, and therefore that the pain the mourner is now experiencing is, in fact, inappropriate. He can therefore consider himself justified in proceeding along this course even if premise 2 is something he would in better circumstances be inclined to defend. After all, this is only a provisional measure, to reverse what is certainly a false conclusion. Another day, when his friend is calmer, he can reopen the discussion and sort everything out more satisfactorily. In the Alcibiades type of consolation, by contrast, there is no intention ever to argue against premise 1, since the version of premise 1 that is now operative is fully in accordance with Stoic ethics. In this kind of case, any attack that is conducted upon premise 2 would need to be motivated by the philosopher's own conviction that premise 2 really is false. For if that premise is true as well, then Alcibiades' anguish is fully justified, and one ought not to proceed with the consolatory venture at all.

The question, then, is whether Cicero's report has given us reason to believe that Chrysippus was himself committed to the rejection of premise 2. As we have seen, the proposed 'Chrysippan' therapy for grief and other emotions does not necessarily imply such a commitment, since that argumentative strategy might be only a temporary expedient for which the therapist's private opposition to premise 1 supplies adequate motivation. If taken seriously, however, the therapy for Alcibiades-type emotions would imply at least a conditional rejection. That is, the philosopher would have to believe at least that the relevant version of premise 2 is false in the present circumstances—say, in view of Alcibiades' pressing obligations to family members or to the state—and might believe something much stronger, viz., that the mere having of psychic pain or other sensations is wrong in and of itself ("the movement itself is a matter of fault"). In this case, the Stoics would have *two* reasons for seeking to eliminate the usual sort of emotions from human life, and not only the reason having to do with mistakes in evaluation. They would be opposed to the *pathē* not only because of the nature of the evaluative judgments they imply, but also because of the nature of the psychic movements they produce.

The status of premise 2

We need therefore to consider whether there is anything in Stoic philosophy which requires Chrysippus, or anyone else, to reject premise 2 outright. For this, it is best to separate the more general version of this premise—the one that is relevant to every type of emotions—from the specific version that is concerned in grief and other distress-type emotions.

P2 (general): 'If something which is either good or evil is either present or
in prospect, it is appropriate for me to undergo some sensed psychophysical
movement.'

P2 (distress-specific): 'If an evil is present, it is appropriate for me to undergo a contraction; i.e., to experience mental pain.'

Neither version is, in my view, a premise which a Stoic thinker either has
to reject or even can reject and still maintain a consistent view. But the reasoning is not quite the same for the narrower as for the broader version.
For ease of handling I will consider the broader version first.

A flat denial of the general version of P2 would be a very strong claim.
One would be saying, in effect, that the psychophysical movements which
constitute the emotions are never appropriate in a human being at all, not
even when confronted with circumstances helpful or harmful to one's
well-being as a moral agent. Such a claim would condemn not only the veridical emotions of an Alcibiades but also the eupathic responses of the
sage, thus reversing a well-attested Stoic position. If walking is inherently
inappropriate, it does not matter whether one walks prudently or impru-
dently; indeed, the very concept of prudent walking begins not to make
sense. By the same token, there could not in this case be any such thing as
'well-reasoned uplift' or 'well-reasoned reaching.' Eupathic love would be
an impossibility. The Stoic sage would indeed live what hostile accounts
have sometimes alleged: the life of a stone.

An important principle is at stake. Central to Stoic thought is the claim
that a rational creature must follow nature, that "nature leads us toward
virtue."[18] This foundational assertion implies that the best philosophical understanding of how a person should live will be one grounded in
observation of the way nature has created us; that is, in the corporeal
and psychological characteristics of our species. Nature does not pass
out characteristics at random: if members of a species regularly exhibit
some significant structural or behavioral feature, then there must be some
way that feature promotes the interests of those species members or of
their biological community. Birds have feathers because they have a use for
feathers; foxes hunt because hunting enables them to survive. The same is
true in human beings. Where there is a significant behavioral capacity that
is found in all people, one should as a rule expect that that capacity will
have some legitimate exercise.

This is not to say that every kind of human behavior is in accordance
with the purposes of nature. Of course it can be said, loosely, that humans

possess many capacities for which we have no legitimate exercise, capacities for murder, false judgment, and so forth. Properly speaking, though, there is no capacity specific to wrongdoing. What is loosely called the capacity for murder is merely a misapplication of a broader functional capacity which also has a legitimate exercise; namely, the capacity to plan and carry out forcible action. Similarly, the supposed capacity for error is better described as a misapplication of our capacity for forming judgments. The possibility of misapplication is just inherent in the nature of that capacity: the making of *any* judgment entails that one can judge either rightly or wrongly. Thus if we are to derive an argument from the presence of certain behavioral capacities in all unimpaired members of our species, we had best be sure that we have identified those capacities correctly.

But the capacities to experience the various psychophysical movements do seem to be human capacities in just this restrictive sense. They are not like the supposed capacity to steal, but more like the capacity to see colors, something that is part of the human being's essential functional endowment. And at least for some genera of feeling, our study of the eupathic responses has shown us what are the occasions in which exercise of these capacities is appropriate. An extension of *pneuma* is appropriate when it impels a person powerfully toward the exercise of the virtues in oneself or in a friend. A retraction is appropriate when it prevents one from behaving badly. Uplift is appropriate when it is a reaction to integral goods in possession. One can, of course, utilize these same capacities in an inappropriate or 'irrational' way: this, for Stoics, is what takes place in the emotions of desire, fear, and delight. But the fact that they are sometimes misused does not in any way impugn the capacities themselves.

In this vein it is worth our while to revisit a passage in Cicero which was mentioned briefly at the beginning of chapter 2. Taken from the opening of Cicero's redaction of the Stoic theory, the passage compares the responses that are natural to humans—that is, the *eupatheiai*—with the four genus-emotions.

> By nature, all people pursue those things which they think to be good and avoid their opposites. Therefore, as soon as a person receives an impression of some thing which he thinks is good, nature itself urges him to reach out after it. When this is done prudently and in accordance with consistency, it is the sort of reaching which the Stoics call a *boulēsis* and which I shall term a 'volition.' They think that a volition, which they define as 'a wish for some object in accordance with reason,' is found only in the wise person. But the

sort of reaching which is aroused too vigorously and in a manner opposed to reason is called 'desire' or 'unbridled longing,' and this is what is found in all who are foolish. Similarly there are two ways we may be moved as by the presence of something good. When the mind is moved quietly and consistently, in accordance with reason, this is termed 'joy,' but when it pours forth with a hollow sort of uplift, that is called 'wild or excessive gladness,' which they define as 'an unreasoning elevation of mind.' And just as it is by nature that we reach out after the good, so also it is by nature that we withdraw from the bad. A withdrawing which is in accordance with reason is termed 'caution,' and this, as they understand it, is found only in the wise person, while the name 'fear' is applied to a withdrawing that is apart from reason and that involves a lowly and effeminate swooning. Thus fear is just caution that has turned away from reason. For present evil the wise person has no affective response, but the foolish person responds with distress. For those who do not obey reason lower and contract their minds in circumstances which they believe to be evil. Hence the first definition for distress is this: 'a contraction of mind contrary to reason.' Thus there are four emotions, but three consistencies [sc. *eupatheiai*], since there is no consistency which corresponds to distress.[19]

Following his Stoic sources, Cicero lays heavy emphasis on the role of providential nature. It is 'by nature' that our minds are such as to be moved by what we perceive as goods or evils, and when they are moved in accordance with reason, the movements meet with full approval from the philosopher. Thus in three of the four affective genera, the movement type itself is unproblematic, although it can be activated in inappropriate ways. However, the fourth genus is anomalous: here only there is a movement type which is never activated in the normative condition.

This is enough to assure us that the generalized version of P2 is at least sometimes true in Stoicism. But the distress-only version must be considered separately, for distress does not have the warrant of a corresponding *eupatheia*. For each of the other emotion-genera, the attainment of wisdom would replace a perverted response type with a proper and natural response of the same type; for the distress genus, though, there is no possible replacement: the wise person simply does not respond in this way. It must be for this reason that Cicero asserts, later in the same book, that "it can never be a right action to contract the spirits," although it can be right to elevate them.[20] Cicero takes it as proven that the narrow, distress-only version of P2 can and should be rejected across the board by one committed to Stoic principles.

And yet it does not follow from what has been said that even the distress-only version of P2 is necessarily false. The fact that the person of perfect understanding never judges 'it is now appropriate for me to contract my spirit' is no reason to conclude that mental pain is somehow inherently inappropriate. In terms of the syllogistic analysis we have used, the primary reason the wise person rejects that conclusion must be that she always rejects the third premise, that an evil is now present. It is still quite possible for her to assert the conditional sentence in P2, that '*if* an evil is present, it is appropriate for me to undergo a contraction.' In her case, the condition is never satisfied. But she is not barred from believing, contrafactually, that it *would* be appropriate to be pained at a genuine evil *if* one were present.

To say that the wise retain this contrafactual belief would be to say that although they never have occasion for any form of mental pain, they are still psychologically equipped to generate that feeling. They are, as it were, set up to respond affectively to present evils, just as the nonwise are, but like burglar alarms in safe neighborhoods, their pain-generating mechanisms never prove their efficacy.

Is this an unheard-of idea to attribute to the ancient Stoics? Not at all, if we remember those claims that were made by Stoics about the momentary 'bitings and small contractions' that occur even in the wise in response to external objects. We noted in chapter 4 that one implication of the Stoic claims concerning 'bitings' or, as they are sometimes called, *propatheiai* is that the person of perfect understanding has the same affective capacities as ordinary humans. In a propathic 'biting,' he or she entertains the notion that an evil may be present, and this brings a twinge of pain even though assent is not given. Since the twinge occurs in connection with an impression concerning present evils, the normative human being must have something in mind that picks out pain as the appropriate response to present evils. Inasmuch as the fleeting pain reaction is said by some Stoics to be 'necessary' and 'natural,' that implied link between stimulus type and response type must be accepted by them as belonging to the normative condition.

The fact is that the school's commitment to a naturalistic perspective makes it awkward, if not impossible, for Stoic thinkers to deny the pain-specific P2 outright. The general principle stated above, that behavioral capacities regularly occurring in a species must have some legitimate exercise, surely applies to painful contraction of spirit just as much as it does to uplift, extension, and retraction of it. The capacity for mental pain is not a specious capacity like stealing; it is a distinct kind of thing the human psyche can do. Of course such pain is disagreeable, just as pain of body is disagreeable. But it may be in our best interests to be able to experience what is disagreeable. Doctors seek to relieve pain of body; they do not seek to make a person impervious to pain. In the same way, a philosopher may at times offer therapy for mental pain without claiming that it would be better not to be able to feel it. He may hold that distress is frequently misdirected but still believe that it has a legitimate function in our lives.

Progressor-pain and moral shame

If one were to consult Philo, or Origen, or any other Jewish or Christian writer of Greco-Roman antiquity, about the proper function of mental distress, an answer would be ready to hand: remorse and repentance bring about a change in one's relationship to god, marked by a fuller awareness of one's responsibilities as a moral agent. This explicitly religious conception of remorse, developed under the influence of the Hebrew *shuv* or 're-turn' (i.e., a return to god), is not to be found in the secular philosophical tradition. However, the notion that mental pain has a role to play in moral progress does make its appearance in the earlier philosophical tradition. It is suggested already by early depictions of the sorrowing Alcibiades, a role model (in this if nothing else) for the beginning student of ethics. And it is also expressed in so many words as a commonplace of therapeutic practice, by philosophers of various schools, Stoics included, who seek to motivate positive change in their hearers.

The terminology and relevant therapeutic assumptions are already in evidence within the practice of the Epicurean school in Athens during the second century B.C.E. A work by Philodemus called *On Frank Criticism*, unearthed in fragments at Herculaneum, gives a striking account of the deliberate use of mental pain by these hedonist philosophers. In order to establish a new way of thinking about ethical matters, it is necessary, says Philodemus, to sting or, literally, to 'bite' the heart of the pupil by sessions of frank criticism (*parrhēsia*). These sessions must be skillfully managed and may be difficult for the teacher to carry off, for the pupil is likely to react with anger as well as shame. But the technique is highly effective in producing a change of habits.[21]

Plutarch sounds a similar note in his ethical treatises, albeit at a later date and from a Platonist standpoint. "Other kinds of distress are removed by reasoning," he writes, "but repentance is produced by reason itself, when the psyche experiences biting pain, along with shame, and is chastised by itself."[22] If, however, the pupil does not experience remorse of his own accord, then it is up to the teacher to express frank criticism of his character and actions and so produce the needed repentance. Plutarch connects this observation with the story of Alcibiades. Socrates, he says, was being a good ethical advisor in that he rebuked Alcibiades rather than flattering him as others did: in so doing he "drew an honest tear from him and turned his heart."[23] Such a gambit is, in Plutarch's judgment, a straightforward application of the Platonist moral psychology which regards each of the emotions as having some practical utility. Consequently he objects to the use of similar techniques by Stoics, claiming that they are at odds with the school's professed commitment to *apatheia*.

> In fact, one can often see them [the Stoics] encouraging young people with praise and checking them with criticism. Of these, one is attended by delight, the other by distress. For criticism and blame bring about repentance and shame, of which one is a species of distress and the other of fear. And they use these a great deal in setting people straight.[24]

A Stoic, he thinks, ought not to proceed in this way but should refrain from generating any kind of emotional fervor in the pupil. Repentance, shame, and even the desire for approbation should all be off limits to the Stoic therapist. For reasons we have seen, however, the therapists criticized here were not bound to agree with him on this point.

Unfortunately Plutarch does not indicate which Stoics he has in mind, whether they are contemporaries whose practice he has observed in person, or Hellenistic Stoics like Zeno and Chrysippus, whose therapeutic practice he knows from books. We can see, however, that his words are an accurate description of some elements in the teaching of Epictetus, whose presence at Rome coincided with his own. Epictetus's manner of speaking, as reported by Arrian, is notably forthright, even abrasive, and his treatment of the self-satisfied is often sarcastic to the point of ridicule. This harshness is entirely deliberate. It is part of the style of discourse which Epictetus calls 'protreptic,' a confrontational style meant to induce his hearers to devote themselves earnestly to self-examination and improvement of life. In his view there are many who fail to realize that there is a contradiction between the thoughts and plans with which they are engrossed and their own most deeply held long-term objectives. The protreptic style benefits these people by awakening them to the logical conflict in which they are, as he puts it, 'enmired.'[25]

Epictetus's remarks on the protreptic style return repeatedly to the need to bring about emotional distress in the learner. If a philosopher's discourse fails to convince the hearer that he is badly off, it is a dead thing. The philosophical classroom is a place for medical treatment: one should leave it not with feelings of pleasure but in pain, like a patient who has just had an operation. The effective lecturer is not one who dresses well or ornaments his speech with vignettes from Homer but one like Epictetus's Stoic teacher Musonius Rufus, who brought people's faults before their eyes. A good speech is one from which the hearer comes away "agonized and examining himself, and saying 'How well the philosopher has taken hold of me! I ought not to act this way any longer.'"[26] This, according to Epictetus, is a long-standing mode of Stoic discourse, going back to Zeno and Cleanthes, and ultimately to Socrates who is the model for all moral philosophers.

Epictetus also allows to progressors a capacity for moral shame, which he calls *aidōs* or the *entreptikon*.[27] Moral shame figures in his teaching as a capacity which all human beings have by nature to blush when they perceive something as degrading. In general Epictetus considers *aidōs* a valuable quality which exercises a check on our behavior. A person who retains it is strongly averse to any kind of conduct which does not accord with his dignity as a rational being. Thus it is a prospective form of affect, rather than reactive as shame often is in English: one blushes when merely thinking of a degrading action and so is prevented from doing it. It is, then, similar to fear, since its objects are prospective evils. It differs from fear, though, in that its concern is not with external evils but with objects within one's own sphere of choice and avoidance.

We know that classical Stoic theory, as reported by Diogenes Laertius, draws a distinction between moral shame and ordinary shame (*aischunē*) on two fronts. On the one hand there is a distinction of objects: whereas ordinary shame is fear of ill repute, an external object, moral shame is directed at justified blame, that is, at a proper evaluation of the agent's own misdeeds in prospect. Second, and crucially, moral shame is a eupathic response, a species of caution rather than of fear.[28] As such it is restricted to the wise, in whom, presumably, it prevents the undertaking of any unworthy action. On this second point Epictetus's usage differs from the classification scheme known to Diogenes Laertius. Epictetus clearly holds that ordinary imperfect people have the capacity to be mortified at the prospect of justified censure for their actions in prospect. That capacity may be underdeveloped or willfully ignored, but in many, perhaps most cases it remains available to us and can assist us in choosing appropriate actions.

Remorse and moral shame occur together in the opening of Seneca's treatise *On Tranquility of Mind*. An innovative prologue represents the addressee, a man named Serenus, as if speaking or writing to Seneca a full disclosure of his personal failings.

> When I examine myself I find some faults so obvious I can reach out and touch them, some hidden away in a corner, and some which are not there all the time but crop up at intervals. These last, I would say, are the most worrisome. They are like guerrilla fighters, attacking when they find opportunity and allowing me neither to remain at readiness, as in wartime, nor to relax my vigilance as in time of peace. But what I detect in myself most of all is a condition neither safe and secure from the things I fear and hate, nor entirely vulnerable to them. Why should I not admit it to you as to a doctor? My state is not the worst, but it is full of moping and complaint; I am neither sick nor well.

Serenus goes on to describe in detail the reactions that worry him. He tries to live simply, not spending much on clothes or household furnishings and choosing inexpensive foods that require little preparation—but when he visits other people's houses he is dazzled by the luxury of his surroundings and wonders, secretly and painfully, whether their choice is not better than his own. He means to devote his career to the service of others, but when the work becomes frustrating or tedious he is all too eager to get away from it and hide away at home. Yet he is not at ease in his legitimate hours of leisure either but keeps wishing to be back in the marketplace, busy and building a reputation. In his writing and his public speaking he intends to keep his style simple and direct, rather than indulging in the fine phrases that bring critical acclaim; often, though, he gets carried away by his own eloquence and ends up doing the very thing he meant to avoid. None of these faults is serious in itself, but collectively they lead Serenus to wonder whether he has not been deceiving himself:

> I fear that I may be deteriorating bit by bit. The worse fear, though, is that I may be just at the point of falling, in greater danger than I myself perceive. For we look upon our own failings with favoritism; bias affects our judgment. Have no doubt: self-adulation is more destructive to us than the adulation of others. Who dares tell himself the truth?

The keynote in this is a kind of horror at one's own possibilities as a moral agent. Serenus knows that he has made some progress and that the faults he has listed are relatively trivial. But he recognizes in them indications of an unstable character, one which in changed circumstances might well prove capable of some thoroughly reprehensible deed. It is this frightening thought which motivates him to seek assistance.

Apatheia revisited

The material we have seen here on remorse and shame gives rise to further reflections on the old ideal of *apatheia* or the disappearance of the *pathē.*[29] Getting a more precise understanding of that ideal has been a major enterprise of this book. I have argued that while the *pathē* Stoics sought to eliminate are indeed cases of emotion in our sense, not everything we now call an 'emotion' was considered by Stoics to be a *pathos* and subject to elimination. The *pathē* are affective responses toward externals, but there are other affect-laden responses that are not *pathē.* Such are the *eupatheiai* of the wise: their joy, their eagerness for what is good, their goodwill, friendship, and love. Thus Jerome is only half right when he complains against the Stoics that achieving *apatheia* would mean becoming "either god or a stone."[30] Being wise and thus free of the *pathē* does mean that one is godlike, for knowledge is a harmonious condition that resembles the harmony of the god-infused cosmos as a whole. But it does not mean that one becomes like a stone, for there are genuine objects to which the wise may respond affectively. Indeed the Stoic understanding of human nature and of the causes of our feelings implies not only that such responses may occur in the normative person but even that they must.

We should remember that the attainment of *apatheia* is not in itself the goal of personal development. For the founding Stoics the endpoint of progress was simply that one should come to understand the world correctly. The disappearance of the *pathē* comes with that changed intellectual condition: one who is in a state of knowledge does not assent to anything false, and the evaluations upon which the *pathē* depend really are false. Thus it seems to me philosophically perverse to think of using Stoic arguments to rid oneself of undesired emotions merely because of the way they feel, without coming to grips with Stoic axiology.[31] That approach may be justifiable on a temporary basis, because of the disruptive nature of emotional judgments. But it misses the central and indispensable point of the Stoics' contribution in ethics and psychology: that no rational being wants to believe what is false.

This chapter has added the observation that even those who are not wise will sometimes respond affectively to integral objects—that is, to features of our own character or conduct. When we do this, it certainly seems possible within Stoic theory that our responses are at least sometimes generated on the basis of true beliefs.[32] These would then have the same status as our other actions have when premised on true beliefs about appropriateness; that is, the status of *kathēkonta,* the ordinary person's 'appropriate actions,' as distinct from the 'fully correct actions' (*katorthōmata*) of the wise. Stoic reasons for believing that the *pathē* would be eliminated in a perfected mind would not apply to them.

This is an interesting point, for the responses treated in this chapter claim no small share of our emotional energy. No doubt it is true, just as the Stoics thought, that many of our emotions are directed at things outside our own control, if not money and fame then health, or the health of a family member, the mere presence of another person, the choices made by others. But the emotions described for Alcibiades, and for Serenus, are also true to life, and there are other reactions, too, that are a mix: times when grief is compounded with remorse, desire with aspiration, fear with moral shame. When we consider these, we may find reason to think that some important components of emotional experience fall within the parameters established by Stoics for appropriate response to integral goods and evils. Many dimensions of our affective lives which common moral intuitions are unwilling to give up might therefore be permitted and even encouraged without departure from Stoic principles.

Like the external-directed *pathē,* these 'Alcibiades' responses are necessarily eliminated with the attainment of wisdom. But the reason for this is quite different from the reason that applies in the external-directed case. Now, it is not a matter of changes in evaluation, for the person of perfect understanding evaluates these integral objects in just the same way as the flawed agent does, though with better justification. Rather, the reason for elimination is that there has been a transformation in the circumstances that are being evaluated. New feelings reflect new facts: that what was inadequate, incomplete, and thus, for Stoics, evil has been replaced by goods in possession.

The Status of Confidence in Stoic Classifications

A minor but not uninteresting problem arises in connection with the following statement made by Cicero in *Tusculan Disputations* 4.66:

> And just as confidence (*confidere*) is proper but fear improper, so also joy is proper and gladness improper—for we make a distinction between 'joy' and 'gladness' for the purposes of teaching.

Taken from Cicero's Stoic-influenced treatment of available therapies for the emotions, the sentence makes use of a familiar Stoic opposition between gladness, one of the four generic emotions and hence an 'improper' response, and joy, a eupathic or 'proper' response. Less obviously Stoic is the first portion of the sentence, where confidence is named as the response opposed to fear. Here there is a puzzle, for according to most Stoic accounts—including Cicero's own earlier in the book—the eupathic response which corresponds to fear is not confidence but *eulabeia* or caution. There is, then, a discrepancy, but it does not follow that Cicero's statement must be emended or set aside. Related witnesses on confidence in the Greek tradition give reason to believe that what we in fact have in *Tusc.* 4.66 is a remnant of an alternative Stoic position on the proper feeling corresponding to fear, which Cicero has not attempted to rectify with his own statements earlier. Taken in conjunction with the rather prominent role played by this emotion in the earlier philosophical tradition, the status here given to confidence offers some limited insight into the principles by which early Stoic authors devised their systems of classification.

The usual way of resolving the inconsistency in Cicero's view has been to remove it by emendation. If Cicero were following a Greek source that mentioned *eulabeia* or the verb *eulabeisthai*, then he would have written *cavere* rather than *confidere*, and it requires only a little exercise of the editorial imagination to believe that *cavere* is what he in fact wrote. The emendation was first proposed by John Davies in 1709 and was accepted by Max Pohlenz and many modern editions; others, by similar reasoning, print *providere*.[1] But *confidere* is the reading of every single manuscript and has impressive support in a fourth-century quotation by the grammarian Nonius Marcellus. That confidence could in fact be treated as a proper feeling within Stoicism was noted by Sven Lundström in 1964 on the strength of Stobaeus, *Ecl.* 2.7.5b and 5g, where *tharros* is twice listed alongside others of the *eupatheiai*.[2] Lundström therefore recommended retaining *confidere* in the text. He did not, however, address the question concerning the status thereby given to confidence among the *eupatheiai*. For Cicero appears to say not merely that confidence is eupathic but that it is the principal or generic *eupatheia* opposed to fear, just as joy is the principal or generic *eupatheia* opposed to gladness. It is this point that now demands our attention.

Both of Lundström's Stobaean passages include confidence in lists meant to illustrate particular points in the classification of psychic goods. In one passage, "joy and cheerfulness and confidence and rational wish and the like" are listed as psychic goods which are not virtues, since they are mental events or movements (*kinēseis*) rather than conditions. A few pages later, "joy and cheerfulness and confidence and prudent walking" are listed as final goods in contrast with the intelligent person and the friend, who are classified as productive goods.[3] On both occasions confidence is clearly being counted as a movement of the virtuous psyche. Further, the fact that it is grouped together with joy, cheerfulness, and in one case rational wish (*boulēsis*) strongly suggests that it is a eupathic response, as distinct from prudent walking, which is this author's usual example of a nonaffective impulse. We can infer also that it is considered by him an important eupathic response, since an obscure item would have little use in illustrating a concept. As examples of virtues in the same context, he chooses the cardinal virtues of prudence, self-control, and courage. His examples of psychic events would be expected to be similarly familiar and important items in the Stoic psychological lexicon.

This expectation is not borne out by what we are told in our major sources on the names of the *eupatheiai*. Confidence is not named as an *eupatheia* either in Diogenes Laertius or in the pseudo-Andronican definition list, and neither is it mentioned in Cicero's main discussion of eupathic response in *Tusc. Disp.* 4.12–14. Joy is named in all of these, and in Diogenes and pseudo-Andronicus—the only two sources that supply us with names for the species-*eupatheiai*—cheerfulness immediately follows joy, as the first of its species. Rational wish is also a genus-*eupatheia*. But in those accounts the third of the genus-*eupatheiai* is not confidence but caution (*eulabeia*), which is not to be found in the Stobaean account.

The Stobaean passages would, however, make good sense if there existed another Stoic classification system in which confidence, rather than caution, figured as the principal eupathic response opposed to fear. In that case the sequence 'joy and cheerfulness and confidence and rational wish and the like' would represent an orderly listing of the principal forms of wise affect: joy and cheerfulness relate to present goods, rational wish to prospective goods, and confidence to future evils. And again, our sentence in Cicero might reflect the same understanding of the classification: confidence and fear are contrasted as the principal affective responses directed at prospective evils, one proper and one improper, exactly the same contrast as between joy and gladness. What I want to suggest, then, is that these three passages, the one in Cicero and the two in Stobaeus, should be read as remnants of an alternative Stoic classification system which otherwise does not survive.

A brief consideration of the philosophical prehistory of confidence will provide some context for this suggestion. There is a good discussion in Plato's *Protagoras,* where the topic is the unity of the virtues.[4] Protagoras concedes that intelligence, justice, self-control, and piety may be much the same but insists that courage is different from the rest, on grounds that in order to be courageous one must also be *tharraleos;* that is, confident or bold. For him, at least initially, it seems that *tharros* is a necessary but not sufficient condition for courage: knowledge may make a person more confident in specific situations, but confidence is not the same thing as knowledge and is also necessary.[5] Divers, chariot fighters, and peltasts behave boldly because they possess knowledge, but people may also be bold without knowledge, if they are 'crazy people.' A related claim is made in *Meno* 88b. There Socrates seeks to establish that qualities of mind are good only when they are forms of knowledge. *Tharros* is his first example: when courage is merely 'a sort of *tharros*' rather than a manifestation of *phronēsis,* it is bivalent, sometimes beneficial to a person and sometimes harmful.

Both the *Meno* passage and the *Protagoras* passage invest *tharros* with some importance in ethics. In neither, though, does Plato make it clear what exactly he takes *tharros* to be. One could easily assume, while reading, that the word refers throughout to a specifically affective response type; that is, to a pattern of behaviors that typically involve some internal feeling that is the inverse of the quivery sensations we associate with fear. But Plato's way of using the verb *tharrein* is also consistent with the assumption that he is referring merely to aggressive or audacious behaviors as viewed by an observer, without consideration of the agent's own inner experience. One cannot really tell in these two dialogues whether Plato has in mind the reckless feeling the diver presumably has as he hurls himself from a cliff, or just the fact that he does sometimes dive from cliffs. Yet these are clearly distinct ways of thinking about boldness.

An extended treatment near the end of book 1 of the *Laws* more clearly represents confidence as an affective response, the inverse experience to fear. There the Athenian stranger suggests, rather playfully, that just as it would be legitimate to use a fear-inducing drug, if any existed, to give people experience with fear and thus train them in courage, so also it might be a good idea for the lawgiver to administer wine, which induces confidence, as a way of training people in modesty.[6] Plato now shows a greater interest in the subjectivity of the agent: the entire discussion of altered mental states implies it, and there are interesting remarks about drinkers' 'fine expectations' and 'capacity for fancy' (*doxa*). There is also an increased interest in the objects toward which *tharros* is felt. Fear, we are told at 644d, is an anticipation of pain or evil, and confidence anticipates the opposite, either good things or the cessation of evils.

At one point, also, Plato makes explicit an idea that was only hinted at in *Protagoras,* that if *tharros* is directed toward the right sorts of objects, it is unimpeachable, a kind of super-*tharros* which cannot go wrong. For the Athenian says that just as there is a kind of fear that is held in honor, so there is a kind of maximal confidence that should be trained into the soul.[7] He does not, however, explain quite how the normative version of confidence is supposed to work. With fear, it is clear enough: there is in this account a correct sort of fear, namely, the fear of "getting a bad reputation when one says or does something dishonorable," and a wrong sort, of which an example would be fear of the enemy in war. So improper fear is directed at externals, while proper fear, ordinarily called 'shame' (*aischunē* or *aidōs*, 647ab), is directed at disgrace due to one's own actions. Conversely, confidence in doing disreputable actions is to be trained out of a person (649c), and so we may be supposed to think that the objects of

irreproachable confidence can only be externals. But the passage never actually makes this last assertion, and perhaps for good reason: would Plato
really want to say that it is always good to be confident about threats to
life and limb? Certainly not: the philosophical reasons to avoid such an assertion had already been made clear in *Meno* and *Protagoras,* and we can
hardly suppose them to have been forgotten here.

Confidence plays a philosophical role also in the writings of Aristotle,
in *Rhetoric* 2.5 and *Nicomachean Ethics* 3.6. For Aristotle, the particular point
of interest is in fitting confidence into a system of multiple feelings and
multiple dispositional states. A list of eleven canonical *pathē* in *Nicomachean Ethics* 2.5 includes *tharros* alongside desire, anger, and fear, and it is
clear in both the *Ethics* and the *Rhetoric* that *tharros* is considered to meet
all Aristotle's criteria for what a *pathos* is and does.[8] Though more systematic than Plato's, his treatment otherwise resembles what we have seen in
Plato: confidence is contrary to fear; it is either good or bad depending on
how it is deployed; it stands in relation to the virtue of courage as an activity to a dispositional state, courage being a disposition to experience both
fear and confidence to the right degree and in the right situations. Also
like Plato, Aristotle shows some interest in the category of objects toward
which confidence is felt. Ordinarily, what he means by *tharros* is that mental experience through which one stands firm against danger from external
threats, especially in a military context. But he also thinks that just as there
are some things one may fear without being a coward—for instance the
possibility that one might abuse a child—so also there are some things one
may be confident about without thereby being courageous. His example is
'being flogged,' presumably for crimes one has committed (*NE* 3.6).

The treatment given to confidence in Plato and Aristotle is thus com-
mensurate with the militaristic values of Greek culture. It is comparable,
for instance, to the frequent references to *tharsos* or *thraseia* in war poetry, above all the *Iliad.* The philosophers do not, of course, accept the
response uncritically but examine and to some extent redefine it, as they
do other ethical concepts. Epicurus, too, invests the term with his own significance, in the *Principal Doctrines* and in his treatise *On the End.* For him,
'confidence' is the attitude a wise person will take toward external threats
and the continued possession of goods.[9] It is therefore indispensable to
happiness in the Epicurean system, since without it present enjoyment is
annulled by anxieties about the future.

Given this rich history, then, it might have been expected that confidence would find some prominent place in the elaborate affective theories
of the early Stoa. For the Stoics were not generally inclined to pass over in

silence terms and concepts which had been invested with significance in earlier moral theory. What we find in the sources, though, is strangely subdued. In the three brief passages presented above, we do catch glimpses of a Stoic profile for *tharros;* in these, and in a handful of other witnesses, confidence is indeed assumed to be an important item in the philosophical lexicon.[10] Yet these run contrary to the prevailing tradition. If one were to look only at the more familiar sources on *pathē* and *eupatheiai,* including the earlier portions of the *Tusculans,* the summary accounts in Diogenes Laertius and Stobaeus, and the pseudo-Andronican definition list, one would think confidence had disappeared altogether. Out of Aristotle's list of eleven, it would be the only one without a Stoic posthistory.[11]

Something must have happened; the disharmony in our sources cannot have arisen without a reason. And so, although the nature of the evidence is not such as to support any very definite historical assertions, I feel I must venture a suggestion. Let us suppose that there was a very early account, one by Zeno or another first-generation author, treating confidence as a genus-*eupatheia,* and that the innovation of Chrysippus or another of the *epigoni* was to remove *tharros* and put *eulabeia* in its place.[12] If that happened, then the innovative classification would be likely to displace most, but perhaps not all, previous versions. This would be especially true if the innovator were Chrysippus himself, for it was his book that librarians generally chose to acquire.

The motivation for getting rid of *tharros* in favor of *eulabeia* might have been simply that confidence does not correspond to fear in quite the way the proposed classificatory system seemed to require. Joy corresponds to gladness in the kind of feeling it is: it is 'rational *eparsis,*' the normative human's psychic uplift. Likewise *boulēsis* or wish, which is the normative version of desire, involves a psychophysical event similar in kind to desire: where desire is 'irrational *orexis,*' *boulēsis* is 'rational *orexis.*' What corresponds to fear, then, should be some rational form of aversion (*ekklisis*). But *tharros* isn't a form of aversion at all, whereas 'caution' fits the slot very neatly.

I suspect, though, that the operative worry did not concern only the nature of the response itself, but had also to do with the objects toward which *tharros* is directed. We have good evidence from Seneca that in what became the standard affective theory, eupathic responses are directed only at objects under one's own control, either actions one performs or traits of character for whose acquisition one is responsible. This is the only position that makes sense for Stoic moral psychology: since normative versions of affect occur only in the normative human mind, the objects with which they are concerned can only be such objects as the person of perfect understanding considers to be genuine goods or evils. Confidence, though, seems like a good thing only when it is a response to external threats. If the object in prospect is something that belongs to one's own agency (as in Aristotle's example, where one considers the possibility that one might molest a child), then the proper response to that object is not confidence but some form of aversion. This is the very line of thinking that we saw begun, but not finished, in Plato's *Laws*.

As evidence that at least one Stoic philosopher did pursue this train of thought on the objects of *tharros,* I cite the following paragraph from Epictetus:

> Although to some people perhaps it seems a paradox what the philosophers claim, still, let us consider as best we can whether it is true that one should do all things at once confidently and cautiously. For it might seem that caution is the opposite of confidence, and that opposites cannot co-occur. But what appears paradoxical to many in this topic depends, it seems to me, on something like this. If we were claiming that caution and confidence were used in relation to the same things, they would be right to charge us with combining incompatibles. But as it is, what is strange about what we are saying? For if the things we frequently assert and prove are sound, that the essence of the good and likewise of evil is in the use of impressions, and that things that do not depend on volition have no share in the nature of either evil or good, then why is it a paradox to say, as do the philosophers, "Where things do not depend on volition, there you should have confidence; where they do, there you should have caution"? For if things which do not depend on volition and are not in our power are nothing to us, then we should exercise confidence toward those things. In this way, we will be cautious and confident at the same time, and even, by god, confident because of our caution. For it is because we are cautious about things that are genuinely evil that we come to be confident about things that are not.[13]

One cannot assume from this passage that Epictetus's position on the objects of *tharros* is derived directly from earlier Stoic authors, for while he speaks of the compatibility of confidence and caution as an assertion already made by 'the philosophers,' the argument he gives to support that assertion may be of his own devising. But Epictetus is very good at working the Stoic system, and here I think he articulates correctly what Chrysippus, too, would want to say about the relation between confidence and caution. Reasoning of this kind could very well have been the motivation for a decision made early in Stoic history to demote *tharros* from its place among the genus-*eupatheiai*.

If so, then what is the status to which confidence is now being relegated? It is not said that it is a eupathic response, only that it can co-occur with one. If it had been so labeled, there would have been a discrepancy, since *eupatheiai* are otherwise always directed at objects determined by the agent; it is fortunate for the coherence of the system, then, that it is not. Neither is it said that *tharros* is an emotion, and this again is fortunate for the coherence of the system, since the wise do not otherwise experience any ordinary form of emotion. But it must be something. There is a third possibility: *tharros* might be simply an instance of 'selection,' an action type defined by Stoics not in terms of its phenomenology as inner experience but in terms of the preference it expresses for one object rather than another.[14] A person who 'has confidence' (*tharrei*) is behaving in a certain way toward indifferents, choosing ones that might in most circumstances be dispreferred, for instance being tortured or killed, on grounds that in these particular circumstances they are in accordance with nature's plan. Such a choice may also be accompanied by feeling, but the choice may be referred to independent of the feeling, as action rather than affect: in the wise, as a 'definitely right action' or *katorthōma,* in the ordinary person who does what the wise person would do, as an 'appropriate action' or *kathēkon.*[15] This is perfectly sound Stoic ethics. It is odd, though, to find a word so central to the older emotion vocabulary taking this role. Thinking, as they did, very deeply and elaborately about the nature of emotion and the relation among emotion concepts, the Stoics seem ultimately to have concluded that the opposite of fear is not an emotion at all.

LIST OF ABBREVIATIONS

D.L.   Diogenes Laertius, *Lives of Eminent Philosophers*

EK   *Posidonius: The Fragments*, ed. Edelstein and Kidd

LS   *The Hellenistic Philosophers*, ed. Long and Sedley

LSJ   *A Greek-English Lexicon*, ed. Liddell, Scott, Jones

OLD   *Oxford Latin Dictionary*, ed. Glare

PG   *Patrologiae cursus completus, Series Graeca*, ed. Migne

PHP   Galen, *On the Precepts of Hippocrates and Plato*, ed. de Lacy

PL   *Patrologiae cursus completus, Series Latina*, ed. Migne

SVF   *Stoicorum veterum fragmenta*, ed. von Arnim

W   *Ioannis Stobaei Anthologium*, ed. Wachsmuth and Hense

NOTES

Introduction

1. The first four examples are from *On the Psyche,* where Chrysippus's intention was to demonstrate that emotions are localized in the heart region (Galen, *PHP* 3.2–3, 3.7.51–52, 4.1). The last three are from *On Emotions,* supporting various points about the causation of emotions and the difficulty of controlling them (Galen, *PHP* 4.6–7).

2. Cf. Inwood (1985, 127–28); Nussbaum (1994, 319). Tieleman (2003, 15–16), although he favors 'affection' to preserve the medical connotations of Chrysippus's catachrestic use of *pathos,* nonetheless grants that 'emotion' is the obvious rendering. The development of the Greek vocabulary of emotion is treated in Konstan (2006).

3. This central assertion, emphasized especially by Nussbaum (1994, 2001, 2004) has been assumed to bring Stoic thought into the camp of 'pure' cognitivist theories like that of Solomon as originally proposed (Solomon 1976) and, especially, of Richard Lazarus (1991). See, for instance, Solomon (2004, 10–11): "If one represents the thought content of every intentional state as a proposition, one cannot account for primitive emotions. One's theory of emotions in that case will be like the theory of the ancient Greek and Roman Stoics. . . . Such a theory is no longer tenable." Nussbaum herself regards the Stoic view as "overly focused on linguistically formulable propositional content" (2001, 37).

4. Like every scholar working in this area I have received much guidance from the annotated collection of fragments made by Long and Sedley (1987), as well as from the older *Stoicorum veterum fragmenta* by von Arnim. For the more obscure authors, my citations include fragment numbers in Long and Sedley (LS) or von Arnim (*SVF*). Translations, except for those from Armenian, are my own throughout.

5. Gill (2005) gives a plausible account of the historical development of this tendency as concerns part-based and monistic models of psyche.

6. In favor of the attribution, see Pomeroy (1999); Inwood (1996); Hahm

(1990); against, Göransson (1995). The material in question matches closely in style and method with other material attributed by Stobaeus, presumably the Arius Didymus mentioned by Gellius. The further identification of Arius Didymus with the Arius known to Augustus is tentative but plausible.

7. See further Graver (2002a, 203–23). A work by Posidonius which is known to have been closely engaged with Chrysippus's treatise shares a number of themes with Cicero's work, but Posidonius's own argument took quite a different tack from Chrysippus, and Cicero, had he relied only on the later work, would surely have shown awareness of this. There could, indeed, have been some other intermediary, unknown to us, which supplied Cicero with his immediate knowledge, but this would have had to be so similar in content to Chrysippus's work that not much would be gained by knowing about it.

8. Perceptions of the Stoic theory within the surrounding culture are treated especially in Konstan (2006); Reydams-Schils (2005); Harris (2002); Nussbaum (1994).

9. Indeed I believe that some of the modifications suggested by those authors were features already present in the ancient position. I have in mind the insistence of Nussbaum (2001, 69–75) that the neo-Stoic should give some role to physiologically based feelings and should distinguish 'background' and 'situational' kinds of judgment, and Becker's view (1998, 97–98, 128–32) that the affective life of the wise should be both intense and expressive.

Chapter 1

1. For examples, see Damasio (1994, 2000, 2003); Rolls (1999); Panksepp (1998); Ekman and Rosenberg (1997); Griffiths (1997); LeDoux (1996).

2. Panksepp (1998, 194).

3. *On the Soul* 1.1.403a.

4. It is noteworthy in this connection that the account of the psyche in Stoic thought comes under the subject matter called 'physics,' which also includes such topics as the nature of the elements and the types of mixture. For a good overview see White (2003); also Furley (1999, 432–51); Sorabji (1988, 79–105); Lapidge (1978); Todd (1978). A more in-depth treatment is Hahm (1977).

5. James (1884); Damasio (1994 and 2000); see Prinz (2004, 5–6, 55–59). Compare Panksepp (1998, 14): "One reason such instinctual states may include an internally experienced feeling tone is that higher organisms possess neurally based self-representation systems. I would suggest that subjectively experienced feelings arise, ultimately, from the interactions of various emotional systems with the fundamental brain substrates of 'the self.'"

6. Galen, *On Incorporeal Qualities* 19.483 (LS 45F); D.L. 7.135 (citing Apollodorus).

7. Nemesius, *On Human Nature* 2.78–79 (LS 45C); known also to Tertullian, *On the Soul* 5 (PL 2, col. 693 [SVF 1.518]). For other Stoic arguments on this point see Nemesius, *On Human Nature* 2.77, 2.81, and Cicero, *Tusc. Disp.* 1.79 (quoting Panaetius), with Hahm (1977, 15–18).

8. Alexander of Aphrodisias, *On the Soul* 2.115 Bruns (SVF 2.785); scholiast on *Iliad* 2.857 (SVF 2.778); Plutarch, *On Common Conceptions* 1084f; see Hahm (1977, 151). The

mingling of soul with body is an instance of 'complete blending' in Alexander of Aphrodisias, *On Mixture* 3.216 (LS 48C); see Long (1992, 38–39); von Staden (2000, 99–100).

9. The four *stoicheia* or basic stuffs are not elements in our sense, material-types of fixed chemical composition; rather, they are just those portions of matter which have come to be characterized, perhaps temporarily, by one of four principal differentiations, hot or cold, dry or wet. Thus any stretch of matter which happens to be hot can be said to have fire mingled with it, and fire is present throughout the universe insofar as anything is hot. Except at the cyclical conflagration, the same is true of the three basic stuffs defined by cold, wet, and dry. See White (2003, 135–36).

10. The biological role of *pneuma* as 'inborn breath' or the life principle was taken over by Zeno from previous Greek thought as known to us through Aristotle and the medical writers. See Hahm (1977, 68–72), citing for instance Aristotle, *On the Generation of Animals* 2.3: "There is present in the semen . . . the substance called the 'hot.' This is not fire or some such power, but *pneuma* . . . and the natural substance which is in this *pneuma,* a substance analogous to the element of the stars."

11. D.L. 7.136, from Zeno's treatise *On the Universe:* "As the seed is carried in the seminal fluid, so also he, being the seminal principle of the cosmos, remains such in the wet [element], making matter a serviceable means for himself to generate things in order." Similarly Stobaeus, *Ecl.* 1.20.1e (171W [*SVF* 1.107]); *Ecl.*1.17.3 (153W [*SVF* 1.497]); Sextus, *Against the Professors* 9.110; Eusebius, *Evangelical Preparation* 15.14.2 (LS 46G); Origen, *Against Celsus* 4.48 (*SVF* 2.1074). See Hahm (1977, 75–76); LS 2.272. In Cleanthes' hymn (LS 54I) the "two-edged" power "by whose strokes all events in nature proceed" is both the active principle and the immanent deity himself.

12. Alexander of Aphrodisias, *On Mixture* 10.224 (LS 47I); Philo, *God's Immutability* 35–36 and *Questions on Genesis* 2.4 (LS 47Q, R); Nemesius, *On Human Nature* 2.70 (LS 47J); Galen, *On Muscular Movement* 4.402–3 (LS 47K).

13. Plutarch, *On Stoic Self-Contradictions* 1053f; *On Common Conceptions* 1085cd (LS 47G); Galen, *Medical Introduction* 14.726 (LS 47N). See Hahm (1977, 153–56, 165–74).

14. D.L. 7.157; Eusebius, *Evangelical Preparation* 15.20.6 (LS 53W); Sextus, *Against the Professors* 9.71–72. This is limited survival rather than immortality, since the *psychai* would be destroyed along with the rest of the cosmos in the next conflagration.

15. This perspective on mind and body sets the rigorous treatment by Hierocles (on which see below) apart from the more casual usage of Seneca. See further Long (1992).

16. The two meanings are distinguished by Sextus, *Against the Professors* 7.234 (LS 53F).

17. The fragments are assembled by von Arnim in *SVF* 2.879–911. Works devoted specifically to the psyche were written also by Chrysippus's pupils Antipater and Diogenes of Babylon (Galen, *PHP* 2.5.7).

18. Eusebius, *Evangelical Preparation* 15.20.2 (*SVF* 1.141). Cf. D.L. 7.156 ('perceptive *phusis*').

19. D.L. 7.157; Nemesius, *On Human Nature* 2.67; Clement, *Stromata* 2.487 (*SVF* 2.714).

20. The need for a single faculty to serve as clearinghouse and command center was recognized also by Aristotle in *On the Movement of Animals* 8–10, 702a–703a, where the single origin of movement is located in the heart and attributed to 'inborn *pneuma*.' For

the integration of sensory input see also *On the Soul* 3.2, 426b17, and Plato, *Theaetetus* 184d–185c.

21. Calcidius, *On the Timaeus of Plato* 220 (LS 53G); see also Aetius, *Views of Philosophers* 4.21 (LS 53H); Iamblichus, in Stobaeus, *Ecl.* 1.49.33 (368W [LS 53K]); Nemesius, *On Human Nature* 15.212.

22. See Tielemann (1996, 144–45, 189–95) and, for the influence of medical writers (including Praxagoras of Cos), Hankinson (2003); Annas (1992, 20–26); von Staden (2000, 96–105); Hahm (1977, 160–65).

23. Calcidius, *On the Timaeus of Plato* 220 (LS 53G).

24. Plutarch, *On Stoic Self-Contradictions* 1052f.

25. Galen, *On the Use of Respiration* 4.502 (SVF 2.783); *On Hippocrates' Epidemics* 6.270 (LS 53E).

26. Chrysippus concedes that the inexactness of anatomical knowledge requires flexibility on such points, and indeed he allows that voluntary motion *might* originate in the brain; so Galen, *PHP* 2.5.68–73.

27. Aristotle, *On the Soul* 3.2.425b12–20.

28. Hierocles, *Elements of Ethics,* col. 4.38–53 (LS 53B). There is an edition by Bastianini and Long (1992) and an earlier one by von Arnim (1906); see further Tielemann (1996, 177–184); Long (1993 and 1992); LS 2.310–12; Inwood (1984).

29. The animate being's capacity for self-perception is discussed also by Seneca, who stresses that the awareness is indirect and thus inexact (*Moral Epistles* 121.12–13).

30. D.L. 7.51; Origen, *On Principles* 3.1.3 (LS 53A). The complexity of animal behavior certainly suggests some access to propositional content. On this issue see Lesses (1998); Sorabji (1993). The principal differences between rational and nonrational intelligence have to do with assent and self-monitoring, on which see further p. 109 below.

31. A proposition is called in Stoic logic an *axiōma,* a species of *lekton* or 'sayable.' See D.L. 7.57, 7.63; Sextus, *Against the Professors* 8.11, 8.70; Seneca, *Moral Epistles* 117.13; with LS 1.198–202.

32. Eusebius, *Evangelical Preparation* 15.20.2 (SVF 1.141). The comparison to the wax seal had been used previously by Plato, *Theaetetus* 191c–195b; more to the point here, though, is Aristotle, *On the Soul* 2.12.424a17–24.

33. Cleanthes' interpretation is quoted by Sextus, *Against the Professors* 7.228, 7.372, 8.400; *Outlines of Pyrrhonism* 2.70. See Sedley (1993, 329–31); Brennan (2005, 53–54).

34. Sextus, *Against the Professors* 7.228–31, from Chrysippus's *On the Psyche* (cf. D.L. 7.50); see LS 2.238.

35. Cicero, *Prior Academics* 2.21.

36. The standard definition, for instance in Aetius, *Views of Philosophers* 4.12 (LS 39B); Sextus, *Against the Professors* 7.161–3.

37. Sextus, *Against the Professors* 8.275; cf. D.L. 7.51, together with the analogy reported in Sextus Empiricus of the mind as a military recruit imitating his training officer (*Against the Professors* 8.409–10).

38. All three terms refer to the endorsing of an impression; however, they are not interchangeable. Stoic usage usually restricts *doxa* and *doxazein* to the beliefs of the nonwise, to contrast with knowledge, which occurs only in the wise. See for instance

Sextus, *Against the Professors* 7.151–57, with LS 1.256–59. In this book I mostly use 'belief' as a general term for the product of assent in either the wise or the nonwise, but I also sometimes employ the word 'opinion' in contexts where the unreliability of nonwise assent is important. Readers should keep in mind that 'belief' in the normative epistemic condition is *always* stable and veridical; 'the wise do not opine.'

39. E.g., Plutarch, *On Stoic Self-Contradictions* 1057b; Stobaeus, *Ecl.* 2.7.11m (111–12W).

40. Stobaeus, *Ecl.* 2.7.9 (86W).

41. On this issue see Inwood (1985, 82–85).

42. Stobaeus, *Ecl.* 2.7.9 (86W), 2.7.9b (88W). On the causation of assent see further pp. 64–65 below.

43. Seneca, *Moral Epistles* 113.23; see further Inwood (1985, 50–51).

44. Stobaeus, *Ecl.* 2.7.10b (90W). The text includes some supplementation; see below, chap. 2, note 13. The Greek words here rendered 'delight' (*hēdonē*) and 'distress' (*lupē*) can also refer indiscriminately to pleasure and pain of body or of mind. In adopting these renderings, I mean to avoid giving the erroneous impression that what one feels in a just-stubbed toe would be counted by Stoics as an emotion. In Stoic authors, there is clear recognition of a conceptual distinction between mental pleasure or pain (i.e., that which has an intentional object) and what would usually be called corporeal pleasure or pain. The latter are morally indifferent and occur also in the normative condition. Compare the definitions cited here with D.L. 7.102 and Stobaeus, *Ecl.* 2.7.7b (81W), and see Cooper (1998, 101); LS 1.421; Nussbaum (1994, 386–87).

45. 'Be contracted' and 'be elevated' are imperfect renderings for the infinitives *sustellesthai* and *epairesthai*. In context these must be middle-voice infinitives; that is, they are intransitive in sense, indicating not that the psyche *is changed* by something else, but just that it *changes*.

46. Galen, *PHP* 5.1.4, 4.3.2, 4.2.4–6. The inclusion of 'lowering' is based on an emended reading (*tapeinōsis*); see de Lacy (1978) on 5.1.4. The same psychophysical movements are also involved in involuntary feelings or *propatheiai*; see pp. 85–93 below.

47. 'Biting': *Iliad* 5.493; Hesiod, *Theogony* 567; Aeschylus, *Persians* 571, 846; Sophocles, *Philoctetes* 378 (LSJ s.v. δακνάζω II, δάκνω III); 'contract' and 'elevate'; Plato, *Republic* 4.434b, 10.608b; Herodotus, *Histories* 5.81, 9.49; Euripides, *Hercules Furens* 1417, *Troades* 108 (LSJ s.v. ἐπαίρω II.1, II.2, συστέλλω I.3). A literal interpretation is defended in Sakezles (1998, 153). For metaphors of emotion in Greek tragedy see further Padel (1994).

48. Cicero, *Tusc. Disp.* 4.15.

49. Cicero, *Tusc. Disp.* 4.14: 'be contracted' is *contrahi;* 'be lowered' is *demitti;* and 'be elevated' is *efferri* (cf. *elatio* in 4.13, 4.67).

50. For pursuit and avoidance generally Stoics had available the terms 'impulse' (*hormē*) and 'counterimpulse' (*aphormē*). So Stobaeus, *Ecl.* 2.7.9 (87W): "For *orexis* is not rational impulse, but a species of rational impulse."

51. For the literal translation see also LS 1.421.

52. Chrysippus in Galen, *PHP* 3.1.25; so also 3.7.3–4, speaking of the feelings associated with joy, confidence, and grief. Both the argument from emotion and the testimony of nonphilosophers are treated at length in *PHP*, book 3.

53. Thus Galen in *PHP* 5.7.29 gives more than one Stoic definition for *orexis*: it may be 'a reasoned impulse toward some object which pleases to the extent that it should'

(in which case it is a eupathic response; cf. *PHP* 4.2.4–5), but it may also figure in the definition of desire as 'an *orexis* which rushes headlong toward acquisition.' It is no wonder that some Stoics objected to an indiscriminate use of the term.

54. There is no implication here that an instance of, for instance, 'well-reasoned reaching' could ever be physically *identical* to an instance of 'ill-reasoned reaching.' Since each of these is also a judgment, and since judgments are physical events, we should assume that there are differences in the substrate, in particular in the ambient tension level of the material. This is consistent with their being instances of the same sort of psychophysical change and having the same sort of "feel" to the one thus moved.

55. For historical as well as philosophical reasons I have not been convinced by the arguments for a substantive difference between Zeno and Chrysippus given in Sorabji (2000, 55–65) and Brennan (1998, 59–60). Uncritical acceptance of Galen's interpretation here would require us to set aside the explicit testimony of Cicero at *Posterior Academics* 1.38 (quoted below, p. 62) and also of Plutarch in *On Moral Virtue* 441cd. The definitions of genus-emotions as 'fresh beliefs' are Zeno's; Galen, *PHP* 4.7.1–5; Cicero, *Tusc. Disp.* 3.74–75. See Price (2005 and 1995, 149), together with Gill (2005, 453–54); Graver (2002b); Inwood (1985, 130–31).

56. This, too, supplied an argument for chest localization, as evidenced (contemptuously) by Galen in *PHP* 2.5.8–20 for Zeno, Diogenes of Babylon, and Chrysippus. Galen (*PHP* 2.4.40) hints at a detailed explanation for speech in which an 'imprint' is said by Stoics to be transmitted from the *pneuma* in the heart to that in the lungs (now clearly 'breath') and thence to the windpipe.

Chapter 2

1. See Striker (1991, 248–61 and 281–97). The point is discussed further in chap. 9 below.

2. Cicero, *On Ends* 3.62.

3. Cicero, *Tusculan Disputations* 4.12; 'reaching' is *adpetitio* (Gr. *orexis*).

4. See, most recently, Solomon (2003b); also Solomon (1976); Lazarus (1991 and 1994); Ben-Ze'ev (2000). Connections between ancient and modern views on this point are explored in Nussbaum (2001, 19–88).

5. The description which includes a verb is the one used in more careful discussions; see Cicero, *Tusc. Disp.* 4.21; Stobaeus, *Ecl.* 2.7.9b (88.4–6W), 2.7.11f (97.22–23W); Seneca, *Moral Epistles* 117, with Brunschwig (1994, 158–69). In more casual contexts, one might speak as if the money itself were the object, and this does no harm as long as it is understood that a clausal formulation is available.

6. D.L. 7.111.

7. Galen, *PHP* 5.2.23, 27.

8. So Brennan (1998, 50; 2003), also Graver (2002a, 152–53, 205). There is some excuse for conflating the two terms. *Pathos* does usually mean 'emotion' in philosophical Greek after Aristotle, but it can also mean 'diseased condition' (like our word 'pathology'), and Chrysippus was not above exploiting the ambiguity for rhetorical purposes.

9. Galen, *PHP* 4.2.1, 4.7.3.

10. Cicero, *Tusc. Disp.* 3.24–25.

11. Frede (1986, 104–7). The explanation given here in terms of background *beliefs* is anticipated by Frede only at one point (105: "if he did not think of the symptomatic paleness as a fatal symptom and of death as an evil . . . there would be no fear"). Earlier portions of his discussion are less apt: where he describes the blind person's conception of a red light, he seems to view differences in one's 'way of thinking' the occurrent propositional content as imagistic or qualitative, whereas what is needed on my view is a linguistically formulable difference in previously existing beliefs.

12. Stobaeus, *Ecl.* 2.7.9 (86W); see p. 27 above. Also note Plutarch, *On Moral Virtue* 449c: "not every judgment is a *pathos*, but only one that is such as to set in motion a forcible and excessive impulse."

13. Stobaeus, *Ecl.* 2.7.10b (90W). The translation renders the text as printed by Pomeroy (1999) and Wachsmuth and Hense (1884–1912), which includes some supplementation based on the parallel texts in Cicero (*Tusc. Disp.* 3.25, 4.14) and ps.-Andronicus (*On Emotions* 1). The term 'fresh' (*prosphaton*) is here included for all four genera, whereas Cicero in *Tusc. Disp.* 3.74–75 and 4.14 reports it only for the two genera concerned with present objects. The difference in wording may reflect two different ways of understanding Zeno's term. The Stoic author behind the Stobaean account understands it to mean what we mean by 'occurrent' ("such as to produce a movement of irrational contraction or uplift," Stobaeus 2.7.10 [88W]), while Cicero (or his source) understands it to mean 'recent'; i.e., that the proposition which is the object of grief or delight is thought of by the emotional person as having recently become the case. See further pp. 54–55 and 100–101 below, together with Graver (2002a, 117–19). For the language of causation see p. 66 below.

14. For the equivalence in a Stoic context compare Galen, *PHP* 4.2.5–6, where *pheukton* and *haireton* are said to have been used by Chrysippus in definitions of distress and delight; that is, interchangeably with *eph' hōi kathēkei* here. A further variation in phrasing can be found in ps.-Andronicus, *On Emotions* 1, which uses the common Greek verb *dei*.

15. Cicero, *Tusc. Disp.* 3.25. The claim is repeated also at 3.64, 3.74, 3.76, and 3.79.

16. Cicero, *Tusc. Disp.* 3.61.

17. Cicero, *Tusc. Disp.* 3.76, 79; cf. 4.59–60.

18. The point is stressed especially by Brennan (1998 and 2003).

19. Cicero, *Tusc. Disp.* 3.63–64, also citing the Demosthenes example; the basis of which is Aeschines, *Against Ctesiphon* 77. See Graver (2002a, 112).

20. This reaction to Lucan's Stoic posture has similarities with that expressed by Sklenář (1999) and Bartsch (1997, 116–17). The perception of Cato as cartoonish is also that of Johnson (1987, 44–45). Of course, Lucan's portrayal of Cato as the 'perfect Stoic' may well be mischievous in intent: it would be naïve to assume that the character we meet in his poem represents the Stoic ideal of virtuous knowledge in the way that Stoic philosophers had in mind. However, some ancient readers were quite serious in interpreting Stoic ethics as inhumane: compare the examples cited by Irwin (1998, 220) from Lactantius.

21. See pp. 196–201 below.

22. Thus Irwin (1998, 224–25) writes, speaking of Stoic theory, "A passion . . . is uncompromising to an extent that is intelligible only if it presents its present concern

as genuinely good, and not simply something to be compared with other things that deserve consideration." This is why Epictetus constantly directs his pupils to withhold these terms from everything for the time being.

23. That is, the object of desire is technically a predicate; see above, note 5.

24. D.L. 7.160; compare Cicero, *On Ends* 3.24.

25. Seneca, *Moral Epistles* 118.11; D.L. 7.103; likewise in the passage just mentioned, where the actor performs 'suitably' to the part. The adverbial formulations may well have been inspired by Plato, *Meno* 78b–78e, 87e–89a, where the mere performance of an action is distinguished from performing it 'justly' or 'intelligently.' Compare also Zeno's use of the adverb in formulating the moral end: *homologoumenōs zēn,* to live 'consistently' as opposed to mere living.

26. Intrinsic value is value *kath' hauto* as in Stobaeus, *Ecl.* 2.7.7f (84.12W); indifferents, by contrast, have only 'selective' value or disvalue.

27. See for instance Stobaeus, *Ecl.* 2.7.5k (73W). Other Stobaean examples include temperate association, acting justly, proper usage of children, joy. It should be noted that the exercise of a virtue is not the same thing as its product; it is the latter that is indicated in Cicero, *On Ends* 3.32; cf. Nussbaum (1994, 362).

28. For value and indifference, see esp. Stobaeus, *Ecl.* 2.6f–7g, 11f (78–84W, 97–98W); Cicero, *On Ends* 3.33–60; D.L. 7.101–7; with Inwood (1985, 194–215); Striker (1991); Irwin (1998). For selection (*eklogē*), see Stobaeus 2.7.7g (84–85W); Cicero, *On Ends* 3.20; D.L. 7.88.

29. D.L. 7.103; compare Cicero, *On Ends* 3.33–34. The thought is similar to *Meno* 87e–89a and *Euthydemus* 280e as noted by LS 2.350; it has much in common also with *Republic* 7.523b–24e and *Phaedo* 102a–107b.

30. The process of intellectual maturation is most clearly described in Cicero, *On Ends* 3.16–21; see chap. 7 below.

31. Plutarch, *On Stoic Self-Contradictions* 1037f–38a, *On Moral Virtue* 449a–b; cf. Philo, *On the Migration of Abraham* 137. The term, as well as the doctrine, is of Hellenistic origin; see Inwood (1985, 173–75). I must insert a caution, however, against Inwood's assertion that "an *eupatheia* is simply the impulse of the fully rational man": the *eupatheiai* are indeed *hormai* of the wise, but the wise also generate other impulses which are noneupathic (viz., responses toward indifferents).

32. Cicero, *Tusc. Disp.* 4.12–15. There is something to be said for the suggestion of Sandbach (which Inwood also endorses) that *constantia* here represents an early Stoic term *eustathia* (Sandbach 1989, 67; Inwood 1985, 305–6); it should be noted, however, that *constantia* more often represents *homologia* (as promised in *On Ends* 3.21).

33. Seneca, *Moral Epistles* 59.2; compare Epictetus, *Discourses* 2.1.1–7 on caution. A recent treatment of this question by Cooper (2004) does not, I think, distinguish sufficiently between responses which conceive of their object as good or evil and 'selective' responses, which conceive of their object only as preferred or dispreferred indifferents. See the response by Kamtekar (2004).

34. Cicero, *Tusc. Disp.* 4.12–13. The point is emphasized in Cooper (2005, 178–79).

35. D.L. 7.115; Alexander of Aphrodisias, *On Aristotle's Topics* 2.6.181 [*SVF* 3.434]). Joy is one kind of right action (*katorthōsis*); Plutarch, *On Stoic Self-Contradictions* 1042f.

36. Seneca, *Moral Epistles* 23.4–6.

37. Foucault (1986, 66–67). For notions of self in antiquity, with particular attention to Seneca, see Inwood (2005, 322–52).

38. The fourfold classification is evident in Stobaeus, *Ecl.* 2.7.10b (90W) (quoted above, p. 42); other principal sources include Cicero, *Tusc. Disp.* 3.24–25; D.L. 7.111–14, ps.-Andronicus, *On Emotions* 2–4. But the classification is very widely attested: it is known, for instance, to Varro (apud Servius, *On the Aeneid* 6.733 [*SVF* 3.387]) and to Aspasius (*On the Nicomachean Ethics* 2.2.44 [*SVF* 3.386]). There is one paragraph in the Stobaean account which gives additional emphasis to the prospective / present distinction. It says, "Desire and fear take precedence (*proēgeisthai*), the one being directed at what seems good, the other at what seems bad. Delight and distress follow upon these (*epigignesthai*), delight when we obtain what we desired or escape what we feared, distress when we fail to obtain what we desired or incur what we feared" (*Ecl.* 2.7.10 [88W]). I take the verb *proēgeisthai* to refer to temporal precedence: since desire and fear view their objects as prospective, while distress and delight view their objects as having occurred, the former necessarily precede the latter in time if considered relative to the same object. Thus my fear of getting a parking ticket precedes my distress at having gotten it, assuming both occur. (This interpretation is intimated in Nussbaum 1994, 386.) Brad Inwood understands the passage rather differently. He takes it to mean that the prospective emotions are also 'primary,' while the present emotions are 'subordinate' to them and are directed at "internal psychic reactions to the results of those endeavors," viz., endeavors to obtain or avoid perceived goods or evils (Inwood 1985, 140; see also Inwood 1997, 62–63). This hierarchical understanding of the genera is defensible insofar as it brings out the Stoics' greater emphasis on behavioral expression where the prospective genera are concerned and on feeling-tone where the present genera are concerned; see pp. 29–31 above. To say that the present genera are 'subordinate,' however, would seem to mean that one is distressed at being ticketed *only* if one previously feared this; in other words, it would make desire-satisfaction or desire-frustration the basis of all affective response. In the absence of further evidence, I am reluctant to attribute such a view to the Stoics.

39. A few texts, discussed in the appendix to this volume, bear traces of an alternative classification system in which confidence (*tharros*) was listed as the *eupatheia* corresponding to fear.

40. There is some variety in terms referring to the prospective genera. Words denoting simple futurity are sometimes found: *mellon* in Philo, *futurus* in some of the Latin texts; but most Greek authors choose the description 'expected' (*prosdokōmenon*), and Stobaeus has 'impending' (*epipheresthai*). Cicero gives both *impendens* and *opinatus* as well as *futurus*.

41. The word 'fresh' (*prosphaton*), in the definitions quoted above, also means 'recent.' See note 13 above, and pp. 100–101 below.

42. For instance in *Discourses* 1.15.

43. Diogenes Laertius lists *kēlēsis* (enchantment) with the definition 'delight which charms through the ears'; so also Cicero, who takes it to cover pleasures through any of the five senses.

44. Examples: our text of Diogenes lacks any definition for rancor but defines hatred

as 'inveterate anger, *rancorous and* biding its time for revenge'; Cicero's list lacks a definition for shame which must have appeared in the original; multiple definitions for some items suggest interpolation.

45. Terms and definitions listed in figure 4 are taken from Stobaeus, *Ecl.* 2.7.10b–c (90–92W) with the omission of three items properly considered *nosēmata* (see pp. 138–139 below). Compare D.L. 7.111–14; Cicero, *Tusc. Disp.* 4.16–21. Some Stoic material is found also in the lists by ps.-Andronicus, *On Emotions* 2–5, and Nemesius, *On Human Nature* 19.229–21.235. The definition given here for erotic love is taken from ps.-Andronicus. The Stobaean account includes *erōs* under the definition, 'an effort to form a friendship through an impression of beauty'; this matches the definition of eupathic love in Cicero, *Tusc. Disp.* 4.72; cf. D.L. 7.129 and 7.114, and see further pp. 185–189 below. The definition given for jealousy (*zēlotupia*) is from Diogenes Laertius; the slightly different Stobaean definition fails to distinguish *zēlotupia* from *zēlos*.

46. *Tusc. Disp.* 4.18; cf. Aristotle, *Rhetoric* 2.8–9.

47. On philosophical treatments of pity in antiquity see Nussbaum (2001, 354–400).

48. The terms listed on figure 5 are those reported in D.L. 7.116, with the addition of erotic love (on which see note 45 above. Definitions are found only in the list by ps.-Andronicus (*On Emotions* 6 [*SVF* 3.432]), again with the exception of the *erōs* definition, which appears in multiple sources. I now think that 'eagerness' (*prothumia*) in Plutarch, *On Moral Virtue* 449a, should probably be termed a *propatheia* (cf. Graver 2002a, 138, and see pp. 91–92 below). For the definition of 'good spirits,' see Brennan (1998), 68n17.

49. Bonhöffer (1890, 287), working from passages in Epictetus, interpreted 'cherishing' and 'welcoming' as glad acceptance of one's present circumstances and possessions; he is followed by Inwood (1985, 173), but cf. Voelke (1973, 60): since 'welcoming,' at least, is defined as a subspecies of 'good intent,' it must be closely tied to the well-being of other people, and the same is true of 'goodwill.' There is no reference to fate in the definitions themselves. See further p. 179 below.

50. See above, note 45.

Chapter 3

1. Galen, *PHP* 4.6.43–45.

2. Cicero, *Posterior Academics* 1.38.

3. Despite the accusations of Galen in *PHP* 4.5.1–5, there is certainly no indeterminist assertion. The view is that the chain of causation runs through oneself, not that it is broken. On this topic in Stoicism see especially Bobzien (1998); also Sedley (1993); Gosling (1990 and 1987).

4. Cicero, *On Fate* 41.

5. Formally, a body is a cause to a body of an incorporeal predicate: the knife is a cause to the meat of the predicate 'being cut' (Sextus, *Against the Professors* 9.211). Thus I myself (a body), in my state of believing that p, am the cause to myself (again a body) of my judging p2 (a predicate).

6. Galen, *On Discerning Faults of Mind* 5.58 (*SVF* 3.172); D.L. 7.46; Stobaeus, *Ecl.* 2.7.11m (111W). See Görler (1977).

7. Galen, *PHP* 4.6.5–6; Stobaeus, *Ecl.* 2.7.5b4 (62W), 5l (73–74W); Plutarch, *On Stoic Self-Contradictions* 1034d; D.L. 7.15.

8. Aulus Gellius, *Attic Nights* 7.2.6–7 (LS 62D); the passage also reports the cylinder analogy. It may be noted that the Latin words *voluntarius impetus* and *voluntas* both occur in Gellius's paraphrase; if the argument given in note 12 is correct, these probably represent *prohairetikē hormē* and *prohairesis* in Chrysippus's Greek.

9. Cicero, *Posterior Academics* 1.38.

10. Cicero, *Tusc. Disp.* 3.64, 3.40, 3.83, 4.65, 4.76, 4.79, 4.82, 4.83; Seneca, *On Anger* 1.8, 2.2.2, 2.3.5; Epictetus, fr. 9 (quoted pp. 85–86 below); Origen, *Commentary on Psalms PG* 12, cols. 1141, 1144. Passages in which the two expressions are used together include *Tusc. Disp.* 3.66, 3.80, 4.65, 4.76; Seneca, *On Anger* 2.3.5. Cicero argues the point on behalf of Chrysippus in *Tusc. Disp.* 3.64–71.

11. For the denial see Pohlenz (1948–49, 1: 319–20, 332ff.; Voelke (1973, 142ff.); Inwood (1985, 240–42; 2005, 137); and see further Kahn (1988, 248, 251–55). Dihle (1982, 133–35, 239) is more circumspect. On the history of the term see also Dobbin (1991).

12. Evidence not previously considered in this context is presented in detail in Graver (2003, 355–60). The essential points are as follows:

1. Herculaneum papyrus 1577 / 1579, probably Philodeman in origin, uses both *prohairesis* and *prohairetikos* in a way that strongly suggests they are taken from the vocabulary of the Stoic author under attack.

2. Comparison between Herculaneum papyrus 1577 / 79 and passages in Cicero's *On the Nature of the Gods* makes clear that the phrase *voluntarios motus,* which Cicero attributes at 2.58 to Zeno, corresponds to *prohairetikai kinēseis* in the Stoic source.

3. Origen in *On Matthew* 11.12.21 (PG 13, col. 939, included by von Arnim as *SVF* 3.523) is shown by comparison with fragments quoted by Plutarch to have quoted almost verbatim from Chrysippus's treatise *On the Law.*

4. Origen insists on the prominence of *prohairesis* in Stoic thought also in *Contra Celsum* 4.45. The witness of Origen appears to have been neglected by von Arnim on the assumption that his knowledge of the term derives solely from Epictetus; in view of points 1–3, however, we do well to question von Arnim's historical analysis. Origen's knowledge of Stoic thought is in general excellent; see Chadwick (1947).

13. Stobaeus, *Ecl.* 2.7.10b (90W), quoted in full above, p. 42. Explicit references to the causal role of beliefs are found also in Cicero, *Tusc. Disp.* 3.24–25, and Galen, *PHP* 4.5.1–2.

14. D.L. 7.110; Stobaeus, *Ecl.* 2.7.1 (39W); Cicero, *Tusc. Disp.* 4.11.

15. Stobaeus, *Ecl.* 2.7.2 (44W), 2.7.10 (88W); Cicero, *On Duties* 1.136, *Tusc. Disp.* 4.11.

16. Stobaeus, *Ecl.* 2.7.1 (39W [*SVF* 1.206]).

17. Galen, *PHP* 4.2.8–18, quoting from book 1 of Chrysippus's *On Emotions; PHP* 4.6.24–46, quoting from book 4, is very similar.

18. Thus Seneca insists, in *On Anger* 1.8, that the mind is not "off by itself" when the emotion is going on, watching it from outside; rather, the mind itself "is changed into the emotion." A very similar explanation, later in date but with explicit attribution to "Zeno, Chrysippus, and other Stoics," is found in Plutarch, *On Moral Virtue* 441c–d: "They hold that the emotional [part or power] is not distinguished from the rational by some difference in its nature, but that it is the same part of the mind—I mean that

which they call the intellect or directive faculty. During emotions and [other] changes in accordance with a condition or state (*diathesis*), this directive faculty is turned and changed throughout its whole, becoming vice and virtue. And it has nothing irrational in itself, but is called 'irrational' when it is carried away by the excessiveness of the impulse toward some ill-suited object contrary to reason's choosing. For emotion, they say, is wicked and uncontrolled reason which gains additional vehemence and strength through a bad and erroneous judgment." (The actual source may be Chrysippus's treatise *On Inconsistency*, cited at 450c as the source of quoted material on mental conflict.)

19. Cicero, *Tusc. Disp.* 4.42. Cicero also offers a nautical version of the image, when he speaks of being "carried out to sea where there is no stopping-place," and, just before, makes a comparison to one who "hurls himself off a cliff."

20. Seneca, *On Anger* 1.7; see also *On Anger* 2.35, *Moral Epistles* 116.6.

21. Euripides, *Medea* 1078–79. Chrysippus's use of the example is reported by Galen in *PHP* 3.3.13–22, 4.6.19–23. See Gill (1983 and 1998); Dillon (1997); Price (1995, 2–5, 160–61). As Gill points out, the second line of Medea's statement can also be taken to mean "anger is ruler of my plans." There is however no reason not to assume that Chrysippus understood the passage in the way that posed the greatest challenge to his explanatory resources.

22. Galen, *PHP* 4.6.7–9.

23. Plutarch, *On Moral Virtue* 446f–447a.

24. Galen, *PHP* 3.3.2–3.

25. For Chrysippus's interest in complex mental processes compare Sextus, *Against the Professors* 7.228–31, quoted above, p. 25.

26. Plato, *Republic* 4.435c–443e; compare also *Phaedrus* 246a–56d.

27. On this point see further Price (1995, 154–57); Gill (2005 and 1998).

28. Galen, *PHP* 5.2.49, from Chrysippus, *On Emotions*, book 4: "Therefore the mind, too, will be called beautiful or ugly by analogy, in reference to the proportion or lack of proportion among some such parts. For the mind does have parts, of which its reason and its condition in reason are composed. And the mind is beautiful or ugly insofar as its directive part is in one condition or the other as concerns its own 'limbs.'" Compare Cicero, *Tusc. Disp.* 4.78.

29. Despite all that has been written about the unitary psyche in Stoicism, it should be obvious that the psyche can hardly be *partless*. The capacity for reason is necessarily a capacity for establishing logical relations among multiple elements. How best to describe these elements—whether as successive judgments, as impressions, or as beliefs residing in memory—does not make any great difference to my argument here, as long as it is understood that Chrysippus's present concern is with the way the *hēgemonikon* functions in practical and theoretical reasoning. There is also another Stoic account of psychic parts, in which the interest is in the multiple capacities of the *psychē* as command center of the living organism; for this see p. 22 above.

30. For Alcinous see Dillon (1993); he is not to be identified with Albinus, the teacher of Galen.

31. Plutarch, *On Moral Virtue* 441d, 446e.

32. Galen, *PHP* 3.3.21–23; cf. 5.7.82–87 on the use of literary examples in philosophy.

For Galen's tendency to oversimplify and compartmentalize positions of earlier philosophers see Tieleman (2003, 80–88).

33. Galen, *PHP* 3.3.15, 5.1.17, etc.; Plutarch, *On Moral Virtue* 442cd, 445bc; Alcinous, *Handbook* 17.4 and 23.3–24.4, the latter also quoting the *Medea* passage. See further Dillon (1997 and 1983); Annas (1999, 117–36). Price (1995, 150), followed by Gill (1998, 136–37) argues on the strength of Stobaeus, *Ecl.* 2.7.10a (89–90W) and Galen, *PHP* 4.2.27, 4.5.18, that Chrysippus too may have made use of this image; in that case, he must have understood it in a way compatible with his own view.

34. Plato, *Timaeus* 69c–71d.

35. Alexandrian vivisection had demonstrated such effects as the loss of capacity for speech or movement due to lesions on the brain or severing of particular nerves. Galen performed his own experiments as well; see *PHP* 1.6.6–12, 2.4.42, 3.6.3. For the research at Alexandria see Hankinson (2003, 296–301); Annas (1992, 20–26); von Staden (1989).

36. Galen, *PHP* 6.2–6. My understanding of this material in Galen has benefited from conversations with Matt Megill.

37. The tensions within Plato's view are stressed in Cooper (1999, 118–37); Price (1995, 30–103); Irwin (1995, 203–22).

38. Tears: Galen, *PHP* 4.7.37 (= Posidonius, fr. 165D EK); music 5.6.20–22 (fr. 168 EK); animals 4.7.35 (fr. 158 EK) and 5.6.37–38 (fr. 33 EK); children 5.1.10 (fr. 159 EK).

39. Galen, *PHP* 4.7.4 (fr. 165A EK).

40. Galen, *PHP* 4.7.7–8 (fr. 165A EK). Posidonius's term *proendēmein* is equivalent to the Latin *praemeditatio futurorum malorum* as explained by Cicero; see p. 79 below, with Graver (2002a, 218–19).

41. Galen, *PHP* 5.6.24–26 (fr. 162 EK).

42. It should be noted that even on Galen's account Posidonius speaks not of multiple parts of the psyche but of multiple capacities (*dunameis*) of "a single substance impelled from the heart" (*PHP* 6.2.5). For reinterpretations of Galen's evidence see especially Gill (2005); Tieleman (2003, 198–287); Cooper (1998). More conservative accounts are given by Sorabji (1998 and 2000, 93–132); Inwood (1993); and Price (1995, 175–78).

43. Zajonc (1984); cf. the strong response to Lazarus (1984, 1994) and related work by Solomon (1976) and others in Griffiths (1997, 21–43). Compare also the responses by Solomon (2003a), Nussbaum (2001, 19–88), and Ben-Ze'ev (2000, 541–42).

44. Greenspan (1988); Stocker (1987). Similar points have been urged also by Frijda (1988) and Leighton (1985).

45. In the main I am impressed with Cooper's arguments (1998) concerning Posidonius's philosophical claims and motives. I must issue a caution, however, concerning the phrase *pathētikē kinēsis,* which according to Cooper serves as a "quasi-technical term" for the nonrational psychic energy which for Posidonius underlies emotion but which is yet distinct from the emotion (the *hormē*) itself. *Kinēsis* is standard for any mental event, and the phrase in question is a viable alternative for *pathos* where there is need to emphasize that one means an occurrent *pathos*. An effort to invest it with a new, specialized meaning would have created nothing but confusion. Posidonius could, however, speak without introducing any special term of the 'movement of the emotive capacity' (*kinēsis tou pathētikou*). This latter is in fact the phrase in *PHP* 5.5.21 (fr. 169E EK) and *PHP* 4.7.33 (fr. 165C EK), two of the three passages Cooper cites in support of his read-

ing; in the third, *PHP* 4.7.28 (fr. 165C EK), the phrase *pathētikē kinēsis* is used merely to refer to the *pathos* of grief, and this may also be the meaning in the more ambiguous *PHP* 4.7.37 (fr. 165D EK).

46. See chap. 2, note 13.

47. Cicero, *Tusc. Disp.* 3.74–75.

48. Nussbaum (2001, 80–85).

49. Cicero, *Tusc. Disp.* 3.52, 3.55.

50. Thus Ben-Ze'ev (2000, 541) remarks in connection with this issue that "imagining is itself a propositional attitude."

51. Griffiths (1997, 26), developing the position taken by Zajonc (1984). It will be noted that Zajonc is content to use the word 'emotion' for the shift in a frog's attention occasioned by a change in light patterns, or, in humans, for the recruitment of carbohydrate from the liver (121). There is some justification for speaking in this way (as Griffiths argues), but one loses purchase on the ethical issues.

52. Solomon (2003b, 232).

53. Bobzien (1998, 338–45).

54. Becker (1998, 131–32), in response to the argument of Posidonius reported in Galen, *PHP* 4.5.26–28 (= Posidonius, fr. 164 EK). Posidonius also remarks in this context on the failure of progressors in moral philosophy to respond emotionally to their own moral shortcomings; on this point, see chap. 9 below.

55. D.L. 7.46; Stobaeus, *Ecl.* 2.7.5l (73–74W); Sextus, *Against the Professors* 7.151; see LS 1.256–59. The position taken here is largely consistent with that of Becker (2004, 265–69): Becker does accept what he calls 'running full tilt' as a feature of wise emotion, but he means by this that such emotions may be powerful, not that they may be at variance with self.

Chapter 4

1. Aulus Gellius, *Attic Nights* 19.1. The work cited is the fifth book of *Discourses*, which is not otherwise extant; the passage is standardly listed as Epictetus fragment 9. Quotation marks in the version given here surround terms which Gellius, in his Latin translation, identifies as technical by retaining the Greek term and sometimes by parenthetical remarks, here omitted.

2. Sorabji (2000, 66–69 and passim). Seneca himself does not make any claim to originality on this point (a point noted in Gill 2005, 458), though he does make such claims elsewhere. The case for earlier origin as argued in Abel (1983) has gained acceptance in Rist (1989); LS 2: 417; Inwood (1985, 180).

3. The point is argued more fully in Graver (1999 and 2002b). For the chronology see further Dillon (1996, 139–40); Griffin (1976, 180–81, 398); Hadot (1969, 133); Pohlenz (1948–49, 2: 154).

4. The passages are *On the Soul* 3.9.432b26–433a1 and *On the Movement of Animals* 11.703b4–11; their relation to Stoic thought is pointed out in Nussbaum (1978 ad loc.); again in Nussbaum (1994, 83–85); Price (1995, 163). For the dependence of emotion on belief see also *On the Soul* 427b21–24: "Besides, when we have come to believe that something is terrible or frightening, we immediately have the corresponding emotion, and similarly when we have come to believe that something is such as to inspire

confidence. But in the case of an impression, it is as if we were looking at the terrible or confidence-inspiring objects in a painting."

5. The rendering 'impression,' which I have used here for the sake of consistency, would in some Aristotelian contexts be better replaced with 'imagination' or 'visualization.' More generally on the relation of Aristotelian *phantasia* to Stoic psychology, see Long (1991) (which uses the term 'representation'); Inwood (1985, 9–17).

6. Galen, *PHP* 4.7.16–17. I omit the negative before 'similar,' on grounds of sense and because it is omitted when the sentence is repeated in 4.7.37. Sorabji (2000, 121–22) offers an interpretation based on the inclusion of the negative in both passages.

7. See pp. 67–68 and 78–79 above. The context in Galen indicates that Posidonius criticized Chrysippus's explanation as insufficient. For Posidonius, the issue is whether emotions in general are adequately explained by Chrysippus's cognitivist approach, and cases of involuntary weeping necessarily count as instances of genuine grief (*PHP* 4.7.37 = Posidonius, fr. 165, lines 156–64 EK). But I think it unlikely that Chrysippus would have employed these vague expressions to deal with a question for which he had a more powerful answer to give. Either Posidonius misunderstands Chrysippus's intent, or Galen brings together discussions which were only tangentially related. See further Tieleman (2003, 122–30).

8. Seneca, *On Anger* 1.16.7 (*SVF* 1.215).

9. Plutarch, *On Moral Virtue* 449a. The word 'troublings' is my rendering of *sunthroēseis,* Sorabji's emendation (2000, 40) for the MS *suneorsis.* For the complaint itself, compare the objections of Augustine in *City of God* 9.4.

10. See p. 233n18 above. Chrysippus is mentioned by name at *On Moral Virtue* 449c.

11. Plutarch, *On Desire and Distress* 4–6 (fr. 154 EK). Both the authorship of the fragment and its relation to Posidonius have been much debated; see Kidd (1988, 560–62); Tieleman (2003, 278–83). Even assuming the reliability of fragment 154, there is no particular reason to name Posidonius as the originator of the *propatheia* or unassented-feelings discussion in Stoicism (cf. Cooper 1998, 99; Holler 1934). Several characteristic elements of that doctrine are lacking here, and Posidonius's other attested concerns point in quite a different direction philosophically. For fuller discussion of the point see Graver (1999, 318–22).

12. For defense of this important point see Graver (2002a, 203–223).

13. Cicero, *Tusc. Disp.* 3.82–83.

14. For this rendering of *sua sponte* see *OLD* s.v. *spons* 2.a. There is no need to alter the received text to include a negative (as does L. D. Reynolds in the Oxford text followed by most translators).

15. Seneca, *On Anger* 2.1.4.

16. Although the word 'impulse' (*impetus*) is used loosely here (as also in *Moral Epistles* 113.18) to mean just 'mental event,' it is also Seneca's regular translation for the Stoic *hormē* and is used by him in that more restricted sense in *On Anger* 2.3.4–5 (quoted below). A distinction between simple and complex forms of *hormē* is otherwise unknown, as Inwood notes (1993, 175). It may be, however, that *hormē* was sometimes used by Greek authors for a preliminary stirring of the mind which does not amount to action; so Stevens (2000).

17. The wording of paragraph 2.3.5 may suggest the latter: the feeling is 'that first

agitation of mind which the impression of injury inflicts (*incussit*)' and seems to be distinguished from the impression itself. Even so we should not assume that the impression and the 'agitation' are numerically different events. They may be alternative descriptions of one and the same event, considered in the one case for its propositional content, in the other for its psychophysical phenomenology.

18. Seneca, *On Anger* 2.2.1–2.3.3.

19. Sorabji (2000, 145–50), referring to research by LeDoux (1996, 138–78).

20. Seneca, *On Anger* 2.3.4–5.

21. In this context neither *putauit* nor *voluit* implies any definite mental commitment. That *voluit* cannot here be interpreted to imply assent (e.g., 'has willed') is clear from the opposition Seneca establishes between the first agitation, which merely "wants revenge," and anger itself, which "presses on toward revenge through a voluntary judgment (*voluntate et iudicio*)."

22. It is interesting to compare this case, which for Seneca is clearly not an instance of emotion, with the Odysseus episode cited by Chrysippus in his treatise (see pp. 71–72 above). In that it takes no immediate action, Odysseus's rage would seem to resemble what Seneca calls a 'preliminary agitation.' However, the repeated association made by Galen between Odysseus and Medea suggests that Chrysippus treated both in the same stretch of text, one in which his primary interest was in the appearance of mental conflict in these literary examples. The involuntary feeling as explained by Seneca and others is not an instance of mental conflict as described by Chrysippus.

23. Seneca, *Moral Epistles* 71.29.

24. Seneca, *Cons. Marc.* 7. The *Consolation to Marcia,* an early work, owes a great deal to the consolatory tradition, where the term 'biting' was also used; in this passage, however, the Stoic criterion of assent is also clearly enunciated: *quantum constituit adficitur.* See further Graver (2002a, 190 and 205).

25. Seneca, *Moral Epistles* 99.18–19. The pairing of 'biting' and 'contraction' is found here as well, in 99.14–15.

26. Philo, *Questions on Genesis* 4.73. The significance of the passage was recognized by Pohlenz (1948–49, 2: 154).

27. The redaction is by Eusebius of Emesus; see Petit (1977, 186–87). As Pohlenz realized, the word *propatheia* here belongs to Procopius, not to Philo, and may reflect Procopius's familiarity with intervening authors (Origen or Eusebius). See also Petit (1978, 168). Still, it is not without significance that Procopius, who seems to have Philo's comments before him, immediately refers the explanation we have here to the *propatheia* doctrine.

28. Philo, *Questions on Genesis* 1.79. There is a slight discrepancy between the Greek fragment and the independently surviving Armenian translation. See further Graver (1999, 304–5); Petit (1978, 73).

29. Philo, *Questions on Genesis* 4.15.

30. On joy see Philo, *On the Migration of Abraham* 137; *The Worse Attacks the Better* 138–39; *Questions on Genesis* 4.16, 4.19, 4.101, etc. See Pohlenz (1948–49, 1: 376).

31. Philo, *Questions on Genesis* 2.57.

32. The pedantic "calque" method used by the Armenian translators permits some confidence in reconstructing the wording of the Greek original. In the paraphrase given here I assume that the second occurrence of 'desire' in the list is in error for 'fear,' *phobos* having been corrupted to *pothos* in the text used by the Armenian translator. See Dillon and Terian (1976–77), with Graver (1999, 316–18). The words 'biting and contraction' are Marcus's literal renderings of Armenian words, supplied in a footnote ad loc.

33. The discussion here is based on two similar passages in his commentaries, one on Psalm 4:5 (*PG* 12, cols. 1141, 1144) and one on Ephesians 4:26, where Paul quotes the same verse (fr. 19.68–75 [Gregg 1902, 420]). See also his comment on Ps. 38:4, *PG* 12, col. 1387. The use of the terms 'up to us' (*eph' hēmin*), 'voluntary' (*proairetikos*), and 'involuntary' (*aproaireton*) in this passage should be compared with passages cited in chap. 3, note 12. On Origen's extensive knowledge of Stoic thought see further Chadwick (1947). On the *propatheia* specifically, see Layton (2000); Sorabji (2000, 353–55).

34. For the moral lesson compare Jerome, *Epistles* 79.9 (*PL* 22, col. 731) and his comments on Ezekiel 18: 1–2 (*PL* 25, col. 176) and Matthew 5: 28 (*PL* 26, col. 39). See Pohlenz (1948–49, 2: 154).

35. *PG* 13, cols. 1741–42. Compare Origen, *On Principles* 2.6, where the agony in Gethsemane is mentioned as a difficulty in understanding the theology of the incarnation.

36. See the very helpful account of the controversy in Kramer and Krebber (1972, 157–58); also Layton (2000). Gesché (1962, 148–99) gives a careful review of the material in the Tura papyrus.

37. Didymus, *Commentary on Psalms* (*Tura-Papyrus*) 221.27–222.14 (on Ps. 34:17), 282.2–7 (on Ps. 39.2), 292.33–293.12 (on Ps. 40:5–6); see also 43.16–25 (on Ps. 21:21), *Commentary on Ecclesiastes* (*Tura-Papyrus*) 221.18–22; texts in Gronewald (1969a, 1969b, 1970); Doutreleau, Gesché, and Gronewald (1969); Kramer and Krebber (1972). Origen's argument is used similarly in Jerome, commenting on Matthew 26:37–38 (*PL* 26, col. 205): "What I said earlier about emotion and pre-emotion (*de passione et propassione*) is shown also in the present verse, that the Lord, to show that he had genuinely taken on the human, was indeed saddened, yet, lest emotion hold sway in his mind, began to be saddened by a pre-emotion. For it is one thing to be saddened and another to begin to be saddened. . . . As for those who suspect that Jesus had taken on an irrational soul, let them explain how he was saddened and knew the time period of his sorrow. For although even dumb animals experience sorrow, they do not know the causes nor the time period for which they must grieve." So also Diodorus of Tarsus, commentary on Psalm 54:4, 54:6, *PG* 33, col. 1592, which argues that the *propatheia* demonstrates Christ's underlying capacity for emotion (*enuparchon pathētikon*).

38. Didymus, *Commentary on Ecclesiastes* (*Tura-Papyrus*) 294.8–23 (on. Eccles. 10:3c–10:4b); text in Gronewald (1979). Cf. Origen, *On Principles* 4.4.2–4. Didymus's insistence that the *propatheia* is not itself a sin is in accordance with the view of other writers of the period. Jerome's remark on Matthew 5:28 (*PL* 26, col. 39) that the pre-emotion "has the fault of the beginning" (*culpam initii habet*) means only that it is at fault as being the beginning of sin. Cf. Sorabji (2000, 353).

39. Didymus, *Commentary on Psalms* (*Tura-Papyrus*) 221.27–33 (on Ps. 34:17), 76.8–17 (text in Gronewald 1968), 293.3–6 (on Ps. 40:5–6).

Chapter 5

1. For assent, perhaps better called 'yielding' (*eixis*), in animals, see Nemesius, *On Human Nature* 35.291 (LS 53O); Alexander of Aphrodisias, *On Fate* 13.182 (LS 62G); Plutarch, *On Stoic Self-Contradictions* 1057a; with Inwood (1985, 70–91) and LS 2: 317. For complex animal behavior see Origen, *On Principles* 3.1.2; Sextus, *Against the Professors* 8.270; *Outlines of Pyrrhonism* 1.69. More generally on the distinction between humans and animals, see Lesses (1998); Sorabji (1993); Cole (1993); Labarrière (1993).

2. Sextus, *Against the Professors* 8.275.

3. Galen, *PHP* 3.7.16, 4.5.4, 5.1.10; Cicero, *Tusc. Disp.* 4.31; Seneca, *On Anger* 1.3.6.

4. Aristotle, *Nicomachean Ethics* 7.1 and 7.5. Aristotle's 'brutishness' includes a variety of subrational or postrational states; it may consist in savagery (as of races which habitually practice cannibalism), disease (*nosos*), mental deficiency (*pērōsis*), or insanity (*mania*).

5. It appears already in *Airs, Waters, Places* 10, and with some frequency from the last third of the fifth century, in Hippocratic texts and at some length in the pseudo-Aristotelian *Problems* (30.1). See Padel (1995, 47–64); Paschall (1939); Müri (1953); for the medical texts see Flashar (1966); for the subsequent tradition, Radden (2000). Aristotle also mentions *melancholia* in *Nicomachean Ethics* 7.7 and 7.10 but treats it as a form of incontinence; he has in mind, apparently, a kind of excitable or peevish temperament in rational persons rather than a loss of rationality.

6. Padel (1995, 48); Dover (1968, 201).

7. A recent treatment of this topic by Tieleman (2003, 178–90) fails to make this distinction; it does, however, supply useful detail on some texts which are treated more briefly here.

8. Aetius, *Views of Philosophers* 4.12 (LS 39B); compare D.L. 7.51. The quotations are from Euripides, *Orestes* 255–59.

9. Sextus, *Against the Professors* 7.243–49.

10. I am not convinced by the arguments of Pigeaud (1987, 102–6) for a Stoic distinction between 'empty' and 'mis-struck' (*paratupōtikas*) impressions. That *phantasma* denotes something less than the object of rational impression is attested also in Aetius, *Views of Philosophers* 4.11.5, where it is the minimal term for mental experience generally including that of nonrational animals, while that of rational animals requires some further qualification. But this is a point on which we should not expect any very great precision.

11. Related witnesses include Cicero, *Prior Academics* 2.51–52, 2.89–91; Plutarch, *Against Colotes* 1123b; Sextus, *Against the Professors* 7.249 (where Bury suspects that Heracles is confused with Pentheus; cf. 7.192). For Alcmaeon (or Alcmeon) see Radt (1971–2004, 4.149–50); Nauck (1964, 379–80); his story is very similar to that of Orestes. Compare also the passing remark by Epictetus at *Discourses* 1.28.33, characterizing the insane (*manikoi*) as 'those who follow every impression that occurs to them.'

12. Plutarch, *On Desire and Distress* 4–6 = Posidonius, fr. 154 EK; see also p. 92 above.

13. D.L. 7.158.

14. Stobaeus, *Ecl.* 3.18.24 (519W [*SVF* 3.713]), citing Chrysippus.

15. D.L. 7.127.

16. Alexander of Aphrodisias, *On the Soul* 2.161 (*SVF* 3.239). Alexander's tone is polemical, and his interpretation of the Stoic view perhaps deliberately distorted. He insists on taking their view to be that one can be virtuous and melancholically insane at the same time, a position which is, as he says, ridiculous: "For how can they possibly say that one who is out of his wits and needs for that reason to be tied up and to have the assistance of friends is acting sensibly at that time?" The misinterpretation does not, however, impair the reliability of the report itself, which is otherwise congruent with that of Simplicius below.

17. Simplicius, *On Aristotle's Categories* 10.402 (*SVF* 3.238). The 'middle condition' is that of a young child who is neither wise nor foolish; so Philo, *Allegory on Laws* 1.93 (*SVF* 3.519).

18. D.L. 7.118.

19. See above, note 16.

20. Quoted by Eusebius, *Evangelical Preparation* 6.264b (*SVF* 3.668).

21. In this the Stoics speak quite differently from Plato in *Timaeus* 86b–d, which medicalizes all forms of suboptimal behavior without distinction. Cf. Tieleman (2003, 187–90).

22. Cicero, *Paradoxes of the Stoics*, pref. 4; Seneca, *Moral Epistles* 87.1.

23. D.L. 7.124.

24. It is 'knowledge of what things are to be done or not to be done or neither'; Stobaeus, *Ecl.* 2.7.5b1 (59W), 5b5 (63W).

25. For instance, the area in which courage is applicable is the endurance of that which it is right to endure; courage is defined as 'knowledge as concerns things to be endured' (D.L. 7.126; Stobaeus, *Ecl.* 2.7.5b5, 2.7.5c, 2.7.11k (63, 69, 106 W).

26. Stobaeus, *Ecl.* 2.7.5b13 (68W).

27. Stobaeus, *Ecl.* 2.7.10 (88W).

28. *To eukinēton tou pathētikou;* Stobaeus, *Ecl.* 2.7.1 (39W). The expression 'by chance' (*eikēi*) was used by Chrysippus (Galen, *PHP* 4.5.6); compare Sextus, *Against the Professors* 7.243–47 above. The 'flutter' terminology is in the modern literature frequently referred to the discussion in Plutarch, *On Moral Virtue* 441c–d, of oscillation between opposing points of view; so, for instance, LS 1: 422. However, the term itself does not appear in that passage, and as oscillation is not always at issue, I am inclined to think that the word is chosen merely to suggest lightness or volatility.

29. Galen, *PHP* 4.6.24–34, quoting from Chrysippus, *On Emotions*, book 4. 'Beside oneself' is *exestēkōs;* 'in an altered state' *parēllachōs;* 'not oneself' *ou par' heautōi.*

30. Galen, *PHP* 4.7.26–27; Origen, *Against Celsus* 8.51; see Graver (2002a, 123).

31. Cicero, *Tusc. Disp.* 4.54.

32. Athenaeus, *Dinner-Sophists* 11.464d (*SVF* 3.667), quoting from Chrysippus's treatise *On Goods and Evils.*

33. Cicero, *Tusc. Disp.* 3.11; see also Graver (2002a, 80–85).

34. D.L. 7.118.

35. Cicero, *Tusc. Disp.* 3.11. Athamas, according to Apollodorus 1.9.2, 3.4.3, pursued and killed his elder son Learchus, believing him to be a stag.

36. Epicurus's statement is reported by Seneca, *Moral Epistles* 18.14. For examples

from Roman poetry see Gill (1997); also the tag from Ennius which makes anger the 'beginning of insanity' (Cicero, *Tusc. Disp.* 4.52). Gill, who argues for Stoic influence in the Roman authors, emphasizes that this etiology is not typically present in Greek tragedy, where madness is regularly god-induced; see further Padel (1994) with Gill (1996). I suggest, on the contrary, that the pattern is potentially present, in that Ajax and Orestes (at least) are represented as undergoing unusually strong passions prior to their insanity, but that Greek tragedy, through the mechanism of divine intervention, excuses the agent of responsibility for his or her condition in a way that the Stoic-influenced poetry of Seneca and Vergil does not allow.

37. Seneca, *On Anger* 2.5.

38. Compare *On Anger* 1.3.3, where Seneca insists, distancing himself from Aristotle, that predatory animals (*ferae*) are not capable of anger.

39. Seneca, *On Anger* 2.5.3. *On Anger* 1.1.3–7 describes the angry expression in detail and observes that every emotion type has a characteristic expression. Seneca's comparison of facial expressions seems especially telling in light of Ekman's work (1982) on the reliability of expressions as indicators of internal states.

40. Seneca, *On Anger* 1.5.2, 1.20.3, etc.

41. Seneca, *On Clemency* 2.4.1–3. (I have not been convinced by the arguments given in Malaspina 2001, 391, for emending the text.) Immediately after the quotation there is another mention of Phalaris, this time as an instance of cruelty in the other sense of the word. Such flexible use of exempla is not uncommon in Seneca's writing; it need not affect my argument here, since there is clear indication of equivalence between *feritas* and the insane type of cruelty.

42. The animalistic conception of cruelty is clearly expressed in Seneca, *On Clemency* 1.25: "Cruelty is an evil which is scarcely human, unworthy of so gentle a spirit. That is the raging of a beast (*ferina rabies*): to rejoice in blood and wounds, to cast off the human being and pass into an animal of the forest." Further examples of usage include Columella, *On Agriculture* 7.12.5; Vergil, *Aeneid* 3.616; and others cited by *OLD* s.v. *crudelis, crudelitas, crudeliter.*

43. Seneca, *Moral Epistles* 83.25–26: "A devotion to drink generally does bring cruelty in its train, for one's soundness of mind then becomes flawed and uneven. Just as long illness causes people to become peevish and difficult and easily offended, so continual drunkenness causes the mind to become brutish. For since they are frequently not themselves, the habit of insanity becomes hardened, and faults acquired under the influence of wine thrive even without it." For Seneca as for other Stoics, drunkenness is itself comparable to insanity; see for instance *On Anger* 1.13.3, *Moral Epistles* 59.15. But Antony was not merely drunk but brutalized by continual drunkenness.

44. Antisocial personality disorder is the term used in the fourth edition of the *Diagnostic and Statistical Manual* (American Psychiatric Association, 1994). For fuller description and examples see Hare (1999).

45. Greenspan (2003, 420).

46. There is a good discussion in Greenspan (2003), with references to additional literature.

47. Seneca, *On Anger* 2.3, quoted p. 97 above.

48. Galen, *PHP* 4.2.16, 4.6.35.

49. Sorabji (2000, 61–63). Older readings include Holler (1934) and Fillion-Lahille (1984, 163–64); countered by Inwood (1993, 153–56). Donini (1995, 206–9) complains that Seneca's view is in Chrysippan terms an 'absurdity.'

50. The view called by Cicero 'Peripatetic'; it is not quite the position Aristotle takes in the *Nicomachean Ethics*. See Graver (2002a, 163–64).

51. Seneca, *On Anger* 1.12. For *eklogē* or 'selection' see p. oo above. It should be remembered that this action on the part of the virtuous person might also have eupathic motivation. The interpretation of the second movement as *eklogē* was suggested to me in a personal communication from Robert Kaster.

52. This is the view of Inwood, in Inwood (1993, 180–81) and personal communications.

53. Seneca, *On Anger* 2.1.4.

54. Seneca, *On Anger* 2.1.3 ('with the mind's approval'), 2.2.2 and 2.3.5 ('volitional'), 2.3.5 ('through judgment').

55. The examples are from Seneca's own usage in *Constancy of the Wise* 12.3; *On Anger* 2.26, 3.34; *On Clemency* 1.16.4 (all concerning animals); *Natural Questions* 3.30.6 (flood waters); *Moral Epistles* 119.2–3 (hunger).

56. For its application to human emotion see Seneca, *On Anger* 1.1.2; *Consolation to Marcia* 8.1; *Consolation to Helvia* 16–17.

57. Taking the verb together with its cognate adjective *efferus* I count at least seventeen occurrences: in the prose works, *On Clemency* 1.13; *Moral Epistles* 83.26 (quoted above, note 43), 88.7, 99.17, 121.4; in the tragedies *Troades* 51; *Hercules* 397; *Medea* 45, 385, 395; *Phaedra* 116, 923, 1221, 1246; *Oedipus* 626; *Phoenissae* 206, 264. Of special interest among these are *Moral Epistles* 83.26, on the brutalizing effects of alcohol, and *Moral Epistles* 99.17, in which a person who faces bereavement courageously is called *efferatus*, i.e., inhuman, by the foolish populace. One passage, *Moral Epistles* 121.4, speaks loosely of our 'most wild emotions' (*adfectus efferatissimos*) as an instance of vice.

58. Another possibility that should be considered is that *efferantur* should be emended by a single letter to read *efferentur*, so that the text reads, in English, "how the emotions begin, how they grow, and how they become brutish." The thought would then have been expressed somewhat more cleanly; the play on words would still be present.

59. Seneca's treatment of *feritas* is similar to Aristotle's treatment of *thēriotēs*, especially in its emphasis on pleasure and also in its mention of Phalaris and the sanguinary vigor of its examples. Nonetheless we should be hesitant to conclude (with Bäumer 1982) that Aristotle's work has influenced him directly. Seneca's knowledge of the *Nicomachean Ethics* does not otherwise extend to details of specific passages. He does mention Aristotle by name in *On Anger*, but the evidence is consistent with his knowing the *Ethics* merely by reputation. (See further Setaioli 1988, 141–50; Laurenti 1979.) A likelier explanation for the resemblance is that an account of *thēriotēs* was by the time of Aristotle a commonplace of Greek thought, available to be developed by different philosophers in ways which suited their differing views in moral psychology. Plato in *Republic* 9 connects the bestial potentialities of human beings with tyrants and with the desiderative part of the psyche. Aristotle, too, takes the topic in his own direction, with a more elaborate treatment of etiology and of the accountability question than appears

in any other ancient source. Theophrastus is known to have linked both brutishness and cruelty (*ōmotēs*) with anger in his treatise *On Emotions,* in a passage dealing with differences of degree (Simplicius, *On Aristotle's Categories* 8.235).

Chapter 6

1. *Iliad* 4.1–36 (paraphrased). The lines about Hera's anger were cited by Chrysippus (*apud* Galen, *PHP* 3.2.11), to illustrate the centralization of psychic function in the heart region.

2. See for instance Jacobs (2001); Sabini and Silver (1998); Moody-Adams (1993); Wolf (1990).

3. Seneca, *On Benefits* 4.27.2 (Seneca concedes the point to his interlocutor).

4. Panaetius is Cicero's source in *On Duties* 1.107–14; see Gill (1990a and 1988).

5. See for instance the definitions of knowledge recorded in Stobaeus, *Ecl.* 2.7.5l (73–74W). I am not saying anything here about what standard of coherence was thought to apply; this issue may or may not have been worked out in the early Stoa.

6. Cicero, *On Ends* 3.48; Plutarch, *On Common Conceptions* 1063a–b.

7. Simplicius, *On Aristotle's Categories* 8.237–238 (LS 47S).

8. The usage is explained in Long (1983).

9. Stobaeus, *Ecl.* 2.7.5f (70–71W); cf. D.L. 7.98.

10. It may be that there are other mere *hexeis* as well: the lists in Stobaeus typically give only representatives of a class. Other possibilities include the lesser or mere faults mentioned in Cicero, *Tusc. Disp.* 4.29–30, and also perhaps the nonintellectual vices in Stobaeus, *Ecl.* 2.7.5b (59W); the latter are analogous to the nonintellectual virtues in *Ecl.* 2.7.5b4 (62W); D.L. 7.90–91; Cicero, *Tusc. Disp.* 4.30.

11. Cicero, *Tusc. Disp.* 4.23–26. The *Tusculans* passage is the earlier report but is somewhat awkward to use, in that Cicero, who thinks the Greek account is overdeveloped, chooses to condense it by conflating the terms he uses to translate *nosēma* and *arrōstēma*. See Graver (2002a, 148–63); Brennan (1998, 39–44).

12. Stobaeus, *Ecl.* 2.7.10e (93W); similarly Seneca, *Moral Epistles* 75.10–12.

13. A general love of humanity (*philanthrōpia*) is however a virtue; see pp. 175–177 below.

14. See p. 48 above.

15. Stobaeus, *Ecl.* 2.7.10e (93W).

16. Cicero, *Tusc. Disp.* 4.28; D.L. 7.115. *Rhōmē* in Stobaeus, *Ecl.* 2.7.5b (58W) is one of the 'virtues which are not types of knowledge,' for which see also Cicero, *Tusc. Disp.* 4.31.

17. See for instance Stobaeus, *Ecl.* 2.7.11m (111–12W); Plutarch, *On Stoic Self-Contradictions* 1057b, with Görler (1977).

18. D.L. 7.111; see p. 39 above. For stubbornness (*akolasia*), compare L. *pervicacia*, labeled a *nosēma* by Cicero at *Tusc. Disp.* 4.26.

19. Galen, *PHP* 5.2.22–24, 5.2.26–27.

20. Cicero, *Tusc. Disp.* 3.7, 3.23; *Posterior Academics* 1.38. For the criticism see Inwood (1985, 126–27); Dougan and Henry (1934 ad loc.); Annas (1992, 104).

21. Stobaeus, *Ecl.* 2.7.10b, 2.7.10c (91W); ps.-Andronicus, *On Emotions* 4 (the misplaced

terms are *philēdonia, philochrēmatia, philotimia, philozōia, philosōmatia, gastrimargia, oinophlugia,* and *lagneia*).

22. Stobaeus, *Ecl.* 2.7.10e (93W). The Stoic author now gives *euemptōsia* as the main term for proclivity using *eukataphoria* (proneness), an obvious synonym, in explanation.

23. Cicero also speaks in *Tusc. Disp.* 4.28 of proclivities to good things, which he terms *facultates.* Without confirmatory evidence I am reluctant to proceed very far in interpretation; tentatively, however, I suggest that while all virtuous people are courageous, some may be especially likely to do brave actions, or that while all virtuous people are susceptible to the *eupatheiai,* one individual wise person might be especially prone to a particular feeling such as joy or reverence.

24. Terms in figure 8 are collated from the following sources: D.L. 7.115 (and cf. *philarguria* and *methē* in 7.111); Stobaeus, *Ecl.* 2.7.10e (93W); Cicero, *Tusc. Disp.* 4.25–26; Plutarch, *On Stoic Self-Contradictions* 1050d; Athenaeus, *Dinner-Sophists* 11.464d (*SVF* 3.667); Chrysippus in Galen, *PHP* 4.5.21–22. For a more detailed list see Graver (2002a, 150–51).

25. Cicero, *Tusc. Disp.* 4.27–28; Galen, *PHP* 5.2.3. (Cicero does not appear to be familiar with Posidonius's treatise; see Graver 2002a, 203–23.)

26. Galen, *PHP* 5.2.2–7 = Posidonius, fr. 163 EK, lines 1–30. The passage as a whole is as follows, beginning with a paraphrase by Galen: "They [Chrysippus and Posidonius] do not give the same explanation concerning what kind of mind inferior persons have during emotions and prior to emotions. For Chrysippus says that it is analogous to bodies which have a tendency to incur fevers or diarrhea or things like that upon a slight and chance pretext. Posidonius criticizes this comparison: he says that the mind of the inferior person should be compared not to such bodies but simply to healthy bodies. For whether they become feverish for large or small causes does not make any difference as concerns their experiencing this, that is, having the *pathos,* at all; rather, they differ only in that some are more prone and others less. For this reason he says that Chrysippus is improperly comparing the health of the mind to that of the body, and the sickness [of the mind] to the condition which falls easily into sickness. For there is a mind which is free of emotions (*pathē*)—that of the sage, obviously—but no body is free of illnesses (*pathē*). It would have been more just to compare the minds of inferior persons 'either to bodily health, which includes a proneness to sickness' (for that is the term Posidonius uses) 'or to sickness itself,' since it is a condition which can only be either disease-ridden or actually diseased. In fact, this is what he says: 'For this reason, also, sickness of mind does not, as Chrysippus thinks, resemble a disease-ridden condition of body through which it is subject to incur irregular nonperiodic fevers; rather, mental "sickness" resembles either bodily health, which includes a proclivity to sickness, or the sickness itself. For bodily illness is a condition already diseased, but the sickness Chrysippus is talking about is more like a proclivity to fevers.'" Note that in this discussion a 'sickness' (*nosos*) is an observable symptom such as fever and is thus analogous to an actual episode of emotion. Hence it cannot be the same as the *nosos* or *nosēma* which is a trait of character. However, a reader who failed to understand this might easily assume that a *euemptōsia* is actually a tendency to acquire a *nosēma* or *arrōstēma* in the technical sense. It may be for this reason that Cicero indicates, in *Tusc. Disp.* 4.28, that a proclivity is properly understood as 'a proclivity to become infirm (*aegrotare*).'

27. Galen, *PHP* 5.2.7 = Posidonius, fr. 163 EK, lines 28–30.

28. Stobaeus, *Ecl.* 2.7.5b11 (67W); similarly 2.7.5k (73W). I here adopt the translation 'habitudes' as being somewhat closer to the Greek term than 'specialties,' my rendering in Graver (2002a). Suggestions by other scholars include 'practices' and 'pursuits.' See LS 1.161–62.

29. As Stobaeus notes, literary study and the management of horses and dogs were 'encyclical skills,' curricular standards in the upbringing of a Greek male of sufficient income.

30. Sextus, *Against the Professors* 7.227, 11.182. On the distinction between skills and forms of knowledge see especially Menn (1995).

31. The cardinal virtues are both skills and forms of knowledge; Stobaeus *Ecl.* 2.7.5b (58W). This applies also to the more specific virtues such as perseverance and kindness in Stobaeus, *Ecl.* 2.7.5b2 (61W). There is also a class of 'nonintellectual' virtues, on which see Graver (2002a, 155–56).

32. The point was argued convincingly by Kerferd (1978).

33. Stobaeus, *Ecl.* 2.7.6d (77W).

Chapter 7

1. Cleanthes, *Hymn to Zeus* 23–29 (LS 54I).

2. Plato, *Republic* 6.492a–493d.

3. D.L. 10.6.

4. Reported in Cicero, *On Fate* 7–9; see p. 170 below.

5. Cicero, *On Ends* 3.16–21; cf. D.L. 7.85; Seneca, *Moral Epistles* 121 and 120; Hierocles, *Elements of Ethics* 1.34–39, 1.51–57 (LS 57C). Plutarch in *On Stoic Self-Contradictions* 1038b indicates that the topic was treated in multiple works by Chrysippus. See further Pembroke (1971); LS 1: 351–52; Long (1993); Striker (1991); Engberg-Pedersen (1990); Brunschwig (1986).

6. Nourishment and places of refuge are specified in the parallel text, Cicero, *On Duties* 1.11, with reference to animals generally.

7. The development of our conception of the good is treated in more detail in Striker (1991); Inwood (2005, 271–301); Frede (1999); Pohlenz (1940, 82–99).

8. Scott (1995, 159–86, 201–10).

9. Aetius, *Views of Philosophers* 4.11 (LS 39E); Sextus, *Against the Professors* 8.56–59.

10. The comparison originates with Descartes; see Scott (1995, 205 and 92).

11. Stobaeus, *Ecl.* 2.7.5b8 (LS 61L): "According to Cleanthes all people have from nature starting points toward virtue. They are like half-lines of poetry, as it were: worthless when incomplete, but worthwhile [or righteous, *spoudaioi*] when completed."

12. Stobaeus, *Ecl.* 2.7.5b3 (62W). A recent article by Jackson-McCabe (2005) convinces me that the *aphormai* are either identical with or closely allied with the 'implanted preconception' (*emphutoi prolēpseis*) in Plutarch, *On Stoic Self-Contradictions* 1041e. The implanted preconceptions, also called 'natural concepts,' are a species of concept (*ennoia*) which differs from other concepts in that they are formed 'naturally' rather than by mental operations based on sense experience. These play an important role in the formation of our concepts of the good and the just.

13. Cicero, *On Duties* 1.11–17 (on the innate tendency toward sociability see further pp. 175–176 below). Striker (1991, 253) argues that this passage of Cicero is "peculiar" both in that it lists innate tendencies to correspond to all four of the cardinal virtues and in that it replaces courage and temperance with magnanimity and propriety. But Stobaeus, too, lists four innate tendencies, in the passage quoted above. Neither can any sharp distinction be drawn between courage and magnanimity (cf. *Tusc. Disp.* 3.15, with Graver 2002a ad loc.) or between propriety (*moderatio = to prepon*) and temperance (*moderatio = sōphrosynē*). So Panaetius (assuming he is the immediate source) is at least not seriously at odds with what we can otherwise determine about early Stoic thought on this issue.

14. Thus I am dissatisfied with the suggestion of Scott (1995, 186) that the reason the Stoics did not consider perverted assent to undermine the reliability of *all* the common notions was simply that they assumed it to be relatively uncommon. My understanding is that perversion affects the formation of some kinds of belief and leaves others to develop properly. Very few people are confused about the proper application of the concept 'horse'; the concept 'good,' though, is misapplied with disconcerting regularity.

15. The problem is recognized by Striker (1991, 253) as a major difficulty within Stoic ethics. "[T]he optimistic assumption that our natural instincts are all for the good makes it hard, if not impossible, for the Stoics to explain why most people in fact turn out to be bad rather than virtuous."

16. D.L. 7.89.

17. It is made quite clear in Galen, *PHP* 5.4.5–17 that the Chrysippan work being criticized is indeed *On Emotions*.

18. Galen, *PHP* 5.5.14.

19. Galen, *PHP* 5.5.14–15, 5.5.19–20; cf. 5.5.21 (= Posidonius, fr. 169E EK).

20. It should be noted that that although Cicero shows knowledge of the twofold cause (as will be argued below), he never offers a clear Latin equivalent either for that phrase or for *katēchēsis*. These omissions are important because they guarantee the independence of the Calcidian report: since the latter has both the key terminology as we know it from Galen and the other details as we know them from Cicero, it is difficult not to conclude that the account as a whole is pre-Ciceronian in origin. Seneca, too, appears to have some knowledge of this Stoic doctrine, given the way he explains human error in the *Moral Epistles*, especially 94.53–54, 115.8–14, 118.7–11. In his case, though, it is possible that the knowledge is derived from Cicero.

21. Among earlier commentaries on the *Timaeus* were some written by authors familiar with Stoic thought: Crantor, Posidonius, Calvenus Taurus, and Galen. But the surviving evidence is meager; see Reydams-Schils (1999, 207–10); Sedley (1997). I differ from Reydams-Schils on the role of Posidonius in the transmission: Chrysippus's own treatise was still widely available for consultation in at least the second century C.E., whereas that of Posidonius was little known; see note 42 in chap. 3. The value of the Calcidius material for understanding Chrysippus's view is urged also in Tieleman (2003, 133–38, 161–62).

22. Calcidius, *On the Timaeus of Plato* 165–66 (*SVF* 3.229); text in Waszink (1962).

23. D.L. 7.86.

24. Stobaeus, *Ecl.* 2.7.7e (83W), 2.7.5l (73W), 2.7.11i (103W). The standard Stoic defini-

tion for *timē*, given in Stobaeus, *Ecl.* 2.7.11i (103W) and in Alexander of Aphrodisias, *On Fate* 35.207 (*SVF* 2.1003), connects it with virtue as Calcidius does: *timē* is 'evaluation as worthy of reward,' with 'reward' being 'the prize for virtue that does good works.'

25. D.L. 7.175.

26. On the sources of *On Laws* 1 see Dyck (2004, 49–52); Zetzel (1999); Ferrary (1995, 67–68). For unacknowledged Stoic influence, compare Cicero's definitions of law at 1.18 and 1.33 with the Chrysippan definitions quoted in Marcian, *Institutions* 1 (*SVF* 3.314). On *Tusculan Disputations* 3 see Graver (2002a, 195–214).

27. For the broader issues see Schofield (1995); Mitsis (1994); Striker (1987 and 1996).

28. Cicero, *On Laws* 1.27: "Now, since it is god who has begotten and adorned the human being, wishing humans to take precedence over all other things, let it now be clearly understood (without exhaustive discussion) that human nature goes on its own beyond that point, and, even without instruction, starting from those things whose kinds it has conceived through its initial and inchoate intelligence, consolidates and per-fects its rationality all by itself." Concept formation is indicated in the phrase "whose kinds it has conceived" (*genera cognovit);* the "initial and inchoate intelligence" precedes and promotes this. Consequently the *intelligentiae* are not themselves concepts formed through experience. It seems to me most natural to take them as equivalent to the *aphormai* treated above. They might, however, be equivalent to the Stoic 'preconcep-tions' (*prolēpseis*), depending on how that term is interpreted; see note 12 above.

29. Cicero, *On Laws* 1.29, reading *vanitas* with the MS; see Dyck (2004, 146).

30. Cicero, *On Laws* 1.33. On the metaphoric implications of 'sparks' and 'seeds' see Graver (2002a, 77); compare 'seeds' in Seneca, *Moral Epistles* 120.4, and the further refer-ences in Dyck (2004, 156–57).

31. Cicero, *On Laws* 1.31–32.

32. The second phrase is in the restatement at *On Laws* 1.47.

33. The translation given here (making *dolor* the subject of *sequi*) is more in ac-cordance with Latin idiom than the rendering preferred by Zetzel and others, making *interitus* (destruction(s)) the subject and inferring *eum* (i.e., pain) as object.

34. Cicero, *Tusc. Disp.* 3.2. For a more detailed explication of the passage see Graver (2002a, 74–78, 206–7).

35. Cicero, *Tusc. Disp.* 3.3.

36. For the personal and political significance of honor and glory in Cicero see especially Long (1995), and compare *On Ends* 2.48–49; *Tusc. Disp.* 1.109–10, 2.63–64; *On Duties* 1.65.

37. Cicero, *Tusc. Disp.* 3.3–4.

38. Despite *On Ends* 3.24, the term 'right actions' (*recte facta*) need not refer in this context to the Stoic *katorthōmata*. The right actions here are performed by ordinary persons on the basis of judgments which are the same in content as the wise person would make. Thus in Stoic terms they are simply 'appropriate actions' (*kathēkonta*).

39. Compare Cicero, *Tusc. Disp.* 1.109: "although glory is not pursued for any intrin-sic reason, still it follows virtue like a shadow."

40. Plato, *Republic* 7.514a1.

41. Stobaeus, *Ecl.* 2.7.10e (93.8–14W); see p. 139 above.

42. Cicero, *Tusc. Disp.* 4.24–25, with minor omissions for the sake of conciseness. Compare Seneca, *Moral Epistles* 75.12: "The emotions . . . when they occur frequently and do not receive any treatment, cause the sickness, just as a single cold in the head, if it is not protracted, brings on nothing more than a cough, but if it happens repeatedly for a long time, it brings on the wasting disease."

43. Epictetus, *Discourses* 2.18.8–10. Epictetus states the rule in the preceding paragraph: "It necessarily happens that from activities the corresponding *hexeis* and capacities either come into being (if they were not in existence before) or are intensified and made strong."

44. So Cicero, in *Tusc. Disp.* 4.24; Stobaeus, *Ecl.* 2.7.110 (113W). But the evidence is contradictory on this point. Cicero in *Tusc. Disp.* 4.32 implies that the *nosēmata* can indeed be removed, albeit with difficulty. Seneca in *Moral Epistles* 75.8–13 is familiar with a Stoic doctrine that makes these conditions *perpetua mala* of the psyche, but at the same time reports that they will be removed in the course of moral progress. As the *nosēmata* are scalar conditions, it would have been reasonable for Stoic theorists to hold that in some advanced cases removal is beyond the limits of practicality and yet insist that it remains theoretically possible in all cases except those of brutish insanity.

45. Bobzien (1998, 19–21); her rendering of the term *sunektikon* is 'cohesive,' rather than 'sustaining,' which I have used here. See also Plutarch, *On Stoic Self-Contradictions* 1053f, with LS 1: 340–42.

46. Bobzien (1998, 303).

47. I.e., disposed in a certain way (*pōs echōn)*; see Simplicius, *On Aristotle's Categories* 4, 66–67, 7.166 (LS 27F, 29B), with LS 1: 177–79. Emotions are specifically cited as *pōs echonta* in Alexander of Aphrodisias, *On the Soul* 2.118 (LS 29A).

48. A comparable case of a body's causing an effect in itself may be seen in Stobaeus, *Ecl.* 1.13.1c (138W [LS 55A]), where a person's possessing prudence counts as the cause of his being prudent (i.e., of his behaving prudently).

49. Bobzien (1998, 290–91).

50. Plutarch, *On Stoic Self-Contradictions* 1050c–e (LS 54T).

51. The point is emphasized in Brennan (2005, 242–69) and Brennan (2001).

52. Nemesius, *On Human Nature* 2.77; Plutarch, *On Stoic Self-Contradictions* 1053d; Bobzien (1998, 292).

53. D.L. 7.158–59. In the reproductive theory of Zeno and Sphaerus the genetic material comes only from the father (D.L. 7.159; Aetius, *Views of Philosophers* 5.4 [*SVF* 1.129]). Why children resemble their mothers is apparently left unexplained.

54. Cicero, *On Fate* 7–9. For detailed treatment of the passage see Bobzien (1998, 296–301); Sedley (1993).

55. As Epictetus likes to point out, in *Discourses* 1.1 and often thereafter.

56. Cicero, *On Fate* 10; compare *Tusc. Disp.* 4.80–81; Alexander of Aphrodisias, *On Fate* 6.171; and see Graver (2002a, 182–84).

57. D.L. 7.173, and see Tsouna (1998); Schofield (1991, 115–18).

Chapter 8

1. Seneca, *Moral Epistles* 118.15–16 (with omissions). For the analogy see also D.L. 7.90–91, following Hecaton of Rhodes.

2. Chrysippus and his predecessors: Plutarch, *On Stoic Self-Contradictions* 1048e. Rarity of the wise: Sextus, *Against the Professors* 9.133; Eusebius, *Evangelical Preparation* 6.264b (*SVF* 3.668); Seneca, *Moral Epistles* 42.1; Alexander of Aphrodisias, *On Fate* 28.199 (LS 61N).

3. Points of similarity between the Stoic material treated here and Aristotle's treatment of friendship in *Nicomachean Ethics* 8–9 include the innate disposition toward other-concern (8.1), the emphasis on similarity (8.1) and mutual awareness (8.2, 8.5), and also the rarity of the wise (8.3). I am inclined to view these resemblances as indications of a shared philosophical heritage rather than of direct influence. For a detailed treatment of the broader philosophical and cultural context see Konstan (1997).

4. See above, p. 153. On the topic see Wright (1995); Blundell (1990); Inwood (1983); Pembroke (1971).

5. Plutarch, *On Stoic Self-Contradictions* 1038b, mentioning in particular the treatise *On Justice.*

6. Cicero, *On Ends* 3.62. Compare especially D.L. 7.85, quoting Chrysippus's own *On Ends* on the orientation to self.

7. Hierocles, *Elements of Ethics*, col. 9: "The <orientation> toward oneself is 'well-intentioned' (*eunoētikē*): that toward one's kindred is 'devoted' (*sterktikē*). . . . For . . . is called . . . by many . . . , and that toward external possessions 'acquisitive' (*hairetikē*). Just as in this regard we are oriented in a devoted way toward our children, and in an acquisitive way toward external possessions, so also the animal is also . . . toward itself, and in a selective way (*eklektikōs*) toward the things which supply the requirements of its system." For the text see Bastianini and Long (1992), together with Long (1993). The condition of the papyrus being very poor, it remains unclear whether Hierocles is speaking of three or four kinds of orientation, and whether, if there are four, he intends them to correspond to the four cardinal virtues as they do in Stobaeus and Cicero's *On Duties*. However the point about devotion to kindred is not in doubt.

8. Stobaeus, *Ecl.* 2.7.11m (109W); similarly Cicero, *On Ends* 3.68; Seneca, *Moral Epistles* 9.18; D.L. 7.123; Epictetus, *Discourses* 1.23.

9. Hierocles, *Elements of Ethics*, col. 11 (LS 57D).

10. Cicero, *On Ends* 3.63.

11. Like the ordinary Greek *polis*, the cosmos is 'a number of persons dwelling in one place governed by law' (Dio Chrysostom 36.20 [LS 67J]); compare Seneca, *On Leisure* 4.1 (LS 67K); Epictetus, *Discourses* 2.10; with Schofield (1991, 57–92).

12. Cicero, *On Ends* 3.62.

13. Hierocles *apud* Stobaeus, *Ecl.* 4.27.23 (672W [LS 67G]).

14. D.L. 7.120, 7.33, quoting Zeno's *Republic.*

15. The example is that of Epictetus in *Discourses* 1.11. For Epictetus's position see further Stephens (1996); Long (2002, 77–79).

16. Epictetus, *Discourses* 3.24–82ff.; cf. also 4.10 and *Handbook* 3. The neo-Stoic Becker (2004, 269–73) offers a thoughtful discussion of the point.

17. D.L. 7.124.

18. Stobaeus, *Ecl.* 2.7.11m (108W).

19. Stobaeus, *Ecl.* 2.7.11m (108W).

20. See pp. 58–59 above.

21. Clement, *Stromata* 5.14 (*SVF* 1.223); Cicero, *On the Nature of the Gods* 1.121.

22. Stobaeus, *Ecl.* 2.7.11i (101–2W); see also *Ecl.* 2.7.11b (93–94W).

23. Seneca, *Moral Epistles* 9.8 and 109.3–6.

24. Stobaeus, *Ecl.* 2.7.11c (94–95W).

25. Stobaeus, *Ecl.* 2.7.5g (71–72W); D.L. 7.96; Cicero, *On Ends* 3.55. See LS 1: 376. I differ from Lesses (1993) on the interpretation of this doctrine. The thought cannot be that the friend is instrumental in the sense that weight training and medical treatment are instrumental, since the wise person himself is likewise a productive good. I take it that the wise person and the friend are productive but not final goods because while they produce good for one another, they do not *constitute* the good for one another.

26. D.L. 7.124; Seneca, *Moral Epistles* 9.12; Cicero, *On Laws* 1.49.

27. Cicero, *On Ends* 3.70.

28. D.L. 7.23.

29. Aristotle, *Nicomachean Ethics* 9.9.1170b6.

30. A similar suggestion is made in Reydams-Schils (2005, 70–71).

31. Stobaeus, *Ecl.* 2.7.11b (93W), 11i (101W); Plutarch, *On Common Conceptions* 1068f. See further Seneca, *Moral Epistles* 109.14–16.

32. For *homonoia* see, in addition to the passages quoted above, Stobaeus, *Ecl.* 2.7.11k (106W), where concord is synonymous with harmony and friendship. Chrysippus wrote a treatise on the topic: Athenaeus, *Dinner-Sophists* 6.267b (LS 67Q).

33. Ps.-Andronicus, *On Emotions* 6 (*SVF* 3.432).

34. Schofield (1991).

35. Seneca, *Moral Epistles* 9.13.

36. Seneca, *Moral Epistles* 9.4. The point is to be connected with the Chrysippan doctrine that everything is of use to the wise person but nothing, including his or her own body, is needful (*Moral Epistles* 9.14).

37. Seneca, *Moral Epistles* 9.5.

38. Cicero, *On Duties* 3.90. For differing reactions to Hecato's argument see Inwood (1984, 182–83); Pembroke (1971, 127–29).

39. D.L. 7.33, 7.36, 7.130, 7.175, 7.178; a more detailed list is in Schofield (1991, 28).

40. Stobaeus, *Ecl.* 2.7.5b9 (65W). The same duality lies behind D.L. 7.113 ("Love is a desire, but not among the virtuous") and also Cicero, *On Ends* 3.68: "they do not think that even holy loves are alien to the wise," where the inclusion of "holy" (*sanctos*) suggests that unholy loves are indeed alien to them.

41. Sappho, fr. 47 Lobel-Page.

42. D.L. 7.130; Alexander of Aphrodisias, *On Aristotle's Topics* 2.2.139 (*SVF* 3.722); Cicero, *Tusc. Disp.* 4.72; Stobaeus, *Ecl.* 2.7.11s (115W).

43. The topic has been well treated; see for instance Thornton (1997); Zeitlin (1996); Halperin (1990); Halperin et al. (1990); Winkler (1990); Dover (1989).

44. Stobaeus, *Ecl.* 2.7.5b9 (65–66W); Seneca, *Moral Epistles* 123.15. Plutarch knows a Stoic definition of *erōs* as 'a chasing after a youth who is undeveloped but well-endowed for virtue' (*On Common Conceptions* 1073b; see further Schofield 1991, 29–31).

45. *Epibolē* is defined in Stobaeus, *Ecl.* 2.7.9a (87.18W) as 'an impulse before an impulse.' The term is discussed in Inwood (1985, 232–33), and Schofield (1991, 29 n. 14).

46. D.L. 7.129–30, reading *epimemptos*, 'subject to blame'; another MS has *theopemptos*, 'god-sent.' Diogenes is unusually explicit about his sources here: for the first sentence quoted he cites Zeno's *Republic*, Chrysippus's *On Lives*, and Apollodorus's *Ethics*; for the last two, Chrysippus's *On Erotic Love*.

47. Stobaeus, *Ecl.* 2.7.11s (115W). Plutarch, *On Common Conceptions* 1072f, is familiar with the same definition.

48. Stobaeus, *Ecl.* 2.7.5b9 (65–66W).

49. There is a full discussion of the usage in Dover (1989).

50. D.L. 7.173.

51. Though some ancient interpreters are inclined to take it that way; so Clement, *Pedagogue* 3.11.74 (*SVF* 1.246). Compare Plutarch, *On Common Conceptions* 1073b, and see Schofield (1991, 115–18).

52. The failure of our attested lists of *eupatheiai* to include *erōs* does not need to be taken as intentional exclusion, since those lists make no pretense of being exhaustive. The discussion concerning erotic love developed separately from the treatment of the passions generally.

53. The view of Schofield (1991, 34), that Stoic love was "desexualized," has not generally been accepted; see Price (2002); Gaca (2000); Inwood (1997); Nussbaum (1995).

54. On the question of age see especially Price (2002).

55. Athenaeus, *Dinner-Sophists* 13.561c (LS 67D).

Chapter 9

1. The portrait of an emotionally engaged Alcibiades, stung by Socrates' criticism and eager to improve himself, appears not only in Plato's *Symposium* but also in the *Greater Alcibiades,* a work which sometimes served as an introduction to the philosophical curriculum (D.L. 3.62), and in the shorter Alcibiades dialogue preserved with the Platonic corpus. An even more emotional portrayal was given by Plato's contemporary Aeschines, whose work seems to have had considerable influence on the later tradition. Dialogues named *Alcibiades* were written also by the Socratic philosophers Antisthenes, Euclides, and Phaedo of Elis. See Giannantoni (1990, 2: 609–10), together with Denyer (2001, 1–29). The version given here combines elements from the principal witnesses: Plato, *Symposium* 215e–216c and *Alcibiades* 118bc, 127d; Cicero, *Tusc. Disp.* 3.77–78; Plutarch, *Life of Alcibiades* 4 and *How to Tell Flatterer from Friend* 69e–f; Aelius Aristides, *Defense of the Four* 576–77; Augustine, *City of God* 14.8.

2. Galen, *PHP* 4.5.26–28 (= fr. 164 EK, lines 12–25). For a partial parallel, compare Cicero, *Tusc. Disp.* 3.68–70, where the point is rather that the emotions described do not occur in every instance and so appear to be under our control.

3. The term is used especially in reference to guilt and shame. See Taylor (1985); more recently Spielthenner (2004); Sabini and Silver (1998, 81–103).

4. Another near equivalent is Bernard Williams's term 'agent-regret' (1981, 27–29). Williams's point in coining the term is that English 'regret' encompasses many attitudes which do not relate specifically to the agent's past actions or decisions but more generally to past events. For a detailed analysis see Rorty (1980).

5. Stobaeus, *Ecl.* 2.7.11i (102–3W). Compare ps.-Andronicus, *On Emotions* 2 (*SVF* 3.414): "Remorse is distress over mistakes in action, that they have come about through one's own agency."

6. Stobaeus, *Ecl.* 2.7.11m (113W). For the interpretation, see Seneca, *On Benefits* 4.34, where the Latin equivalent for Gr. *metameleia* is *paenitentia*. After repeating the Stoics' "proud boast" in words very similar to those above, Seneca continues: "The wise person does not alter his view so long as all the circumstances remain that were in force when he adopted it. The reason he does not ever experience repentance is that it was not possible at that time for him to do anything better than what he did, nor to make a better decision than the one he made."

7. This is sometimes called 'impulse with reservation': see Epictetus, *Discourses* 2.6.9–10 (quoting Chrysippus); Seneca, *On Benefits* 4.34; Stobaeus, *Ecl.* 2.7.11s (115W [LS 65W]), with Inwood (1985), 119–26; Brennan (2000).

8. The two are distinguished sharply by Kaster (2005, 66–83), looking toward the usage of Latin *paenitentia*. However, the two terms are virtually indistinguishable in the usage of most Greek authors; see Thompson (1908).

9. Compare Aristotle, *Nicomachean Ethics* 9.4.1166a29: "the good person is without remorse." One could perhaps try to argue that the wise might regret actions performed before they became wise, since epistemic perfection develops out of imperfection. But the attainment of perfect understanding is such a radical transformation of the circumstances of agency that it is questionable whether the wise would regard errors of their flawed former selves as evil for their present selves.

10. Stobaeus, *Ecl.* 2.7.11i (102–3W).

11. Again the Stoic view resembles that of Aristotle in *Nicomachean Ethics* 9.4; see Irwin (1998, 233). Likewise in Plato, *Republic* 9.577e: "the soul that rules a tyrant is full of disturbance and remorse." See further Alexandre (1995, 22); Martin (1990).

12. On consolation in antiquity see Graver (2002a, 187–94); Scourfield (1993); Johann (1968); Kassel (1958).

13. Cicero, *Tusc. Disp.* 3.77.

14. Cicero, *Tusc. Disp.* 3.76; cf. 4.59–61, and see further Graver (2002a, 121–23, 171–73); Sorabji (2000, 175–80). The significance of the Alcibiades example is noted in White (1995) and Brennan (1998, 50–51).

15. Origen, *Against Celsus* 8.51 (*SVF* 3.474), from Chrysippus, *On Emotions*, book 4. Compare Cicero, *Tusc. Disp.* 4.62.

16. Galen, *PHP* 4.7.26–27, from Chrysippus, *On Emotions*, book 2. The inflammation metaphor is a commonplace of consolatory treatises: cf. Plutarch, *Consolation to Apollonius* 102a–b, and see Graver (2002a, 191–92).

17. Cicero, *Tusc. Disp.* 4.60–62.

18. D.L. 7.87. See esp. Striker (1991, 248–61 and 281–97).

19. Cicero, *Tusc. Disp.* 4.12–15. For the term 'consistencies' see p. 51 above. A similar statement can be found in Epictetus, *Discourses* 3.3.2–4.

20. Cicero, *Tusc. Disp.* 4.67.

21. Philodemus, *On Frank Criticism*, frs. 7, 13, 22, 32, 71; columns VIIIb, XVa, XVIIa, XXIb, XXIIa; tab. IV I. See the edition by Konstan et al. (1998) and, for Epicurean therapy more generally, Nussbaum (1994, 102–39).

22. Plutarch, *Tranquillity of Mind* 476f; see also *How to Tell Flatterer from Friend* 56a.

23. Plutarch, *Life of Alcibiades* 4.1–2, 6.1; *How to Tell Flatterer from Friend* 69e–f.

24. Plutarch, *On Moral Virtue* 452c–d.

25. Epictetus, *Discourses* 3.23.34. On the protreptic style see Long (2002, 52–66); on Epictetus's manner of speaking see also Sorabji (2000, 216–18); Knuuttila (2004, 78–79). For the verb *kulindesthai*, 'to tumble about' or 'to wallow in the mire,' cf. Plato, *Phaedo* 82e, *Statesman* 309a. I would like to thank Enrica Ruaro for calling my attention to the philosophical resonance of this verb.

26. Epictetus, *Discourses* 3.23.37.

27. On this topic I differ from Kamtekar (1998) chiefly in that I see *aidōs* in Epictetus as at all times an affective response. It is not *merely* an inclination to judge certain actions appropriate or inappropriate in relation to one's self-conceived role in life, but also, and fundamentally, a disposition to experience a certain feeling which is manifested in blushing as well as aversion. On my understanding Epictetus does not at this point advocate suspending the terms good and evil: the fact that seeing one's own act-in-prospect as degrading (*aischron*) arouses this visceral response indicates that degradation is regarded (correctly for Epictetus) as an evil.

28. D.L. 7.116; definition in ps.-Andronicus, *On Emotions* 6; see pp. 58–59 above. Similarly, the virtue of shamefastness (*aidēmosunē*) is defined in Stobaeus, *Ecl.* 2.7.5b2 (61W), as 'knowledge which is disposed to caution regarding justified blame.' The reference to caution in the definition makes it clear that *aidōs* is a species of caution for the Stobaean author as well as for D.L. and ps.-Andronicus.

29. The norm is not exclusively Stoic; see Spanneut (1994).

30. Jerome, *Epistle* 133.3 (PL 22, col. 1151), against the Stoic-influenced view of Evagrius Ponticus.

31. The rationale for this approach is explored in Sorabji (2000, 159–93).

32. But only sometimes, because an imperfect intellect always lacks the epistemic guarantee.

Appendix

1. For a review of other suggestions see Dougan and Henry (1934); Pohlenz and Heine (1957); Giusta (1984); Lundström (1964, 1986).

2. Lundström (1964, 159).

3. Stobaeus, *Ecl.* 2.7.5b (58W), 2.7.5g (72W); with the latter cf. D.L 7.96.

4. *Protagoras* 349e–351a, 359a–360e. *Tharros* is also treated briefly in *Laches* 197a–b and is listed among the disturbances of the mortal psyche in *Timaeus* 69d. The *Protagoras* does not use the noun form, preferring the adjective *tharraleos* or the verb *tharrein*. I have assumed lexical equivalence among all these forms and also among the variants of the noun (*tharros, tharsos, thrasutēs,* and *thraseia*); cf. however LSJ s.v. θράσος fin.

5. Protagoras's reluctance to relinquish this position at 360d–e suggests that Plato

finds his position attractive. Compare the *Republic*'s definition of courage at 4.430b as 'knowledge of what is and is not to be feared.'

6. Plato, *Laws* 644c–650b.

7. Plato, *Laws* 647a, 649b; cf. *Protagoras* 360b.

8. See further Fortenbaugh (2002).

9. Epicurus, *Principal Doctrines* 6, 28, 39, 40; D.L. 10, 140, 148, 154; *On the End apud* Cicero, *Tusc. Disp.* 3.41.

10. *Tharros* appears also in the *Iliad* scholiast (ad *Iliad* E 2 [*SVF* 3.287]), citing a Stoic definition, 'unshakeable certainty that one will not incur any terrible thing'; in a syllogistic argument using the incompatibility of fear and confidence as a premise at Cicero, *Tusc. Disp.* 3.14; and in an interesting but poorly preserved discussion at *Tusc. Disp.* 4.80 (on which see Graver 2002a, 182–84).

11. Hence Aspasius, who is familiar with the dominant Stoic tradition, complains of the omission (*On the Nicomachean Ethics* 2.2.46). The passage is pointed out in Sorabji (2000, 136).

12. In *Cicero on the Emotions*, not having considered all the parallels listed here, I made the opposite suggestion, that the classification using *eulabeia* is earlier, with *tharros* being substituted for it in a later version.

13. Epictetus, *Discourses* 2.1.1–7; compare *Discourses* 2.12.13, where it is *eulabeia* that causes one to refrain from overzealous dialectical examination of someone who is not likely to benefit.

14. Stobaeus, *Ecl.* 2.7.7g (84.24–85.11W); Cicero, *On Ends* 3.20. It is worth noting that while the virtue of shamefastness is defined by the Stobaean author in a way which clearly derives it from the *eupatheia* of moral shame (see p. 00 above), the same author's definition for the virtue called *tharraleotēs* (i.e., the disposition to exhibit *tharros*) lacks any affective component: it is just 'knowledge by which we are sure that we will incur nothing terrible' (*Ecl.* 2.7.5b2 [61W]).

15. That confidence has an affective dimension is indicated by Chrysippus's remark, reported in Galen, *PHP* 3.7, that *chara* and *tharsos* take place in the heart region. A view like the one I am suggesting is nonetheless implied by the distinction drawn by Chrysippus *apud* Galen, *PHP* 7.2.9, among the four terms *haireteon, poiēteon, tharrēteon, agathon*. Galen takes it as obvious that there is synonymy between what one faces with confidence and what one takes for a genuine good, but this is not Chrysippus's view.

BIBLIOGRAPHY

Abel, K. 1983. Das *Propatheia*-Theorem: Ein Beitrag zur stoischen Affektenlehr. *Hermes* III, 78–97.

Alexandre, M. 1995. Le lexique des vertus: vertus philosophiques et religieuses chez Philon: μετάνοια et εὐγένεια. In *Philon d'Alexandrie et le langage de la philosophie,* ed. Carlos Lévy. Turnhout: Brepols. 17–46.

Algra, K., J. Barnes, J. Mansfield, and M. Schofield, eds. 1999. *Cambridge History of Hellenistic Philosophy.* Cambridge: Cambridge University Press.

American Psychiatric Association. 1994. *Diagnostic and Statistical Manual.* Washington, D.C.

Annas, J. 1999. *Platonic Ethics, Old and New.* Ithaca, N.Y.: Cornell University Press.

———. 1992. *Hellenistic Philosophy of Mind.* Berkeley: University of California Press.

Barnes, J., and M. Griffin, eds. 1997. *Philosophia Togata II: Plato and Aristotle at Rome.* Oxford: Oxford University Press.

Bartsch, S. 1997. *Ideology in Cold Blood.* Cambridge: Harvard University Press.

Bastianini, G., and A. A. Long, ed. 1992. *Ierocle.* In *Corpus dei papiri filosofici greci e latini,* vol. 1.1**. Florence: Olschki. 268–451.

Bäumer, Ä. 1982. *Die Bestie Mensch: Senecas Aggressionstheorie, ihre philosophischen Vorstufen und ihre literarischen Auswirkungen.* Frankfurt am Main: Lang.

Becker, L. 2004. Stoic Emotion. In Strange and Zupko 2004, 250–75.

———. 1998. *A New Stoicism.* Princeton: Princeton University Press.

Ben–Ze'ev, A. 2000. *The Subtlety of Emotions.* Cambridge: MIT Press.

Blundell, R. 1990. Oikeiosis and Stoic Friendship. *Ancient Philosophy* 10, 221–42.

Bobzien, S. 1998. *Determinism and Freedom in Stoic Philosophy.* Oxford: Oxford University Press.

Bonhöffer, A. 1890. *Epiktet und die Stoa.* Stuttgart: Ferdinand Enke.

Boudouris, K. J., ed. 1993. *Hellenistic Philosophy.* Vol. 1. Athens: International Center for Greek Philosophy and Culture.

Braund, S., and C. Gill, eds. 1997. *The Passions in Roman Thought and Literature.* Cambridge: Cambridge University Press.

Brennan, T. 2005. *The Stoic Life: Emotions, Duties, and Fate.* Oxford: Oxford University Press.

———. 2003. Stoic Moral Psychology. In Inwood 2003, 257–94.

———. 2001. Fate and Free Will in Stoicism. (Review of Bobzien 1998.) *Oxford Studies in Ancient Philosophy* 21, 259–86.

———. 2000. Reservation in Stoic Ethics. *Archiv für Geschichte der Philosophie* 82, 149–77.

———. 1998. The Old Stoic Theory of Emotions. In Sihvola and Engberg-Pedersen 1998, 21–70.

Bruns, I. 1887a. *Alexander Aphrodisiensis: De Anima cum Mantissa* (= *Commentaria in Aristotelem Graeca, Supplementum Aristotelicum,* 2.1). Berlin: Reimer.

———. 1887b. *Alexander Aphrodisiensis: Scripta Minora* (= *Commentaria in Aristotelem Graeca, Supplementum Aristotelicum,* 2.2). Berlin: Reimer.

Brunschwig, J. 1994. *Papers in Hellenistic Philosophy.* Cambridge: Cambridge University Press.

———. 1986. The Cradle Argument in Epicureanism and Stoicism. In Schofield and Striker 1986, 113–44.

Brunschwig, J., and M. Nussbaum, eds. 1993. *Passions and Perceptions: Studies in Hellenistic Philosophy of Mind.* Cambridge: Cambridge University Press.

Bury, R. G. 1935. *Sextus Empiricus: Against the Logicians.* Cambridge: Harvard University Press.

Chadwick, H. 1947. Origen, Celsus, and the Stoa. *Journal of Theological Studies* 48, 34–49.

Cole, E. B. 1993. The Soul of the Beast in Stoic Thought. In Boudouris 1993, 42–50.

Cooper, J. 2005. The Emotional Life of the Wise. In *Ancient Ethics and Political Philosophy: Proceedings of the Spindel Conference 2004,* ed. Tim Roche. *Southern Journal of Philosophy,* supplement 43, 176–218.

———. 1999. *Reason and Emotion.* Princeton, N.J.: Princeton University Press.

———. 1998. Posidonius on Emotions. In Sihvola and Engberg-Pedersen 1998, 71–112. Also in Cooper 1999, 449–84.

Damasio, A. 2003. *Looking for Spinoza: Joy, Sorrow, and the Feeling Brain.* Orlando, Fla.: Harcourt Brace.

———. 2000. *The Feeling of What Happens: Body and Emotion in the Making of Consciousness.* New York: Harcourt Brace.

———. 1994. *Descartes' Error: Emotion, Reason and the Human Brain.* New York: Grosset / Putnam.

De Lacy, P., ed. 1978. *Galen: On the Doctrines of Hippocrates and Plato. Corpus Medicorum Graecorum,* vol. 5, no. 4.1.2. Berlin: Academy of Sciences.

Denyer, N., ed. 2001. *Plato: Alcibiades.* Cambridge: Cambridge University Press.

Diels, H., ed. 1917. *Philodemos Über die Götter. Drittes Buch.* Berlin: Academy of Sciences.

————, ed. 1879. *Doxographi Graeci*. Berlin. Rpt. Berlin and Leipzig: Walter de Gruyter, 1929.

Dihle, A. 1982. *The Theory of Will in Classical Antiquity*. Berkeley: University of California Press.

Dillon, J. 1997. Medea among the Philosophers. In *Medea: Essays on Medea in Myth, Literature, Philosophy, and Art*, ed. J. Clauss and S. Johnston. Princeton, N.J.: Princeton University Press. 211–18.

————. 1996. *The Middle Platonists*. Ithaca, N.Y.: Cornell University Press.

————, ed. 1993. *Alcinous: The Handbook of Platonism*. Oxford: Oxford University Press.

————. 1990. *The Golden Chain: Studies in the Development of Platonism and Christianity*. Aldershot: Ashgate.

————. 1983. Metriopatheia and Apatheia: Some Reflections on a Controversy in Later Greek Ethics. In *Essays in Ancient Greek Philosophy*, vol. 2, ed. J. Anton and A. Preus. Albany, N.Y.: SUNY Press. 508–17. Rpt. Dillon 1990.

Dillon, J., and A. Terian. 1976–77. Philo and the Stoic Doctrine of *Eupatheiai*: A Note on *Quaes. Gen.* 2.57. *Studia Philonica* 4, 17–24. Rpt. Dillon 1990.

Dobbin, R. 1991. Προαίρεσις in Epictetus. *Ancient Philosophy* 11, 111–35.

Donini, P. 1995. *Pathos* nello Stoicismo Romano. *Elenchos* 16, 195–216.

Dougan, T., ed. 1905. *M. Tulli Ciceronis Tusculanarum disputationum libri quinque*, vol. 1. Cambridge: Cambridge University Press. Rpt. Salem, N.H.: Ayer, 1988.

Dougan, T., and R. Henry, eds. 1934. *M. Tulli Ciceronis Tusculanarum disputationum libri quinque*. 2 vols. Cambridge: Cambridge University Press. Rpt. Salem, N.H.: Ayer, 1988.

Doutreleau, L., A. Gesché, and M. Gronewald. 1969. *Didymos der Blinde: Psalmenkommentar*, pt. 1. Papyrologische Texte und Abhandlungen 7. Bonn: Habelt.

Dover, K. J. 1989. *Greek Homosexuality*. 2nd ed. Cambridge: Harvard University Press.

————. 1968. *Aristophanes: Clouds*. Oxford: Oxford University Press.

Dyck, A. 2004. *A Commentary on Cicero, De Legibus*. Ann Arbor: University of Michigan Press.

Edelstein, L., and I. G. Kidd, eds. 1989. *Posidonius: The Fragments*. Cambridge: Cambridge University Press.

Ekman, P. 1982. *Emotion in the Human Face*. 2nd ed. Cambridge: Cambridge University Press.

Ekman, P., and E. L. Rosenberg, eds. 1997. *What the Face Reveals: Basic and Applied Studies of Spontaneous Expression Using the Facial Action Coding System*. New York: Oxford University Press.

Engberg-Pedersen, T. 1990. The Stoic Theory of *Oikeiosis*. Aarhus: Aarhus University Press.

Ferrary, J.-L. 1995. Statesman and Law in Cicero's Political Philosophy. In Laks and Schofield 1995, 48–73.

Fillion-Lahille, J. 1984. *Le De ira de Sénèque et la philosophie stoïcienne des passions*. Paris: Klincksieck.

Flashar, H. 1966. *Melancholie und Melancholiker in den medizinischen Theorien der Antike*. Berlin: Walter de Gruyter.

Forschner, M. 1995. *Die stoische Ethik: über die Zusammenhang von Natur-, Sprach- und Moralphilosophie im altstoischen System*. 2nd ed. Darmstadt: Wissenschaftliche Buchgesellschaft. First published 1981.

Fortenbaugh, W. W. 2002. *Aristotle on Emotion*. 2nd ed. London: Duckworth.

———, ed. 1983. *On Stoic and Peripatetic Ethics: The Work of Arius Didymus*. New Brunswick and London: Duckworth.

Foucault, M. 1986. *The History of Sexuality*, vol. 3: *The Care of the Self*. Trans. R. Hurley. New York: Random House.

Frede, M. 1999. On the Stoic Conception of the Good. In *Topics in Stoic Philosophy*, ed. K. Ierodiakonou. Oxford: Oxford University Press. 71–94.

———. 1986. The Stoic Doctrine of the Affections of the Soul. In Schofield and Striker 1986, 93–110.

Frijda, N. H. 1988. The Laws of Emotion. *American Psychologist* 43, 349–58.

Furley, D. 1999. Cosmology. In Algra et al. 1999, 412–51.

Gaca, K. 2000. Early Stoic Eros: The Sexual Ethics of Zeno and Chrysippus and Their Evaluation of the Greek Erotic Tradition. *Apeiron* 33, 201–38.

Gesché, A. 1962. *La christologie du "Commentaire sur les Psaumes" découvert à Toura*. Gembloux: Duculot.

Giannantoni, G. 1990. *Socratis et Socraticorum Reliquiae*. 4 vols. Naples: Bibliopolis.

Gill, C. 2005. Competing Readings of Stoic Emotions. In Salles 2005, 445–70.

———. 1998. Did Galen Understand Platonic and Stoic Thinking on Emotions? In Sihvola and Engberg-Pedersen 1998, 113–48.

———. 1997. Passion as Madness in Roman Poetry. In *The Passions in Roman Thought and Literature*, ed. C. Gill and S. Morton Braund. Cambridge: Cambridge University Press. 213–41.

———. 1996. Mind and Madness in Greek Tragedy: A Discussion of R. Padel, *In and Out of the Mind* and *Whom Gods Destroy*. *Apeiron* 29, 249–66.

———. 1990a. The Character-Personality Distinction. In *Characterization and Individuality in Greek Literature*, ed. C. B. R. Pelling. Oxford: Oxford University Press. 1–31.

———, ed. 1990b. *The Person and the Human Mind: Issues in Ancient and Modern Philosophy*. New York: Clarendon Press.

———. 1988. Personhood and Personality: The Four-*Personae* Theory in Cicero, *De Officiis* Book 1. *Oxford Studies in Ancient Philosophy* 6, 169–200.

———. 1983. Did Chrysippus Understand Medea? *Phronesis* 28, 136–49.

Giusta, M., ed. 1984. *M. Tulli Ciceronis Tusculanae Disputationes*. Turin: Paravia.

Glare, P. G. W., ed. 1982. *Oxford Latin Dictionary*. New York: Oxford University Press.

Glibert-Thirry, A., ed. 1977. *Pseudo-Andronicus de Rhodes* περὶ παθῶν. Leiden: E. J. Brill.

Göransson, T. 1995. *Albinus, Alcinous, Arius Didymus*. Göteborg: Ekblad.

Görler, W. 1977. ἀσθενὴς συγκατάθεσις: Zur Stoischen Erkenntnistheorie. *Würzburger Jahrbücher*, n.s. 3, 83–92. Rpt. in *Kleine Schriften zur hellenistisch-römischen Philosophie*, ed. C. Catrein. Leiden: Brill, 2004. 1–12.

Gosling, J. C. B. 1990. *The Weakness of Will*. London: Routledge.

———. 1987. The Stoics and ἀκρασία. *Apeiron* 20, 179–202.

Graver, M. 2003. Not Even Zeus: A Discussion of A. A. Long, *Epictetus: A Stoic and Socratic Guide to Life. Oxford Studies in Ancient Philosophy* 24, 343–59.

———. 2002a. *Cicero on the Emotions: Tusculan Disputations 3–4.* Chicago: University of Chicago Press.

———. 2002b. Review of Sorabji 2000. *Ancient Philosophy* 22, 225–34.

———. 1999. Philo of Alexandria and the Origins of the Stoic προπάθειαι. *Phronesis* 44, 300–325.

Greenspan, P. S. 2003. Responsible Psychopaths. *Philosophical Psychology* 16, 417–29.

———. 1988. *Emotions and Reasons: An Enquiry into Emotional Justification.* New York: Routledge.

Gregg, J. A. F. 1992. The Commentary of Origen upon the Epistle to the Ephesians. *Journal of Theological Studies* 3, 233–44, 398–420, 554–76.

Griffin, M. 1976. *Seneca: A Philosopher in Politics.* Oxford: Oxford University Press.

Griffin, M, and J. Barnes, eds. 1989. *Philosophia Togata: Essays on Philosophy and Roman Society.* Oxford: Oxford University Press.

Griffiths, P. E. 1997. *What Emotions Really Are: The Problem of Psychological Categories.* Chicago: University of Chicago Press.

Gronewald, M. 1979. *Didymos der Blinde: Kommentar zum Ecclesiastes,* pt. 5. Papyrologische Texte und Abhandlungen 9. Bonn: Habelt.

———. 1970. *Didymos der Blinde: Psalmenkommentar,* pt. 5. Papyrologische Texte und Abhandlungen 12. Bonn: Habelt.

———. 1969a. *Didymos der Blinde: Psalmenkommentar,* pt. 3. Papyrologische Texte und Abhandlungen 8. Bonn: Habelt.

———. 1969b. *Didymos der Blinde: Psalmenkommentar,* pt. 4. Papyrologische Texte und Abhandlungen 6. Bonn: Habelt.

———. 1968. *Didymos der Blinde: Psalmenkommentar,* pt. 2. Papyrologische Texte und Abhandlungen 4. Bonn: Habelt.

Hadot, I. 1969. *Seneca und die griechisch-römische Tradition der Seelenleitung.* Berlin: Walter de Gruyter.

Hahm, D. 1990. The Ethical Doxography of Arius Didymus. In *Aufstieg und Niedergang der römischen Welt.* Vol. 2.36.4. Berlin: Walter de Gruyter. 2935–3055.

———. 1977. *The Origins of Stoic Cosmology.* Columbus: Ohio State University Press.

Halperin, D. M. 1990. *One Hundred Years of Homosexuality, and Other Essays on Greek Love.* New York: Routledge.

Halperin, D. M., J. Winkler, and F. Zeitlin, eds. 1990. *Before Sexuality: The Construction of Erotic Experience in the Ancient Greek World.* Princeton: Princeton University Press.

Hankinson, R. J. 2003. Stoicism and Medicine. In Inwood 2003, 295–309.

Hare, R. D. 1999. *Without Conscience: The Disturbing World of the Psychopaths among Us.* New York: Guilford Press.

Harris, W. 2002. *Restraining Rage: The Ideology of Anger Control in Classical Antiquity.* Cambridge: Harvard University Press.

Heylbut, G., ed. 1889. *Aspasii.* In *Ethica Nicomachea quae supersunt commentaria* (= *Commentaria in Aristotelem Graeca,* vol. 19). Berlin: G. Reimer.

Holler, E. 1934. *Seneca und die Seelenteilungslehre und Affektpsychologie der Mittelstoa.* Kall-
münz: M. Lassleben.

Inwood, B. 2005. *Reading Seneca.* Oxford: Clarendon Press.

———, ed. 2003. *Cambridge Companion to the Stoics.* Cambridge: Cambridge University
Press.

———. 2000. The Will in Seneca the Younger. *Classical Philology* 95, 44–60. Rpt. Inwood
2005, 132–56.

———. 1997. Why Do Fools Fall in Love? In *Aristotle and After* (*BICS* Supplement 68),
ed. R. Sorabji. London: Institute of Classical Studies. 55–69.

———. 1996. Review of Göransson 1995. *Bryn Mawr Classical Reviews* 7, 25–30. (Elec-
tronic publication 95.12.8 [1995].)

———. 1993. Seneca and Psychological Dualism. In Brunschwig and Nussbaum 1993,
150–83. Rpt. Inwood 2005, 23–64.

———. 1985. *Ethics and Human Action in Early Stoicism.* Oxford: Oxford University Press.

———. 1984. Hierocles: Theory and Argument in the Second Century a.d. *Oxford Studies in Ancient Philosophy,* 151–83.

———. 1983. The Two Forms of *Oikeiosis* in Arius and the Stoa. In Fortenbaugh 1983,
190–201.

Irwin, T. H. 1998. Stoic Inhumanity. In Sihvola and Engberg-Pedersen 1998, 219–42.

———. 1995. *Plato's Ethics.* Oxford: Oxford University Press.

Jackson-McCabe, M. 2005. The Stoic Theory of Implanted Preconceptions. *Phronesis* 49,
323–47.

Jacobs, J. 2001. *Choosing Character: Responsibility for Virtue and Vice.* Ithaca: Cornell University Press.

James, W. 1884. What Is an Emotion? *Mind* 9, 188–205.

Johann, H. 1968. *Trauer und Trost, Eine quellen- und strukturanalytische Untersuchung der
philosophischen Trostschriften.* Munich: W. Fink.

Johnson, W. R. 1987. *Momentary Monsters: Lucan and His Heroes.* Ithaca: Cornell University Press.

Joyce, R. 1995. Early Stoicism and *Akrasia. Phronesis* 40, 315–35.

Kahn, C. 1988. Discovering the Will. In *The Question of Eclecticism,* ed. J. M. Dillon and
A. A. Long. Berkeley: University of California Press. 234–59

Kalbfleisch, K., ed. 1907. *Simplicii In Aristotelis Categoriis commentarium. Commentaria in
Aristotelem Graeca,* vol. 8. Berlin: G. Reimer.

Kamtekar, R. 2004. Good Feelings and Motivation: Comments on John Cooper, "The
Emotional Life of the Wise." In *Ancient Ethics and Political Philosophy: Proceedings of
the Spindel Conference 2004,* ed. Tim Roche. *Southern Journal of Philosophy,* supplement
43. 219–29.

———. 1998. αἰδώς in Epictetus. *Classical Philology* 93, 136–60.

Kassel, R. 1958. *Untersuchungen zur griechischen und lateinischen Konsolationsliteratur.*
Munich: Beck.

Kaster, R. 2005. *Emotion, Restraint, and Community in Ancient Rome.* Oxford: Oxford
University Press.

Kerferd, G. B. 1978. What Does the Wise Man Know? In *The Stoics*, ed. J. Rist. Berkeley: University of California Press. 125–36.

Kidd, I. G. 1988. *Posidonius II: The Commentary.* 2 vols. Cambridge: Cambridge University Press.

Knuuttila, S. 2004. *Emotions in Ancient and Medieval Philosophy.* Oxford: Clarendon Press.

Konstan, D. 2006. *The Emotions and the Ancient Greeks: Studies in Aristotle and Classical Literature.* Toronto: University of Toronto Press.

———. 1997. *Friendship in the Classical World.* Cambridge: Cambridge University Press.

Konstan, D., et al., eds. 1998. *Philodemus: On Frank Criticism.* Atlanta: Society of Biblical Literature.

Kramer, J., and B. Krebber. 1972. *Didymos der Blinde: Kommentar zum Ecclesiastes,* pt. 4 Papyrologische Texte und Abhandlungen 16. Bonn: Habelt.

Labarrière, J.-L. 1993. De la 'nature phantastique' des animaux chez les Stoïciens. In Brunschwig and Nussbaum, 1993, 225–49.

Laks, A., and M. Schofield, eds. 1995. *Justice and Generosity: Studies in Hellenistic Social and Political Philosophy.* Cambridge: Cambridge University Press.

Lapidge, M. 1978. Stoic Cosmology. In *The Stoics*, ed. J. Rist. Berkeley: University of California Press. 161–85.

Laurenti, R. 1979. Aristotele e il De ira di Seneca. *Studi Filosofici* 2, 61–91.

Layton, R. 2000. Propatheia: Origen and Didymus on the Origin of the Passions. *Vigiliae Christianae* 54, 262–82.

Lazarus, R. S. 1994. *Passion and Reason : Making Sense of Our Emotions.* New York : Oxford University Press.

———. 1991. *Emotion and Adaptation.* New York: Oxford University Press.

———. 1984. On the Primacy of Cognition. *American Psychologist* 39, 124–29.

LeDoux, J. 1996. *The Emotional Brain: The Mysterious Underpinnings of Emotional Life.* New York: Simon and Schuster.

Leighton, S. R. 1985. A New View of Emotion. *American Philosophical Quarterly* 22, 133–41.

Lesses, G. 1998. Content, Cause, and Stoic Impressions. *Phronesis* 43, 1–25.

———. 1993. Austere Friends: The Stoics and Friendship. *Apeiron* 26, 57–75.

Liddell, H. G., R. Scott, and H. S. Jones, eds. 1996. *A Greek-English Lexicon.* Oxford: Oxford University Press.

Long, A. A. 2002. *Epictetus: A Stoic and Socratic Guide to Life.* Oxford: Oxford University Press.

———. 1996. *Stoic Studies.* Cambridge: Cambridge University Press.

———. 1995. Cicero's Politics in *De Officiis.* In Laks and Schofield 1995, 213–40.

———. 1993. Hierocles on Oikeiosis and Self-Perception. In Boudouris 1993, 93–104. Rpt. Long 1996, 250–63.

———. 1992. Soul and Body in Stoicism. *Phronesis* 27, 34–57. Rpt. Long 1996, 224–49.

———. 1991. Representation and the Self in Stoicism. In *Companions to Ancient Thought,* vol. 2: *Psychology,* ed. S. Everson. Cambridge: Cambridge University Press. Rpt. Long 1996, 264–85.

———. 1983. Arius Didymus and the Exposition of Stoic Ethics. In Fortenbaugh 1983, 41–66. Rpt. Long 1996, 107–33.

———, ed. 1971. *Problems in Stoicism*. London: Athlone Press.

Long, A. A., and D. N. Sedley, eds. 1987. *The Hellenistic Philosophers*. 2 vols. Cambridge: Cambridge University Press.

Lundström, S. 1986. *Zur Textkritik der Tusculanen*. Stockholm: Almqvist & Wiksell.

———. 1964. *Vermeintliche Glosseme in den Tusculanen*. Uppsala: Almqvist & Wiksell.

Malaspina, E. 2001. *L. Annaei Senecae De Clementia Libri Duo*. Turin: Edizioni dell'Orso.

Marcus, R., ed. 1953. *Philo, Questions and Answers on Genesis*. Cambridge: Harvard University Press.

Martin, C. F. J. 1990. On an Alleged Inconsistency in the *Nicomachean Ethics* (IX.4). *Journal of Hellensitic Studies* 110, 188–91.

Menn, S. 1995. Physics as a Virtue. *Proceedings of the Boston Area Colloquium in Ancient Philosophy* 11, 1–34.

Migne, J.-P., ed. 1800–1875. *Patrologiae cursus completus, Series Graeca*. Paris: Migne.

———, ed. 1844–64. *Patrologiae cursus completus, Series Latina*. Paris: Migne.

Mitsis, P. 1994. Natural Law and Natural Right in Post-Aristotelian Philosophy: The Stoics and Their Critics. In *Aufstieg und Niedergang der römischen Welt*. Vol. 2.36.7. Berlin: Walter de Gruyter. 4812–50.

Moody-Adams, M. 1993. On the Old Saw That Character Is Destiny. In *Identity, Character, and Morality*, ed. O. Flanagan and A. O. Rorty. Cambridge: MIT Press. 111–32.

Morani, M. 1987. *Nemesius De Natura Hominis*. Leipzig: Teubner.

Müri, W. 1953. Melancholie und schwarze Galle. *Museum Helveticum* 10, 27–38.

Nash, R. A. 1989. Cognitive Theories of Emotion. *Nous* 23, 481–504.

Nauck, A. 1964. *Tragicorum Graecorum Fragmenta: Supplementum*. Hildesheim: G. Olms.

Nussbaum, M. 2004. Emotions as Judgments of Value and Importance. In Solomon 2004, 183–99.

———. 2001. *Upheavals of Thought: The Intelligence of Emotions*. Cambridge: Cambridge University Press.

———. 1995. Eros and the Wise. *Oxford Studies in Ancient Philosophy* 13, 231–67. Rpt. Sihvola and Engberg-Pedersen 1998, 271–304.

———. 1994. *Therapy of Desire: Theory and Practice in Hellenistic Ethics*. Princeton: Princeton University Press.

———. 1993. Poetry and the Passions: Two Stoic Views. In Brunschwig and Nussbaum 1993, 97–149.

———. 1978. *Aristotle's De motu animalium*. Princeton: Princeton University Press.

Nussbaum, M., and A. O. Rorty, eds. 1992. *Essays on Aristotle's De anima*. Oxford: Clarendon Press.

Nussbaum, M. and J. Sihvola, eds. 2002. *The Sleep of Reason: Erotic Experience and Sexual Ethics in Ancient Greece and Rome*. Chicago: University of Chicago Press.

Padel, R. 1995. *Whom Gods Destroy: Elements of Greek and Tragic Madness*. Princeton: Princeton University Press.

———. 1994. *In and Out of the Mind: Greek Images of the Tragic Self.* Princeton: Princeton University Press.

Panksepp, Jaak. 1998. *Affective Neuroscience: The Foundations of Human and Animal Emotions.* New York: Oxford University Press.

Paschall, D. M. 1939. *The Vocabulary of Mental Aberration in Roman Comedy and Petronius.* Baltimore: Linguistic Society of America.

Pembroke, S. G. 1971. Oikeiōsis. In Long 1971, 114–49.

Petit, F., ed. 1978. *Philon d'Alexandrie, Quaestiones in Genesim et in Exodum, fragmenta Graeca.* Paris: Editions du Cerf.

———, ed. 1977. *Catenae Graecae in Genesim et in Exodum.* Corpus Christianorum Series Graeca, vol. 2. Turnhout: Brepols.

Pigeaud, J. 1987. *Folie et cures de la folie chez les médecins de l'antiquité gréco–romaine.* Paris: Belles Lettres.

Pohlenz, M. 1948–49. *Die Stoa: Geschichte einer geistigen Bewegung.* Göttingen: Vandenhoeck and Ruprecht.

———. 1940. *Grundfragen der stoischen Philosophie.* Göttingen: Vandenhoeck and Ruprecht.

Pohlenz, M., and O. Heine, eds. 1957. *Ciceronis Tusculanarum Disputationum libri V.* Stuttgart: A. M. Hakkert.

Pomeroy, A. J., ed. 1999. *Arius Didymus, Epitome of Stoic Ethics.* Atlanta: Scholars Press.

Price, A. 2005. Were Zeno and Chrysippus at Odds in Analyzing Emotion? In Salles. 2005, 471–88.

———. 2002. Plato, Zeno, and the Object of Love. In Nussbaum and Sihvola 2002, 170–99.

———. 1995. *Mental Conflict.* London: Routledge.

Prinz, J. 2004. *Gut Reactions: A Perceptual Theory of Emotion.* New York: Oxford University Press.

Radden, J., ed. 2000. *The Nature of Melancholy: From Aristotle to Kristeva.* Oxford: Oxford University Press.

Radt, S. 1971–2004. *Tragicorum Graecorum Fragmenta.* Göttingen: Vandenhoeck and Ruprecht.

Reid, J., ed. 1885. *M. Tulli Ciceronis Academica.* London: Macmillan.

Reydams-Schils, G. 2005. *The Roman Stoics: Self, Responsibility, and Affection.* Chicago: University of Chicago Press.

———. 1999. *Demiurge and Providence: Stoic and Platonist Readings of Plato's Timaeus.* Turnhout: Brepols.

Reynolds, L. D. 1977. *L. Annaei Senecae Dialogorum Libri Duodecim.* Oxford: Clarendon Press. New York: Oxford University Press.

Rist, J. 1989. Seneca and Stoic Orthodoxy. In *Aufstieg und Niedergang der römischen Welt.* Vol. 2.36.3. Berlin: Walter de Gruyter. 1993–2012.

Rolls, Edmund T. 1999. *The Brain and Emotion.* Oxford: Oxford University Press.

Rorty, A. O. 1980. Agent-Regret. In *Explaining Emotions*, ed. A. O. Rorty. Berkeley: University of California Press. 489–506.

Rosini, C. M., et al., eds. 1862–76. *Herculanensium Voluminum Quae Supersunt. Collectio Altera,* ed. J. Minervini. 11 vols. Naples: Typographia Regia.

Royse, J. 1991. *The Spurious Texts of Philo of Alexandria.* Leiden: E. J. Brill.

Runia, D. 1993. *Philo in Early Christian Literature: A Survey.* Assen: Van Gorcum. Minneapolis: Fortress Press.

Sabini, J., and M. Silver. 1998. *Emotion, Character, and Responsibility.* New York: Oxford University Press.

Sakezles, P. 1998. Aristotle and Chrysippus on the Physiology of Human Action. *Apeiron* 31, 127–66.

Salles, R., ed. 2005. *Metaphysics, Soul and Ethics: Themes from the Work of Richard Sorabji.* Oxford: Oxford University Press.

Sandbach, F. H. 1989. *The Stoics.* 2nd ed. Indianapolis: Hackett.

Schofield, M. 1995. Two Stoic Approaches to Justice. In Laks and Schofield 1995, 191–212.

———. 1991. *The Stoic Idea of the City.* Cambridge: Cambridge University Press.

Schofield, M., M. Burnyeat, and J. Barnes, eds. 1980. *Doubt and Dogmatism: Studies in Hellenistic Epistemology.* Oxford: Oxford University Press.

Schofield, M., and G. Striker, eds. 1986. *The Norms of Nature: Studies in Hellenistic Ethics.* Cambridge: Cambridge University Press.

Scott, D. 1995. *Recollection and Experience: Plato's Theory of Learning and Its Successors.* Cambridge: Cambridge University Press.

Scourfield, J. 1993. *Consoling Heliodorus: A Commentary on Jerome, Letter 60.* Oxford: Oxford University Press.

Sedley, D. 1997. Plato's *Auctoritas* and Rebirth of the Commentary Tradition. In Barnes and Griffin 1997, 110–129.

———. 1993. Chrysippus on Psychophysical Causality. In Brunschwig and Nussbaum 1993, 313–31.

Setaioli, A. 1988. *Seneca e i greci: Citazioni e traduzioni nelle opere filosofiche.* Bologna: Pàtron.

Sherman, N. 2005. *Stoic Warriors: The Ancient Philosophy behind the Military Mind.* Oxford: Oxford University Press.

Sihvola, J., and T. Engberg-Pedersen, eds. 1998. *The Emotions in Hellenistic Philosophy.* Dordrecht: Kluwer.

Sklenář, R. 1999. Nihilistic Cosmology and Catonian Ethics in Lucan's *Bellum civile. American Journal of Philology* 120, 281–96.

Solomon, R. C., ed. 2004. *Thinking about Feeling: Contemporary Philosophers on Emotions.* Oxford: Oxford University Press.

———. 2003a. Emotions, Thoughts, and Feelings: What Is a 'Cognitive Theory' of the Emotions and Does It Neglect Affectivity? In *Philosophy and the Emotions,* ed. A. Hatzimoysis. Royal Institute of Philosophy supplement 52. Cambridge: Royal Institute of Philosophy. 1–18.

———. 2003b. *Not Passion's Slave: Emotions and Choice.* Oxford: Oxford University Press.

———. 1976. *The Passions.* New York: Doubleday. 2nd ed. Indianapolis: Hackett, 1993.

Sorabji, R. 2000. *Emotion and Peace of Mind: The Stoic Legacy.* Oxford: Oxford University Press.

———. 1998. Chrysippus—Posidonius—Seneca: A High-Level Debate on Emotion. In Sihvola and Engberg-Pedersen 1998, 149–70.

———. 1993. *Animal Minds and Human Morals: The Origins of the Western Debate.* Ithaca: Cornell University Press.

———. 1988. *Matter, Space, and Motion.* Ithaca: Cornell University Press.

Spanneut, M. 1994. Apatheia ancienne, apatheia chrétienne. In *Aufstieg und Niedergang der römischen Welt.* Vol. 2.36.7. Berlin: Walter de Gruyter. 4641–4717.

Spielthenner, Georg. 2004. Moral Emotions. *Disputatio* 1, no. 17, 3–15.

Stephens, W. O. 1996. Epictetus on How the Stoic Sage Loves. *Oxford Studies in Ancient Philosophy* 14, 193–210.

Stevens, J. 2000. Preliminary Impulse in Stoic Psychology. *Ancient Philosophy* 20 (2000): 139–68.

Stocker, M. 1987. Emotional Thoughts. *American Philosophical Quarterly* 24, 59–69.

Stocker, M., and E. Hegeman. 1996. *Valuing Emotions.* Cambridge: Cambridge University Press.

Strange, S., and J. Zupko, eds. 2004. *Stoicism: Traditions and Transformations.* Cambridge: Cambridge University Press.

Striker, G. 1996. *Essays in Hellenistic Epistemology and Ethics.* Cambridge: Cambridge University Press.

———. 1991. Following Nature: A Study in Stoic Ethics. *Oxford Studies in Ancient Philosophy* 9, 1–73. Rpt. Striker 1996, 221–80.

———. 1987. Origins of the Concept of Natural Law. *Proceedings of the Boston Area Colloquium in Ancient Philosophy* 2, 79–94. Rpt. Striker 1996, 209–20.

Taylor, G. 1985. *Pride, Shame, and Guilt: Emotions of Self-Assessment.* Oxford: Clarendon Press.

Thompson, E. F. 1908. μετανοέω and μεταμέλει in Greek Literature until 100 A.D. Ph.D. diss, University of Chicago.

Thornton, B. 1997. *Eros: The Myth of Ancient Greek Sexuality.* Boulder: Westview Press.

Tielemann, T. 2003. *Chrysippus' On Affections: Reconstruction and Interpretation.* Leiden: Brill.

———. 1996. *Galen and Chrysippus on the Soul: Argument and refutation in the De Placitis Books II–III.* Leiden: Brill.

Todd, R. B. 1978. Monism and Immanence: The Foundations of Stoic Physics. In *The Stoics,* ed. J. Rist. Berkeley: University of California Press. 137–60.

Tsouna, V. 1998. Doubts about Other Minds and the Science of Physiognomics. *Classical Quarterly* 48, 175–86.

Voelke, A.-J. 1973. *L'idée de volonté dans le Stoicisme.* Paris: Presses Universitaires de France.

von Arnim, H. 1906. *Hierocles: Ethische Elementarlehre.* Berlin: Weidmann.

———, ed. 1903–24. *Stoicorum veterum fragmenta.* Leipzig: Teubner.

von Staden, H. 2000. Body, Soul, and Nerves: Epicurus, Herophilus, Erasistratus, the Stoics, and Galen. In *Psyche and Soma: Physicians and Metaphysicians on the Mind-Body Problem from Antiquity to Enlightenment,* ed. J. P. Wright and P. Potter. Oxford: Clarendon Press. 79–116.

———. 1989. *Herophilus: The Art of Medicine in Early Alexandria.* Cambridge: Cambridge University Press.

Wachsmuth, C., and O. Hense, eds. 1884–1912. *Ioannis Stobaei Anthologium.* 4 vols. Berlin: Weidmann.

Wallies, M., ed. 1881. *Alexander Aphrodisiensis: In Aristotelis topicorum libros octo commentaria* (= *Commentaria in Aristotelem Graeca,* vol. 2, part 2). Berlin: Reimer.

Waszink, J., ed. 1962. *Timaeus, A Calcidio translatus commentarioque instructus. Plato Latinus,* ed. R. Klibansky. Vol. 4. London: Warburg Institute.

White, M. 2003. Stoic Natural Philosophy (Physics and Cosmology). In Inwood 2003, 124–52.

White, S. 1995. Cicero and the Therapists. In *Cicero the Philosopher: Twelve Papers,* ed. J. G. F. Powell. Oxford: Oxford University Press. 219–46.

Williams, B. 1981. *Moral Luck.* Cambridge: Cambridge University Press.

Winkler, J. 1990. *The Constraints of Desire: The Anthropology of Sex and Gender in Ancient Greece.* New York: Routledge.

Wolf, S. 1990. *Freedom within Reason.* Oxford: Oxford University Press.

Wright, M. R. 1995. Cicero on Self–Love and Love of Humanity in *De Finibus* 3. In *Cicero the Philosopher,* ed. J. G. F. Powell. Oxford: Clarendon Press. 171–95.

Zajonc, R. B. 1984. On the Primacy of Affect. *American Psychologist* 39, 117–23.

Zeitlin, F. 1996. *Playing the Other: Gender and Society in Classical Greek Literature.* Chicago: University of Chicago Press.

Zetzel, J. G. 1999. *Cicero: On the Commonwealth and On the Laws.* Cambridge: Cambridge University Press.

INDEX LOCORUM

Page numbers in bold indicate where passages are quoted.

GENERAL INDEX

Abraham, 102–4
Achilles, 61, 134, 198
action, 26–28, 63–66, 140; appropriate actions (*kathēkonta*), 220, 248n38; emotions as, 5–6, 38–39, 94–98, 68–69, 229n12; pursuit and avoidance, 31, 139, 227n50; right actions (*katorthōmata*), 211, 220, 230n35, 248n38; tendencies toward, 142–43, 145. *See also* impulse; selection
activities. *See* movements
Admetus, 61
adverbial formulations, 48, 230n25
Aeschines, 252n1
aesthetic responses, 95–97
Ajax, 110, 114, 121, 242n36
Alcibiades, 191, 196–97, 206–7, 252n1, 253n14
Alcinous, 234n30
Alcmaeon, 117, 121, 240n11
alcohol. *See* drunkenness
Alexander of Aphrodisias, 9, 11, 241n16
ambition (*doxomania*), 119–20
anger, 56–57; and brutishness, 122–23, 125–32; causes of, 94–98, 238n21–22; in Origen, 105–6; physical sensation of, 31; in Plato, 72–73; as temporary insanity, 111, 118–19, 122, 130. *See also* irascibility
animals: complex behavior in, 109–110, 176, 240n1, 242n38; cross-species

comparisons, 15, 176; feelings of, 75, 78, 96; impressions of, 24, 226n30, 240n10; limitations of, 51, 109–110; souls do not survive death, 20
Antipater, 225n17
Antony, Mark, 124, 242n44
anxiety, 56, 57
apatheia (impassivity), 5, 87, 210–11, 254n29; objections to, 45, 202, 207
aphormai. See virtue, starting points toward
Apollinaris of Laodicea, 107, 239n36
Apollodorus, 11, 122–23, 252n46
appraisals, 37, 38–41. *See also* evaluations
appropriateness: appropriate actions (*see* actions); beliefs concerning, 41–46; terminology of, 42, 229n14; arch analogy, 173–74, 250n1
Arianism, 106
Aristides the Just, 134
Aristo (of Chios): analogy to drama, 48
Aristotle: on basics of psychology, 16–17, 21, 23, 31, 225n20; on brutishness, 110, 112, 240n4, 243n59; on emotions, 57–58, 61, 217, 253n9, 253n11; on friendship, 175, 250n3; on impressions, 89, 226n32, 236n4; influence on Seneca, 131, 243n59; on involuntary feelings, 88–89, 236n4; later Aristotelians, 128, 243n50; on melancholy, 240n4; on *pneuma*, 225n10, 225n20

courage: and magnanimity, 247n13; in Plato, 215–17, 255n5; starting point for, 153

cruelty, 122, 123–25, 242n41–42

cylinder analogy, 64, 134, 149, 233n8

Damasio, Antonio, 17

Davies, John, 214

death: mistaken for evil, 160–61; survival of souls after, 20, 225n14

delight, 28, 53–54, 204; as physical change in psyche, 28, 32–33; vs. pleasure of body, 227n44; species of, 55–57

delirium, 115–16, 121

Demosthenes, 45, 229n19

Descartes, René, 246n10

desire, 227n53; and erotic love, 185–88, 251n36; as genus emotion, 53–54, 57, 204; as physical change in psyche, 30–31; species of, 56

determinism, 62, 80, 81, 169, 232n3

diatheseis. See conditions

Didymus Caecus, 11, 107–8, 239n36–37

Diodorus of Tarsus, 239n37

Diogenes of Babylon, 11, 225n17, 228n56

Diogenes Laertius, 10, 11

Diogenianus, 116–17

directive faculty, 21–24; in Aristotle and Plato, 225n20; in emotions, 233n13; located in chest, 34, 223n1, 227n52, 228n56

disease (*morbus*), as rendering for *pathos*, 141

dispositions, 37, 40–41. *See also* traits of character

distress, 39–40, 53–54; distinguished from pain of body, 227n44; as natural capacity of humans, 204, 205–6; no analogue in the wise, 53–55, 194, 204; as physical change in psyche, 28 (*see also* biting; contraction); species of, 55–58; toward integral objects, 191–93, 196, 199–200. *See also* grief; remorse

doxa. See opinion

doxographic tradition, 10

dreams, 114

drunkenness: and brutishness, 124, 242n43, 243n57; as character trait, 39, 141; and confidence, 216; and loss of virtue, 114, 115–16;

duty, 43

eagerness (*prothumia*), 92, 232n48

education: as bad influence, 150, 158, 161; eroticized, 8–9, 186–89; in ethics (*see* therapy)

ekklisis. See withdrawing

eklogē. See selection

elements: four-element physics, 19, 225n9

elevation: associated with delight, 28, 29, 30, 229n13, 227n45, 227n47; irrational vs. well-reasoned, 32–33, 52, 204, 227n49; natural capacity for, 36, 204

emotionlessness. See *apatheia*

emotions: as actions, 38–39, 66–69, 85–93, 94–99, 229n12; analogues in animals and children, 78, 110; capacity for, as natural, 6–7; causation of, 42–46, 63–66, 68–69, 75–80, 140, 237n7; as causes, 111–12, 120–23, 131–32, 164–67, 169, 242n36, 249n47; and character traits, 133–35, 140–41, 164–67; definitions of, 4–5, 28–34, 38–46, 67, 86–87; classified by genus, 53–55, 104–5, 203–4, 231n38; classified by species, 55–58, 231n43, 232n45; as contumacious, 130, 243n55–56; distinguished from feelings, 7, 33–34, 35, 86–87; elimination of (see *apatheia*); examples of, 2–3, 55–58, 231n43–44, 232n45; good emotions (see *eupatheiai*); toward integral objects, 191–93, 195, 196, 199–200, 208, 210–11, 216–17, 254n28; moderation in (*metriopatheia*), 102, 128, 243n50; modern theories, 15–16, 37, 80–81, 97, 223n3, 224n1, 228n4, 235n43–44, 236n51, 236n54–55; moral emotions, 193, 252n3, 253n4; overwhelming, 5, 61–70, 127–28, 118–20, 130–31; as physical events, 18, 28–34, 121–22; physical sensations of, 4–5, 18, 227n52; and simple ascriptions of value, 37–41. *See also* feelings

enviousness, 142

environment, influence on traits, 170, 249n54

envy (*phthonos*), 56

eparsis. See elevation

epibolē (effort or resolve), 186, 252n45

Epictetus: as source, 11, 12; on caring for family, 177–78, 250n15–16; on caution and confidence, 219, 230n33; on development of character traits, 165, 249n43; on insanity, 240n11; on moral failings of others, 55; on moral shame, 208, 254n27; on

as source of examples, 3, 31, 61, 70–72,
110, 234n21, 235n33, 244n1; Stoic influence
in Roman, 45, 121, 229n20, 241n36. *See also*
names of specific characters and index of
passages cited
Pohlenz, Max, 214, 238n27
politics. *See* communities
Posidonius, 10–11, 82, 143, 224n7; on causes
of emotion, 75–77, 235n40, 235n45, 236n54,
237n7; on involuntary feelings and
impressions, 92, 114; on origins of error,
154–55, 247n21; on proclivities, 143–44,
245n26; on remorse, 192, 252n2; reinterpretations of, 235n42
pourings (*chuseis*). *See* outpourings
power, natural orientation toward, 153, 157
praise, and moral development, 155–58,
162–63
Praxagoras of Cos, 226n22
preconceptions, 246n12
predicates, 27, 28–33, 47, 230n33
pre-emotions, 7–8, 85–108, 205; 'beginnings,'
86, 90–91, 96–98, 106–7, 127, 239n38;
criticism, 91–92, 237n9; implications,
87–88, 108; involuntary 'bitings,' 92–93,
105, 239n32, 205; origins of Stoic concept,
78, 87–88, 88–93, 236n2–3, 237n7, 237n11;
preliminary or simple 'impulse,' 94–95,
237n16–17, 238n21–22; in Scriptural exegesis, 102–8, 239n33; term *propatheia*, 87, 98,
102, 104, 106, 238n27–28. *See also* feelings
prerehearsal of future ills, 76, 79, 235n40
present objects, 54–55, 231n38
Price, Anthony, 235n33
proclivities, 137–38, 142–45; development of,
165; toward goods, 245n23; terminology
of, 245n22
Procopius of Gaza, 104, 238n27
Progressors, pain of, 191–95, 206–210, 236n54
prohairesis, 66, 233n8, 233n11–12, 239n33
propatheiai. *See* pre-emotions
proper characteristic (*idion*), 49
propositions, 23–28, 49–50, 226n31, 226n37
proprioception. *See* self-perception
proskopē. *See* aversions
prospective objects, 54–55, 231n38, 231n40
prosphaton. *See* freshness
prudence (*phronēsis*), 117, 153, 241n24, 249n48

psyche, 20–24, 225n16–18; part-based and
monistic models, 23, 69, 72–75, 223n5,
233n13, 234n28–29; self-perception, 23–24,
28, 31–32, 226n29; tension in, 20–21, 26,
64–65, 71, 114–16, 141. *See also* mind
psychopathy, 124–25, 242n44
ptoia. *See* fluttering.
pursuit. *See* action, pursuit and avoidance

rancor, 56, 231n44
rationality: descriptive vs. normative
accounts, 24, 36; in eupathic response,
7–8, 32–33, 36, 203, 218; and the human
good, 48–51, 202, 210; and human nature,
18, 109–10, 152, 248n28; loss of, 115–16,
120–125, 131–32, 241n16–17; of loved ones,
181, 190; and moral responsibility, 5, 68,
168–71 (*see also* assent); and pre-emotions,
95, 99, 102, 107–8; rational soul of Jesus,
107, 239n36–37; reasoning 'part' according
to Plato, 72–73; required for emotion,
111–12, 129–30. *See also* human nature
rational wish. *See* wish
reaching (*orexis*), 30–31, 227n50–51, 227n53;
natural capacity for, 36, 203–4. *See also*
actions, pursuit and avoidance; desire;
feelings
reader emotions, 95–97
reason. *See* rationality
reflexes, 61, 94–97
regret, 253n4. *See also* remorse
remorse, 8–9, 191, 193–95, 253n5; appropriateness of, 195, 200–201; and moral progress,
206–7, 208–10; in Plato and Aristotle,
253n9, 253n11; religious conception of,
206; vs. repentance, 194, 253n8
repentance, 193–94, 253n6, 206. *See also*
remorse
reputation, 156–58, 162–63
reservation, 194, 253n7
respiration, 22, 34
responsibility, moral: for actions and
emotions, 5–8, 62–66, 80–82, 109–10,
232n3; for character, 134, 149–51, 167–71;
in psychopaths, 125, 242n46; set aside,
110–11, 116
reverence, 58
Reydams-Schils, Gretchen, 247n21